Understanding Finance *with the* FINANCIAL TIMES

Understanding Finance *with the* FINANCIAL TIMES

Terry Byland

HARRAP
LONDON

For Magda

First published in Great Britain 1988
by HARRAP Ltd
19-23 Ludgate Hill, London EC4M 7PD

ISBN 0–245–54509–3

Designed by Roger King Graphic Studios

Phototypeset by Falcon Graphic Art Ltd
Wallington, Surrey

Printed and bound in Great Britain by
Mackays of Chatham Ltd, Chatham, Kent

Contents

Understanding Finance *with the* FINANCIAL TIMES

FINANCIAL TIMES

LONDON – FRANKFURT – NEW YORK

No. 30,399 Thursday November 26 1987 40p

WORLD NEWS

Six Israelis killed in Arab raid

At least six Israeli soldiers were killed and seven wounded in the most daring Arab guerrilla raid for years on an army base in northern Israel.

The raiders flew across the heavily guarded border with Lebanon in a glider or light aircraft.

Civilians were also injured. It was unclear which Arab group was responsible for the attack. **Back Page**

Belfast halted by bomb alerts

More than 20 bomb alerts brought Belfast traffic to a standstill last night. Hijacked vehicles were abandoned near police stations and army bases.

Army bomb disposal teams were busy dealing with suspect vehicles, but a number of alerts were declared hoaxes.

Earlier in the evening, Paul Kane, 32, the man at the centre of an Anglo-Irish extradition tangle, was held by Irish police on assault charges after a car chase. Sinn Fein leader Gerry Adams, MP, was in the car. **Page 8**

North Sea dumping deal

Agreement to ban dumping or burning of toxic waste and dumping of ships' waste in the North Sea to reduce pollution was reached at an eight-nation ministerial meeting in London. **Page 8**

Heart boy's operation

Six-week-old David Barber, the postponement of whose hole-in-heart operation prompted his parents to take court action, had a successful operation at Birmingham.

US Army team at jail

The US Army flew in a team of Special Operations soldiers to Atlanta, Georgia, where Cuban prisoners resisting repatriation seized 25 more hostages, taking the total held to 94. Life behind bars, **Page 6**

Chicago mayor dies

Mayor Harold Washington, 65, the first black mayor of Chicago, died of a heart attack after collapsing at his City Hall desk. **Page 6**

East Germans raid church

East German security forces raided a church in East Berlin and seized printing equipment and literature. Five people from an environmental group were detained. **Page 2**

Commons backing for FT

MPs on all sides of the House of Commons welcomed the strongest indication yet given by the Government that any attempt by Rupert Murdoch to secure control of the Financial Times would be referred to the Monopolies and Mergers Commission. **Page 14**

Equality chairman

Mrs Joanna Foster, who heads the Pepperell Unit, The Industrial Society's equal opportunities division, has been appointed chairman of the Government's Equal Opportunities Commission. **Page 8**

Soviet airliner held

A Soviet airliner remained grounded at Manchester airport last night after six Russian engineers, who had come to replace an engine, were refused entry because they had no visas.

Ashdown Forest sold

East Sussex county council is buying the 6,400-acre Ashdown Forest from the De la Warr family for just over £1m. **Page 10**

Qadir routs England

Spin bowler Abdul Qadir took nine wickets for 56 to help Pakistan dismiss England for 175 in the first Test at Lahore. Pakistan reached 15-0.

BUSINESS SUMMARY

Abolition of steel quotas proposed

THE EUROPEAN Commission proposed yesterday that output quotas on most of the steel production under its control be ended by next July, with the rest liberalised by 1990.

The plan - a serious blow to the EC steelmakers' organisation Eurofer - is likely to be supported by most member states but opposed by Britain, which wants an immediate return to a free market. **Back Page**

NICKEL PRICES climbed to six-year highs in dollar terms on the London Metal Exchange, helped by speculative demand and strong buying by Japan's stainless steel industry. The cash position rose £160 to £3,585 a tonne. The cash price for Grade A copper reached a record £1,610 a tonne in London. **Commodities, Page 38**

Nickel
Cash Metal (£ per tonne)

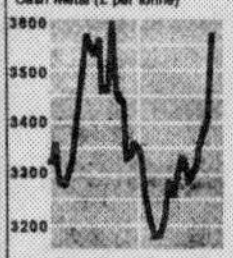

S.G. WARBURG Group, large independent City investment bank, said it had been hit by unspecified losses since last month's stock markets crash. **Back Page and Lex**

SIR IAN MACGREGOR, 75, former chairman of British Steel and the former National Coal Board, is to become chairman of North Sea Assets, an Edinburgh-based investment company specialising in oilfield services. **Men and Matters, Page 26**

BRITISH TELECOM'S monopoly on public telephone boxes is expected to be broken. Trade and Industry undersecretary John Butcher said the company had to face competition. **Page 8**

MAGNET, kitchen and bedroom furniture group, is to cut up to 600 jobs by the end of the year because of a shortfall in forecast demand. **Page 19**

SAUDI ARABIA has invited bids from three European groups, including Vosper Thornycroft of the UK, for eight minehunting ships. **Back Page**

BRAZILIAN Government is preparing an economic package to raise revenues and reduce public spending. **Page 6**

STATOIL, Norway's state oil company, is to have Jan Erik Langangen, 37, president of Norway's largest insurance company Storebrand, as chairman.

ELECTROLUX of Sweden, world's leading white goods manufacturer, showed a 35 per cent rise in profits (after financial items), to SKr604m (£56.6m) in the third quarter, helped by recent acquisitions. **Page 33**

AACHENER und Muenchener, West German insurance group, reported an "extraordinarily good" year, based on figures to September. **Page 32**

CABLE and Wireless, telecommunications group, blamed currency movements for a rise of just 3 per cent to £165m in interim taxable profits. **Page 29; Lex, Back Page; Hong Kong Telephone results, Page 34**

BAT INDUSTRIES, tobacco-based multinational, boosted pre-tax profits 16 per cent to £1.02bn in the nine months to end-September. **Page 28; Lex, Back Page**

COURTAULDS, textiles, chemicals and industrial products group, saw first-half pre-tax profits rise 25 per cent to £102.2m, slightly up on forecasts. **Page 30; Lex, Back Page**

MARKETS

DOLLAR	STERLING
Tokyo opening Y134.75	New York ($1.79225)
New York:	London: $1.795 (1.7725)
DM 1.671 (1.6695)	DM 2.9925 (2.99)
FFr 5.66625 (5.6715)	FFr 10.155 (10.135)
SFr 1.3715 (1.37)	SFr 2.46 (2.455)
Y134.9 (134.65)	Y241.75 (240.25)
London:	Sterling index 75.8 (75.4)
DM 1.6675 (1.6875)	
FFr 5.6575 (5.7175)	
SFr 1.3705 (1.3855)	
Y134.7 (135.5)	
Dollar index 95.9 (96.5)	

LONDON MONEY
3-month interbank:
closing rate 8¹⁵⁄₁₆% (8⅞)

NORTH SEA OIL
Brent 15-day Dec (Argus)
$17.70 (17.90)

US CLOSING RATES
Fed Funds 6¾% (same)
3-month Treasury Bills:
yield: 5.85% (5.95)
Long Bond: 98⅝ (98¾)
yield: 9.05% (9)

STOCK INDICES
FT Ord 1,316.6 (-18.6)
FT-A All Share 834.85 (-1.2%)
FT-SE 100 1,664.1 (-25)
FT-A long gilt yield index:
High coupon: 9.38 (9.3)
New York:
DJ Ind Av 1,946.95 (-16.58)
Tokyo:
Nikkei 23,219.69 (+363.67)

GOLD
New York: Comex Dec
$476.9 (475.4)
London: $476.75 (473.75)

Chief price changes yesterday, Back Page

SELLING PRICE IN IRELAND 60p

Health authorities to be allowed to sell services in hospitals

BY MICHAEL DIXON

HEALTH AUTHORITIES are to be freed to introduce commercial activities in hospitals and clinics under a government bill published yesterday.

The bill and an accompanying White Paper also propose charges for eye tests for all except children and young people in full-time education, adults on low incomes and people registered as blind or partly sighted.

There would also be charges for dental checks, with similar exceptions, and higher fees for dental treatment.

The scheme came under immediate criticism from Tory backbenchers as well as Opposition MPs, and from the majority of health service associations.

Under the bill, health authorities, in addition to leasing space to shops and other commercial operations, could set up fee-charging health clubs and supply services such as operating facilities for private patients at a profitable price.

The Health and Medicines Bill and the White Paper spell out a wide range of measures intended by ministers to develop primary health care services, with particular emphasis on preventative action against illness.

These include incentives to family doctors, dentists, pharmacists and others to concentrate more on providing people with advice on preventing illness instead of merely treating it.

Mr Tony Newton, Health Minister, said he hoped the new options for health authorities to make money through commercial enterprise would generate about £60m next year increasing to £70m by around 1990.

The price for eye tests could be up to £10, with an estimated fee of less than £3 for dental examinations.

The White Paper says the increases and extensions to charges will raise substantial sums. They are described as indispensable to the Government's plan for developing primary health care.

In addition, the Government plans to increase spending on the family practitioner service - now running at £5.08bn a year - by a total of £570m over the three years to 1991.

The intention, the White Paper says, is to keep charges to a minimum by promoting sharper competition between NHS medical and dental practitioners.

This will be achieved by linking their pay more closely to per-

Continued on Back Page
Details, Page 8; Editorial comment, Page 26

THE MAIN POINTS

THE BILL

POWERS for health authorities to make money.
COMPULSORY retirement at 70 for NHS family doctors.
CHARGES for eye-tests and dental checks.
OPTICIANS must give eye tests without insisting they supply any spectacles needed.
GENERAL PRACTICE Finance Corporation, making loans for family doctors' surgeries, to be privatised.

THE WHITE PAPER

FAMILY DOCTORS: Pay to be more dependent on performance; negotiations to permit advertising; incentive payments for preventative services; extra funds for in-service training.
DENTISTS: Changes to pay system to encourage greater commitment to NHS.
PHARMACISTS: Incentives to keep records of medicines used by NHS customers, and to help train other workers in community health services.
NURSES: Consideration of allowing limited powers to prescribe, and to decide timing and dosage of pain-relieving drugs prescribed by doctors.
HEALTH AUTHORITIES: Greater managerial responsibilities and powers for Family Practitioner Committees, Dental Estimates Boards etc.

British Gas faces probe over industrial prices

BY MAURICE SAMUELSON

THE MONOPOLIES and Mergers Commission is to investigate British Gas's treatment of large industrial customers after complaints that its contract prices are up to 50 per cent higher than those on the continent.

The inquiry, which will last nine months, was ordered by Sir Gordon Borrie, Director General of Fair Trading.

Sir Gordon said it was not for him to judge whether prices were reasonable "but the material that has been submitted to me by industrial customers and others is in my opinion such as to justify a thorough investigation."

It is the first time that British Gas, privatised 18 months ago, has faced the commission, although it was scrutinised in the late 1970s by the now disbanded Price Commission.

Sir Denis Rooke, British Gas chairman, welcomed the speed of the inquiry - most of the commission's inquiries last much longer - and promised the group's full co-operation. British Gas has previously resisted any reference to the commission.

The Chemical Industries Association, one of the leading complainants, welcomed the move and also the speed of the inquiry. The chemicals industry is among direct energy intensive sectors, including [illegible] and paper, which also want UK gas prices to be investigated by the European Commission.

The Office of Fair Trading said the inquiry had been called because of its director's concern over four issues:

- The lack of a clear basis for different contracts and of a clear relationship to changes in the price of alternative fuels or British Gas's own costs. Users had, therefore, complained of great difficulty in estimating their future costs.
- The "wide differences" in prices said to be paid by customers with similar requirements.
- Contracts were for three months or less, adding to the complaints about the difficulty of estimating costs;
- British Gas's unwillingness to quote a price for interruptible supplies until the customer had installed dual-fired equipment, making it difficult for him to judge whether such investment was worthwhile. Such customers pay less if they agree to have their supplies cut off at short notice when demand is high.

British Gas said its gas contract pricing policy had operated for 20 years with the full approval of successive governments, and had not been changed with privatisation or subsequently.

The policy had been able to cope with huge changes in the price of competing energy sources brought about by the collapse in crude oil prices.

In the highly competitive industrial energy market, contract prices for gas were related to oil product prices. There had been 22 changes to scheduled oil prices in the 12 months to the end of October. This caused uncertainties in the industrial market, but the group had done what it could to help its contract customers.

Icahn buys Holmes a Court stake

BY JAMES BUCHAN IN NEW YORK

MR ROBERT Holmes a Court, the Australian entrepreneur who has liquidated large parts of his business empire since stock markets crashed last month, has lost US$100m (£56.5m) in selling half his 10 per cent holding in Texaco to Mr Carl Icahn, the US corporate raider.

The $348m deal again suggests that the Australian may be conducting a fire sale of assets to meet debt payments at his highly borrowed companies. It also brings fresh uncertainty to Texaco, the beleaguered US oil group which has taken refuge in bankruptcy from a colossal $10.3bn damages judgment.

Mr Icahn, who controls about 76 per cent of Trans World Airlines, said yesterday that TWA had bought 12m shares of Texaco from Mr Holmes a Court's Bell Resources for $29 a share. TWA said it had a right of first refusal and a voting proxy over the remaining 12.1m Bell shares in Texaco.

The purchase gives Mr Icahn, one of the most aggressive and successful US takeover specialists, voting control over 12.3 per cent of Texaco. He is believed to have cash and liquidity of around $1bn available for stock purchases.

Disposal of the Texaco stock, which Mr Holmes a Court bought in the summer at an average $37.50 a share, takes to more than A$1bn (£381m) the cash he has raised from asset sales since the world-wide fall in share prices began on October 19. The stock prices of Mr Holmes a Court's main companies, Bell Group and Bell Resources, have plummeted on Australian exchanges amid fears that he faces a liquidity squeeze.

Analysts said that the Texaco stake was expensive to hold because the bankrupt company was not permitted to pay dividends. The company decision this month to appeal to the Supreme Court against the damages awarded to its rival, Pennzoil, raised the prospect of a long delay before a solution, the analysts added.

However, the Icahn stake is expected to increase the pressure on Texaco to settle with Pennzoil, which was awarded the judgment on the grounds that Texaco interfered with its contract to buy an interest in Getty Oil in 1984. Mr Icahn was left with spare financing of $800m when he dropped a plan to buy the remaining TWA shares after the crash. Texaco stock rose $1¼ to $30¼ yesterday.

CONTENTS

For London market and latest share index 01-246 8026; overseas markets 01-246 8086

Economic institute calls for interest rate cuts

By Philip Stephens, Economics Correspondent

A CALL for further sharp cuts in interest rates to cushion the deflationary impact on Britain's economy of the stock market crash and of the recent rise in sterling's value is made today by a leading independent economics research group.

The National Institute of Economic and Social Research says in its latest Economic Review that the Government should reduce borrowing costs from 9 per cent to 8 per cent immediately. A further cut to 7 per cent by the end of the year, or soon after, should then be considered.

The institute's call comes against the background of its forecast of an abrupt slowing in the pace of growth in the economy next year. By the end of 1988, output is projected to be rising only by an annual 1.5 per cent compared with the current 4 per cent.

Britain's exporters are likely to be hit by slower growth in world trade as well as by the loss of competitiveness resulting from the pound's gains this year against both the dollar and the D-Mark.

Last month's slump in British equity prices is not expected to be the major factor behind the economic slowdown. But, combined with a previously-expected deceleration from the present rapid pace of growth and with the impact of sterling's appreciation, it could depress the growth rate to a level at which unemployment would start to rise again, the review says.

Mr Nigel Lawson, the Chancellor, has taken a cautious approach to any further reduction in borrowing costs, and has suggested that such a move would need to be part of a wider international package to stabilise the dollar.

The institute, however, says that a reduction should not be contingent on similar action elsewhere. Lower borrowing costs are needed to underpin the momentum of the domestic economy and to prevent sterling from becoming excessively overvalued.

In a series of articles covering the performance of Britain's manufacturing industry, the institute suggests that the sector's importance to the economy will increase over the next few years.

It argues that despite the strong growth in output and productivity over the past few years, Britain's manufacturing sector is still lagging behind those of its key competitors in a number of respects.

Details, Page 12; Stoltenberg speech, Back Page

Nato to halt deployment of INF missiles

BY QUENTIN PEEL IN BRUSSELS

THE US has agreed with its Nato allies that no further intermediate-range nuclear missiles will be deployed in western Europe from December 8, the date when President Ronald Reagan and Mr Mikhail Gorbachev will sign the treaty to scrap such weapons over the next three years.

European governments yesterday welcomed the accord, despite some doubts in West Germany about its contents and disagreements within Nato about what the next step in arms control should be.

Mr George Shultz, the US Secretary of State, announced the decision on deployment in Brussels yesterday, where he flew to brief Nato foreign ministers and ambassadors on the outcome of his talks in Geneva with Mr Eduard Shevardnadze, the Soviet Foreign Minister.

The decision to call a halt to deployment even before the US Congress has ratified the treaty on intermediate nuclear forces (INF) will remove a major political problem for those countries providing bases for the cruise missiles - in particular Belgium and the Netherlands, but also the UK, Italy and West Germany.

The Molesworth base in Cambridgeshire, scheduled to take 64 cruise missiles, will now not be used. There are 96 launchers in place at Greenham Common, Berkshire.

The question of further missile deployment has been an important election issue in Belgium, where the Government goes to the polls on December 13. Both Belgium and the Netherlands have been strongly resisting US pressure to deploy missiles.

The decision to halt deployment was not matched by any similar Soviet agreement, Mr Shultz said. The Soviets could continue to deploy new SS20s until the date of ratification of the INF treaty by the US Senate.

Mr Shultz came to Nato seeking a solid endorsement of the INF treaty from the allies, which he won from all sides.

Lord Carrington, the Nato Secretary-General, said the organisation's council "enthusiastically welcomed the INF agreement, and looked forward to its signature and early ratification."

There was a widespread welcome from the Europeans on three fronts: for the decision not to insist on further missile deployment, for the success of the US in negotiating a deal with the Soviet Union, which is removing more than four times as many warheads than the US; and for the verification measures agreed to allow for inspection of missile sites and missile manufacturing facilities.

Sir Geoffrey Howe, Britain's Foreign Secretary, welcomed the agreement and said in a statement that Nato had achieved everything it wanted under the proposed pact.

The terms of the pact justified the decision taken in 1979 by the North Atlantic alliance to deploy US-built cruise and Pershing missiles and "bears witness to the determination and unity of the Nato countries."

The West German Government, elements of which only seven months ago were firmly opposed to the INF deal in its present form, put on a brave smile and welcomed the Geneva agreement.

Chancellor Helmut Kohl said he greeted the news of the accord "with extraordinary satisfaction." In June, Mr Kohl was refusing to include West German Pershing 1A missiles - which carry US warheads - in an INF deal. Now these, too, form part of the Geneva package, which he

Continued on Back Page
Editorial Comment, Page 26

Minister admits poll tax may hit 3m households

BY PETER RIDDELL, POLITICAL EDITOR

THE GOVERNMENT admitted last night that 3m households might face an increase of more than 50 per cent in their local tax bills as a result of the proposed new system of local government finance.

In a Commons written answer, Mr Michael Howard, the Local Government Minister, also revealed that about 1.8m households might have to pay 80 per cent or more above their existing domestic rate payments.

These figures are for 1990-91, the first year of the proposed community charge or poll tax, and assume current levels of spending.

However, Mr Howard stressed that this outcome need not arise if local authorities immediately started to reduce expenditure.

Last week's announcement of transitional arrangements for the replacement of domestic rates by the new charge enables the figures to be calculated now.

The size of increase for a large number of households is certain to provide ammunition for Labour and Tory critics of the bill, which is due to be published at the end of next week and will receive its second reading in the Commons in three weeks.

1 Reading the FT

The *Financial Times* is widely regarded as a 'specialist' newspaper — aimed at readers with a close affinity to the City of London and its various financial and commodity markets. Like most assumptions, this is half true and therefore half untrue. It *is* true that the paper has always given a high priority to economic and business affairs, but in this it has been followed by the other 'quality' UK newspapers. The FT still provides comprehensive lists of UK share and commodity prices daily — but the readership for such information has expanded nationally and internationally. It is also true, however, that the FT has, over the past thirty years, widened its area of coverage far beyond the business field. The paper's reviews of the Arts have a long-established and world-wide reputation. Fishing, farming, cooking and shopping, all have their place in the newspaper. Most readers, however, see the FT as a source of news and comment on the world of finance and business, so any assessment of the paper's content must start there.

The *Financial Times*, or the FT — or even the Pink 'Un if you prefer — sets out to inform its readers of all the events of the day which are likely to affect or to be reflected in the world financial and business community. A pretty tall order in today's volatile world. Investors now need to keep an eye on a wide variety of political and social developments in just about every part of the globe, as well as scrutinizing the tea-leaves of the major stock markets. So the FT front page carries most of the news-stories to be found in the other leading newspapers. But then comes the great mass of small print towards the back of the FT, where eye-boggling lists of share prices are accompanied by mystifying hieroglyphics explained in brisk but minuscule footnotes.

Markets, and the prices that are quoted in them, are the lifeblood of the world's business, so it is inevitable that the FT should be full of them. Every market and every price is of importance to some portion of the FT readership, and must therefore offer valuable information for the investor. This mass of figures published every day in the paper may be the best place to start looking at the FT.

FT Ordinary Share Index

Everyone has heard of the FT Index, as the Ordinary Share Index is usually known. It is quoted all the time on the television and radio news, as well as in the national and international press, as a handy indicator of the day's progress of the UK stock market.

The index is simply the combination of the share prices of 30 major companies which are always actively traded on the market. As these 30 shares trade, their prices are captured electronically and incorporated into a mathematical formula which calculates the index minute by minute.

This is a very quick and fairly simple way of showing the changing moods in the market. The index has been doing this job for more than fifty years — since 1935. This has taken it through stirring times, and it is no surprise that the index hit its all-time low in the summer of 1940 as Britain awaited a Nazi invasion force. This long track record is one of the index's great strengths, for it gives it credence as an investment tool. The managers of the big investment funds like to know what cycles the market has passed through over a substantial period of time.

CONSTITUENTS OF THE FT 30 SHARE INDEX

Allied Lyons	Arthur Guinness
Assoc. Dairies	Hanson Trust
BICC	Hawker Siddeley**
BOC INT.	I.C.I.**
BTR	Lucas Ind.
Beecham GP.	Marks & Spencer
Blue Circle**	P & O Defd.
Boots	Plessey
British Telecom	National Westminster Bank
BP	Royal Insurance
Cadbury Schweppes	Tate & Lyle
Courtaulds**	Thorn EMI
General Electric**	Trusthouse Forte
Glaxo	B. Gas
Grand Met.	
GKN**	** *Original Constituent*

A recent list of constituents of the FT Ordinary Share Index, which is updated at intervals.

Like many elderly servants, however, the index shows some weaknesses. When it was created, it was intended to reflect the industrial section of the British economy — indeed, the word 'industrial' remained in the title until a few years ago. But the economy has changed shape significantly in recent years. Financial, retailing and service companies are now very important in the nation's business life. Moreover, some of the original 30 companies have simply vanished either through takeovers or through the general decline of the great giants which dominated manufacturing industry in the Thirties. More recently, privatization has brought into the index such names as British Telecom and British Gas, both heavily traded in the market but neither even in quoted share form when the index was first formulated.

Choosing new constituents for the index is a delicate task, which is carried out by the FT's editor and some of his senior colleagues.

Where to find the FT Index

The index is included in the Markets statistics table on page one and

MARKETS

DOLLAR

Tokyo opening Y134.75
New York:
DM 1.671 (1.6695)
FFr 5.66625 (5.6715)
SFr 1.3715 (1.37)
Y134.9 (134.65)
London:
DM 1.6675 (1.6875)
FFr 5.6575 (5.7175)
SFr 1.3705 (1.3855)
Y134.7 (135.5)
Dollar index 95.9 (96.5)

US CLOSING RATES

Fed Funds 6¾% (same)
3-month Treasury Bills:
yield: 5.85% (5.95)
Long Bond: 98½ (98⅝)
yield: 9.05% (9)

GOLD

New York: Comex Dec
$476.9 (475.4)
London: $476.75 (473.75)

STERLING

New York ($1.79225)
London: $1.795 (1.7725)
DM 2.9925 (2.99)
FFr 10.155 (10.135)
SFr 2.46 (2.455)
Y241.75 (240.25)
Sterling index 75.8 (75.4)

LONDON MONEY

3-month interbank:
closing rate 8 15/16% (8[illegible])

NORTH SEA OIL

Brent 15-day Dec (Argus)
$17.70 (17.90)

STOCK INDICES

FT Ord 1,316.6 (-18.6)
FT-A All Share 834.85 (-1.2%)
FT-SE 100 1,664.1 (-25)
FT-A long gilt yield index:
High coupon: 9.38 (9.3)
New York:
DJ Ind Av 1,946.95 (-16.58)
Tokyo:
Nikkei 23,219.69 (+363.67)

Chief price changes yesterday: Back Page

Page one Markets table.

FINANCIAL TIMES STOCK INDICES

	Nov. 25	Nov. 24	Nov. 23	Nov. 20	Nov. 19	Year Ago	1987 High	1987 Low	Since Compilation High	Since Compilation Low
Government Secs	89.80	90.45	90.61	91.03	90.89	81.08	93.32 (8/5)	83.73 (19/10)	127.4 (9/1/35)	49.18 (3/1/75)
Fixed Interest	95.54	95.73	95.91	95.64	95.28	88.34	99.12 (15/6)	90.23 (2/1)	105.4 (28/11/47)	50.53 (3/1/75)
Ordinary ♥	1316.6	1335.2	1309.4	1285.7	1289.9	1286.3	1926.2 (16/7)	1232.0 (9/11)	1926.2 (16/7/87)	49.4 (26/6/40)
Gold Mines	327.8	312.3	293.0	287.2	296.9	299.7	497.5 (4/8)	261.6 (6/11)	734.7 (15/2/83)	43.5 (26/10/71)
Ord. Div.Yield	4.71	4.64	4.73	4.82	4.80	4.44				
Earnings Yld. %(full)	11.64	11.47	11.71	11.93	11.86	10.28				
P/E Ratio (net)(*)	10.50	10.66	10.43	10.25	10.30	11.88				
SEAQ Bargains (5pm)	21,955	24,801	24,205	28,924	22,180	25,721				
Equity Turnover (£m)	-	-	674.89	903.81	888.29	1259.76				
Equity Bargains	-	-	27,515	30,167	25,130	38,101				
Shares Traded (ml)	-	-	349.0	481.4	437.9	427.0				

S.E ACTIVITY

Indices	Nov.24	Nov.23
Gilt Edged Bargains	-	121.5
Equity Bargains	-	178.3
Equity Value	-	1364.1
5-Day average		
Gilt Edged Bargains	-	116.6
Equity Bargains	-	185.0
Equity Value	-	2166.0

♥ Opening	10 a.m.	11 a.m.	Noon	1 p.m.	2 p.m.	3 p.m.	4 p.m.
1323.2	1321.8	1319.2	1316.8	1316.8	1314.8	1314.3	1319.1

Day's High 1327.3 Day's low 1313.3

Basis 100 Govt. Secs 15/10/26, Fixed Int. 1928, Ordinary 1/7/35, Gold Mines 12/9/55, S E Activity 1974, * Nil=10.35.

LONDON REPORT AND LATEST SHARE INDEX: TEL. 01-246 8026

in a panel in the Lex Column on the back page. The main display is to be found in a box on the London Stock Exchange report page towards the back of the paper. This table includes other useful information:

1) The index level over the previous five days and a year ago; the year's high and low, and the high and low since the index started in 1935.

2) Hourly movements over the previous day and the day's high and low points.

3) The dividend yield, earnings yield and price earnings ratio of the 30 companies in the index. (These measures are explained in Chapter 2.)

4) The FT Gold Mines Index. This is based on 25 South African mines and calculated in the same way as the 30-Share index.

5) Indices for Government securities and fixed interest stocks.

6) Various indicators of recent levels of business on the London Stock Exchange. These give a picture of the volume and value of shares traded over the previous days, which is helpful in judging both the mood and liquidity of the market-place.

7) These rather crude indices are another way of measuring the level of activity in different sectors of the market.

Calculation of the FT Index

The index is calculated by multiplying the 30 share prices (with each share divided by its value at the chosen base date) and taking the thirtieth root. The index is unweighted and geometric in form.

The way in which the index is constructed means that it can be seriously distorted if the shares of one or two components fall — or rise — sharply and permanently out of line with the rest. For example, the collapse of British Leyland and, later, of Rolls-Royce, had a lasting impact on the index, partly because their successors had to enter at the same depressed level. Because of the way the formula works, if one share actually fell to zero, then the whole index would register zero as well. Thus, the paper has to keep a sharp eye on the constituents of its most widely-quoted index.

In the mid-Seventies, as it became clear that the nature of the British economy was shifting permanently away from heavy industry and toward service and retailing, it became a problem to find new shares for the index which were as representative as the older names had been in their heyday. It was decided that the share components must be those most actively traded and widely held on the market. British Petroleum was included in 1977, filling a glaringly obvious gap in the index, which until then included no oil shares. And in 1984, when the word 'industrial' was dropped from the index title, the change was affirmed by the inclusion of National Westminster Bank.

By the early 1980s, the need for another market index started to become apparent. In particular, the futures and traded options markets (both described later in this book), wanted an index which was more representative of the entire stock market yet could still be calculated electronically, minute by minute, like the traditional FT Index. The options market knew that if they had such an index they could create new trading products which would allow investors to hedge, or take a view on future trends in the market by means of a single transaction.

In this debate, the FT Ordinary Share Index was judged to be too narrowly-based, and also unacceptably volatile due to its geometric construction.

So in January 1984 came the FT-SE 100 Share Index, which quickly became known as the 'Footsie'. As the name indicates, this index is calculated on the basis of the 100 largest quoted companies, with prices taken directly from the Stock Exchange Automated Quotations System (SEAQ). The prices are fed into a computer that

FT – SE 100 COMPANIES

Amstrad Consumer Electronics PLC
Allied-Lyons
Argyll group
Associated British Foods
ASDA-MFI Group
BAA PLC
B.A.T. Industries
BET PLC
BOC Group
BPB Industries
BTR PLC
Barclays Bank
Bass PLC
Beecham Group
Blue Arrow PLC
Blue Circle Industries
Boots Company
British & Commonwealth
British Aerospace
British Airways
British Gas PLC
British Petroleum
British Telecommunications
Britoil PLC
Bunzl PLC
Burton Group
Cable & Wireless
Cadbury Schweppes
Coats Viyella PLC
Commercial Union Assurance
Consolidated Gold Fields
Cookson Group PLC
Courtaulds
Dee Corporation
Dixons Group
English China Clays
Fisons PLC
General Accident
General Electric Company
Glaxo Holdings
Globe Invst. Trust
Granada Group
Grand Metropolitan
Great Universal Stores
Guardian Royal Exchange
Guinness PLC
Hammerson Properties
Hanson Trust
Hawker Siddeley Group
Hillsdown Holdings PLC
Imperial Chemical Industries
Jaguar PLC
Ladbroke Group
Land Securities
Legal & General Group
Lloyds Bank
MEPC PLC
Marks & Spencer
Maxwell Communications
Midland Bank
National Westminster Bank
Next PLC
Peninsular & Oriental Steam Navigation Co.
Pearson PLC
Pilkington Brothers
Plessey Co.
Prudential Corp.
Racal Electronics
Rank Organisation
Rank, Hovis, McDougall
Reckitt & Colman
Redland PLC
Reed International
Reuters Holdings
Rio Tinto Zinc
Rolls Royce
Rothmans International PLC
Rowntree Mackintosh
Royal Bank of Scotland Group
Royal Insurance
Sainsbury (J.)
Sears Holdings
Sedgwick Group
Shell Transport & Trading Co.
Smith & Nephew Associated Companies
Standard Chartered Bank
Standard Telephones & Cables
Storehouse PLC
Sun Alliance & London insurance
TSB Group PLC
Tarmac PLC
Tesco PLC
THORN EMI
Trafalgar House
Trusthouse Forte
Unilever PLC
United Biscuits (Hldgs.)
Wellcome PLC
Whitbread & Co.
Woolworth Hldgs.

calculates the Footsie Index minute by minute from 9.01 in the morning to around 5.30 pm. The link between the Footsie and the SEAQ network has proved a winning hand for the new index. The 100 Footsie stocks, as well as the running Footsie Index itself, are permanently displayed and updated in real time on the SEAQ screens which have dominated market trading since the move to electronics on Big Bang Day in October 1986.

Since market traders spend the day keeping a close eye on the Footsie screen, it is inevitable that market commentaries are now expressed in terms of the Footsie, rather than the old FT Ordinary Share Index. The Footsie, in fact, is beginning to look like the cuckoo in the market index nest, shouldering the FT Ordinary Share Index ever further aside.

The 100 shares of the Footsie Index add up to nearly 70 per cent of the total value of the UK equity market. Companies are added or deleted as their position in the league table of major companies rises or falls. Here again, changes in the index constituents are decided at quarterly meetings of experts.

The latest list of companies making up the Footsie Index is shown in the table opposite.

For the ordinary investor, it does not matter whether the Footsie or the 30-Share index is used to track the market — provided you know which is which. Institutional investors, however — that is to say, the professional managers of the pension funds, unit trusts and the like — need a market index which is more sophisticated than either the FT 30-Share or the Footsie. They use the FT-Actuaries indices which, added together, represent more than four-fifths of the total value of the companies listed on the Stock Exchange. The flagship is the FT-Actuaries All-Share Index, which began life in 1962 and now includes the share prices of more than 700 major companies. When fund managers talk of 'beating the index', or 'matching the index', it is usually the FT All-Share Index they are talking about.

The All-Share is calculated only once a day, just after the official close. It is not quite as sensitive to short-term movements as the 30-Share index, but it has proved better suited to those long-term trend measurements that fund managers need to track. This is partly because the All-Share includes many stocks which may not be actively traded in every session but which may respond to deeper shifts in investment perceptions.

Private investors should bear in mind one significant reason why

FT-ACTUARIES INDICES

These Indices are the joint compilation of the Financial Times, the Institute of Actuaries and the Faculty of Actuaries

	EQUITY GROUPS & SUB-SECTIONS	Tuesday November 24 1987						Mon Nov 23	Fri Nov 20	Thu Nov 19	Year ago (approx)
	Figures in parentheses show number of stocks per section	Index No.	Day's Change %	Est. Earnings Yield% (Max.)	Gross Div. Yield% (Act at (27%)	Est. P/E Ratio (Net)	xd adj. 1987 to date	Index No.	Index No.	Index No.	Index No.
1	**CAPITAL GOODS (213)**	672.07	+1.5	10.47	4.24	12.01	19.71	661.84	647.72	654.49	672.94
2	Building Materials (30)	874.32	+0.2	10.79	4.21	11.59	23.87	872.77	852.77	863.49	827.34
3	Contracting, Construction (33)	1231.42	+0.8	10.12	4.05	13.21	34.54	1221.61	1211.73	1222.60	1138.02
4	Electricals (14)	1886.28	+3.9	9.65	4.93	13.47	64.72	1815.77	1805.31	1808.04	1713.27
5	Electronics (33)	1483.98	+2.8	10.73	3.41	12.20	36.02	1444.17	1391.52	1407.21	1472.48
6	Mechanical Engineering (60)	328.24	+1.8	11.25	4.94	11.19	11.92	322.48	318.92	321.85	373.95
8	Metals and Metal Forming (7)	392.71	+1.0	10.03	4.21	12.14	11.55	388.94	377.47	381.98	399.61
9	Motors (14)	240.89	+0.7	12.62	4.81	9.21	7.36	239.27	236.05	239.87	263.62
10	Other Industrial Materials (22)	1174.47	+1.5	8.85	4.42	13.43	37.40	1157.01	1131.29	1141.76	1196.78
21	**CONSUMER GROUP (183)**	991.88	+1.8	8.58	3.60	14.83	23.47	974.61	959.10	964.72	921.95
22	Brewers and Distillers (21)	924.94	+1.3	11.00	4.02	11.47	18.46	913.03	894.38	888.81	949.21
25	Food Manufacturing (23)	784.37	+1.8	9.63	4.07	13.40	22.49	770.53	760.65	766.71	718.00
26	Food Retailing (17)	2003.81	+0.1	7.68	2.97	17.36	40.77	2000.85	1977.21	1987.13	1816.14
27	Health and Household Products (10)	1784.19	+3.2	6.48	2.52	18.14	33.67	1728.83	1687.46	1686.61	1482.27
29	Leisure (30)	1054.15	+1.1	7.70	4.33	16.22	29.45	1042.95	1012.57	1024.48	955.30
31	Packaging & Paper (16)	455.30	+1.5	9.16	3.97	14.38	12.53	448.37	443.37	450.03	471.27
32	Publishing & Printing (15)	3161.11	+0.6	6.89	4.62	18.33	97.34	3142.54	3125.91	3129.30	2579.95
34	Stores (35)	829.94	+2.1	9.00	3.63	14.91	20.18	812.56	807.63	817.28	836.02
35	Textiles (16)	588.73	+3.6	10.69	3.93	10.82	15.46	568.45	550.46	566.81	539.68
40	**OTHER GROUPS (87)**	822.62	+2.2	10.62	4.34	11.72	21.23	805.21	791.41	796.59	786.60
41	Agencies (17)	969.46	+4.2	6.33	2.36	20.75	16.91	930.33	909.28	937.15	0.0
42	Chemicals (21)	992.91	+2.6	10.04	4.71	12.17	33.31	968.05	959.36	966.26	975.26
43	Conglomerates (13)	1090.61	+1.4	9.69	4.33	11.81	22.43	1075.19	1059.04	1064.62	0.0
45	Shipping and Transport (11)	1663.56	−0.3	10.23	4.95	12.82	56.73	1667.92	1640.21	1646.73	1580.12
47	Telephone Networks (2)	888.67	+2.9	11.41	4.55	11.69	18.98	864.02	844.11	846.24	779.98
48	Miscellaneous (23)	1151.36	+1.8	13.04	4.12	9.15	33.80	1130.89	1111.98	1117.52	1107.02
49	**INDUSTRIAL GROUP (483)**	870.43	+1.8	9.61	3.96	13.11	22.29	854.85	839.81	845.84	831.11
51	Oil & Gas (17)	1617.51	+2.2	10.27	6.08	12.00	65.74	1582.99	1597.15	1583.75	1420.74
59	**500 SHARE INDEX (500)**	933.75	+1.9	9.71	4.28	12.94	26.04	916.56	904.02	908.39	880.62
61	**FINANCIAL GROUP (120)**	600.55	+0.9	-	5.19	-	21.37	594.95	588.29	597.48	603.74
62	Banks (8)	613.73	+1.0	21.74	6.34	6.08	25.98	607.57	602.15	607.60	658.19
65	Insurance (Life) (8)	888.59	+0.4	-	5.18	-	32.56	884.73	868.08	885.83	840.68
66	Insurance (Composite) (7)	479.77	+0.4	-	5.74	-	20.16	477.86	474.48	474.07	442.01
67	Insurance (Brokers) (8)	794.01	+3.6	13.99	7.22	9.15	39.63	766.21	756.72	765.74	1246.98
68	Merchant Banks (11)	329.39	+2.1	-	4.27	-	8.77	322.68	320.06	329.51	354.84
69	Property (49)	889.64	+0.8	5.58	3.37	23.10	18.92	882.29	874.39	898.39	797.69
70	Other Financial (29)	371.08	+0.9	9.89	4.34	12.81	11.96	367.78	359.98	368.99	366.79
71	Investment Trusts (88)	787.11	+1.6	-	3.17	-	17.14	774.56	766.24	780.15	835.75
81	Mining Finance (2)	410.64	+7.9	11.07	4.16	10.17	12.77	380.62	364.13	370.56	332.42
91	Overseas Traders (10)	889.78	+3.0	10.22	5.49	11.46	37.00	863.67	838.70	847.43	760.19
99	**ALL-SHARE INDEX (720)**	844.66	+1.8	-	4.38	-	24.49	829.64	818.26	824.11	806.11
		Index No.	Day's Change	Day's High	Day's Low	Nov 23	Nov 20	Nov 19	Nov 18	Nov 17	Year ago
	FT-SE 100 SHARE INDEX ♦	1689.1	+31.4	1694.4	1659.8	1657.7	1633.4	1639.1	1663.7	1660.1	1619.3

FIXED INTEREST

	PRICE INDICES	Tue Nov 24	Day's change %	Mon Nov 23	xd adj. today	xd adj. 1987 to date
	British Government					
1	5 years	124.22	+0.06	124.15	-	10.03
2	5-15 years	142.25	−0.15	142.46	-	12.14
3	Over 15 years	150.05	−0.43	150.69	-	12.41

	AVERAGE GROSS REDEMPTION YIELDS		Tue Nov 24	Mon Nov 23	Year ago (approx.)
	British Government				
1	Low	5 years	8.48	8.49	9.95
2	Coupons	15 years	9.16	9.12	10.69
3		25 years	9.08	9.03	10.70
4	Medium	5 years	9.10	9.12	11.43
5	Coupons	15 years	9.37	9.31	11.07
6		25 years	9.30	9.19	10.69
7	High	5 years	9.15	9.16	11.52
8	Coupons	15 years	9.49	9.44	11.26

fund managers concentrate on the All-Share Index. This index makes an excellent tool with which to measure the performance of share portfolios. If a fund fails to match the All-Share Index, its manager will have some explaining to do next time he appears before the bosses. So, if you want to know how your own portfolio is performing, or whether you have chosen the best unit trust, it is a good idea to measure it against the All-Share over a twelve-month or two-year period.

LONDON SHARE SERVICE

AMERICANS – Contd

[illegible]

CANADIANS

[illegible]

BANKS, HP & LEASING

[illegible]

Hire Purchase, Leasing, etc.

[illegible]

BEERS, WINES & SPIRITS

[illegible]

BUILDING, TIMBER, ROADS

[illegible]

BUILDING, TIMBER, ROADS – Contd

[illegible]

CHEMICALS, PLASTICS

[illegible]

DRAPERY AND STORES

[illegible]

DRAPERY AND STORES – Contd

[illegible]

ELECTRICALS

[illegible]

ENGINEERING

[illegible]

ENGINEERING – Contd

[illegible]

FOOD, GROCERIES, ETC

[illegible]

HOTELS AND CATERERS

[illegible]

INDUSTRIALS (Miscel.)

[illegible]

INDUSTRIALS (Miscel.) – Contd

[illegible]

INDUSTRIALS (Miscel.) – Contd.

[illegible]

INSURANCES

[illegible]

2 The London Share Information Service

It is hardly possible to refer to the FT at all without referring to the pages of share prices which dominate the back half of the paper. Indeed, the lists of share prices provided the FT's chief *raison d'être* when it was first published. For many readers these lists still do, and 'the price in the FT' is often referred to in the City as if it were an official source. This is at least half true. The FT share prices are often taken as an official source for probate purposes, for example. But for workaday purposes, the FT prices are just the reported prices from the previous day's trading session. No stock market trader is required to deal at any price just because it has been printed in a newspaper. However, the FT share prices coverage is much wider than any of its rivals. Around 3,000 stocks are quoted daily, providing just about all the active sectors of the market. There is exhaustive coverage of daily prices in the British Government bond sector (see Chapter 4). There is a substantial list of unit trust prices in the paper, sub-divided into Authorised Unit Trusts, Insurance and property bonds and Offshore and Overseas Funds. And, as securities trading becomes increasingly global in scope, the FT carries an ever widening range of share prices from other world markets.

The heart of the share price coverage, the London Share Service, has undergone a transformation since October 1986 when the London Stock Exchange changed its entire trading system. Among its other provisions, Big Bang set up an electronic market-place where electronic screens replaced the trading stands of the traditional Stock Exchange. In fact, the rapid depopulation of the old trading floor proved to be the first and most dramatic outcome of Big Bang. This posed a problem for the FT, whose reporters had traditionally collected the share prices directly from the old-style trading stands. Now, the FT collects its daily share prices directly from the Stock Exchange electronic network. This means that the FT prices are a very accurate reproduction of the business transacted on the stock market. Since it does not need a constant flow of prices, the FT takes a prices sample three times a day, culminating in the closing prices which are taken when the Stock Exchange Automated Quotations network closes down, and are the prices published in the newspaper.

The FT divides its share prices into the different sectors of the market, making it easier for readers to find a specific share and to compare it with other stocks operating in the same business and therefore likely to respond to similar factors. With so many stocks quoted, an alphabetical list would be impossibly unwieldy. The table below shows the full range of information which the FT offers on each share price. Reading from the left:

1) High and low of the share for the year. A switch is made to the new year around April — from January to April, the data spans fifteen months or so. This is useful information. There is all the difference in the world between a price holding steady at the

LONDON SH

TIMBER, ROADS — Contd

...k	Price	+ or –	Div Net	C'vr	Y'ld Gr's	P/E
.0p........	115	+7	L2.7	2.2	3.2	19.2
t 10p.....	116	–4	R3.85	3.4	4.5	8.9
lliams....	229	–1	N9.5	2.3	5.7	12.8
....	108	....	6.75%	–	8.6	–
....	259	....	†h7.5	2.9	4.0	11.8
gs. 10p...	58	–3	h0.98	4.5	2.3	13.2
isen.........	132	–2	h3.0	3.9	3.1	10.3
Cpn.......	20	....	–	–	–	–
....	675	+25	♦†10.0	1.7	2.1	(34.5)
A$.50.......	73	–2	Q20%	2.1	5.4	8.9
s Pts. 10p	125	+3	d4.77	2.6	5.2	10.1
p. F100....	£119	+1	Q21%	♦	1.8	♦
)............	228	....	†h5.67	5.2	3.4	7.7
) £1.........	275	–5	h8.25	3.2	4.1	9.6
W.).........	92	–½	†4.0	2.6	6.0	8.9
nvRdPf £1.	125	+3	8½%	–	9.3	–
C.)...........	38½	....	–	–	–	–
lydeside.....	95	....	5.7	2.0	8.2	8.2
J.)...........	205	....	†h4.0	3.6	2.7	14.1
(Alfred).....	385	....	†14.5	3.0	5.2	9.5
Stone 20p.	385	....	†3.31	7.1	1.2	16.3
lin & H.....	185	+5	†7.0	2.1	5.2	12.4
....	170	–2	†6.0	2.5	4.9	11.1
Hldg).........	315	....	†10.0	2.1	4.3	15.2
....	140	–3	†4.1	2.0	4.0	16.4
Halifax......	263	–3	†6.25	2.5	3.3	16.7
(John) 20p	213	....	5.7	4.9	3.7	7.7
....	302xd	+3	†7.0	4.5	3.2	9.5
	59		1.25	1.1	2.9	41.0

DRAPERY AND STORES — Cont

1987 High	Low	Stock	Price	+ or –	Div Net	C'vr	Y'ld Gr's
220	105	T & S Stores 5p........	130	+5	†h1.75	4.0	1.8
267	140	Tibbet & Britten 5p..	190	+5	L3.5	2.8	2.5
201	92	Tie Rack 5p.............	112xd	....	L1.1	4.2	1.3
252	83	Time Prods. 10p.......	140xd	–1	†3.0	3.5	2.9
193	76	Tip Top 10p.............	80	....	2.0	1.0	3.4
*135	66	Top Value Inds 10p...	78	–2	2.5	3.4	4.4
264	109	Underwoods 10p.......	111	–1	2.5	2.5	3.1
*155	111½	Upton (E.)...............	75	....	–	–	–
228	95	✠Usher (Frank) 5p....	163	–2	†5.5	2.6	4.6
*302	114	Vivat Hldgs..............	167	–2	†gh2.5	4.4	2.1
437	257	Ward White.............	313	–3	†7.5	3.0	3.3
161½	99	Do Cnv Red Prf 10p	115	–2	6.0	–	7.1
275	73	Wassall (J. W.).........	100	....	1.0	1.9	1.4
355	255	Wickes.....................	265	–5	2.5	5.1	1.3
315	153	Wigfalls....................	178	–1	2.5	0.3	1.9
295	135	Wilding Off. Eqp. 10p...	175	–5	u3.25	2.3	2.5
142	68	Windsmoor 5p...........	85	....	2.0	4.3	3.2
215	80	✠Wooltons B'ware10p..	106	....	dR3.7	2.3	4.7
461	266	Woolworth Hldgs......	275	–12	†8.0	2.5	4.0
£206	£117½	Do. 8½pc Ln 2000..	£128½	–3	8½%	–	f6.
153	95	World of Leather 10p...	98	....	d3.0	3.3	4.

ELECTRICALS

High	Low	Stock	Price	+ or –	Div Net	C'vr	Y'ld Gr's
*486	284	AB Electronic..........	285	....	12.5	1.9	6
83	43	AMS Inds 5p...........	46	....	1.5	3.3	4
74	28	✠Acorn Cmptr 10p....	39	....	–	–	
180	113	Admiral Computing 5p..	113	....	u2.13	3.6	2
170	78	Alba 10p..................	87	....	L3.8	2.2	6
			275	–5	†2.5	6.4	

year's high and another price trying to struggle up from the year's low. Comparing the high/low with that of the relevant data in the FT-Actuaries Index is a useful exercise. Just one point to watch. If the company has made a scrip or rights issue over the year, then the high/low will have been adjusted and marked with an asterisk.

2) Title of the security and nominal value if other than 25p. Shares almost always trade substantially above face value. It is bad news if they fall below it because company law forbids the sale of new shares by the company below nominal value.

Against some names are symbols referring readers to the notes published at the end of the share price lists. These disclose

RE SERVICE

ENGINEERING – Contd

1987 High	Low	Stock	Price	+ or –	Div Net	C'vr	Y'ld Gr's	P/E
5	151	✠Atlas Conv Equ 5p..	223xd	+8	L4.9	2.6	3.0	17.6
8	48	Aurora10p................	63	....	†1.75	3.8	3.8	8.9
8	205	BM Group 10p..........	293	....	2.3	6.2	1.1	17.9
3	180	Babcock Intl............	280	....	♦8.7	2.2	4.3	(12.3)
1	15	Bailey (C. H.)..........	21	−1	–	–	–	♦
254	138	Banro Inds. 20p........	195	....	†h6.34	2.3	4.5	12.2
73	71	Beauford 10p............	100	....	†3.5	2.9	4.8	10.0
89	139½	Birmid Qualcast........	200	−2	†4.75	2.7	3.3	15.4
*278	140	Birmingham Mint......	140	....	g6.75	2.8	6.6	7.7
81	34½	Blackwood Hodge.....	40½	−1	†1.0	4.1	3.4	8.3
65	135	Booth Industries........	200	....	3.0	4.4	2.1	13.6
50	148	Braithwaite £1..........	205	−3	–	–	–	–
72½	15	Brasway 10p............	46	....	h0.67	3.7	2.0	18.4
45	6½	Bristol Ch.Ship10p....	12½	−½	–	–	–	27.3
190	72	Bromsgrove Inds 5p..	113xr	....	†1.65	3.3	2.0	20.6
34	23	Bronx Eng. 10p.........	34#	....	a0.3	0.7	1.2	–
66	26	Brooke Tool 5p.........	33	....	†1.45	2.3	6.0	10.0
545	335	Bullough 20p............	365	+5	†10.6	2.9	4.0	12.0
94	27½	C.I. 10p....................	40	−1	†1.05	2.7	3.6	13.9
260	88	Camford Eng.............	123	−2	2.5	3.6	2.8	12.7
210	87½	Carclo Eng. 5p..........	135	−2	3.75	2.6	3.8	13.7
200	101	Castings 10p.............	133	....	3.75	3.3	3.9	10.6
46½	14	Cauldon Group 5p......	19	....	–	–	–	–
176	98	Chamberlin & Hill.....	100	+2	4.0	2.8	5.5	8.7
895	583	Chemring Group 5p...	605	....	†16.5	2.3	3.7	15.6
182	114	Do.Cnv.Rd.Pf 5p......	115	−3	6.0	–	7.2	–
*139	23	Christy Hunt..............	53	−2	0.55	♦	1.4	♦
335	125	Clayton Son 50p........	225xd	−5	9.0	3.2	5.5	7.5
845	500	Cohen (A) 20p..........	500	....	†12.1	3.9	3.3	8.2
281	103	Concentric 10p..........	188xd	−2	6.5	♦	4.7	♦
*269	100	Cook (Wm.) 20p.......	100xd	....	5.0	2.0	6.8	8.7
			144	+3	2.35	♦	2.3	♦

INDUSTRIALS (Mis

1987 High	Low	Stock	Price
290	101	✠Airsprung Group 10p..	160
265	165	Alexander(W) 10p....	165
268	124	Alexandra W'kwear 10p...	155
£36⅛	£21½	Alfa-Laval AB'B'Sk50	£22
88	27	Allied Part. 5p..........	41
460	192	Alumasc....................	300
234½	118	Amari.......................	149
563	303	Amber Ind. 10p.........	315
150	60	✠Amer. Bus. Syst.5p.	75
*£36¾	£20½	Amer Group Free A...	£2
56	15	Anglo Nordic............	2
196	110	✠Antler 5p................	13
112	50	Arenson 10p.............	7
79	30	Armour Trust 10p.....	3
*128	28	Ashley Ind. Tst. 5p....	4
*21	5½	Assoc. Br. Eng. 1p....	
*960	243	Do. 8pcCumCvRdPf...	35
677	315	Assoc Brit Ports........	39
65	25	✠Assoc. Energy 5p....	2
£30¾	£16¼	Astra AB B Sk12½...	£
425	226	Avis Europe..............	2
885	363	Avon Rubber £1........	5
152	87	BAA..........................	
*249	109	BBA Group...............	1
311	197	BET..........................	2
		For BETEC see	
559	300	BOC Group...............	
109½	48½	BSG Int. 10p............	
448	242	BSS Group 20p.........	
374	228	BTR..........................	
625	190	BTR Nylex A$0.50....	
555	290	Baird (Wm.) £1........	

whether the company is involved in a merger or reorganization which could mean an impending change in the share price data. Alternatively, the symbol may indicate that the stock is not officially listed in the UK, or that it is listed on the USM (Unlisted Securities Market), discussed in Chapter 6.

3) The share price. This is the closing price, and will take account of any late dealings. Since Big Bang, when the stock market switched mostly to telephone dealing, late trading has become more difficult to track. However, the FT tries to do so, and will always change a price if the trading screens show very late deals.

The quoted price is a 'middle price', half-way between the buying and selling price made by the marketmaker. Once again, Big Bang has shifted the guidelines a little. Most major stocks are now quoted by a dozen or more marketmakers, so market prices can stray some distance from the FT middle price.

If trading in a share is suspended, usually because of the announcement of merger negotiations, the symbol beside the price will draw attention to the appropriate entry in the notes.

4) The change in the price measured against the FT quote for the previous trading session.

5) Rate of dividend paid in the latest year, expressed in pence per share and with tax deducted at the basic rate of income tax. Various symbols point to notes explaining further information on dividends. In particular, note that an increase in the half-time payment is sometimes regarded as a sign that the final dividend will also be raised.

Dividends are shown net of tax because companies usually declare them that way, subtracting the standard tax rate from each shareholder's payment. Individual shareholders paying less than standard rate income tax can then reclaim the excess from the Internal Revenue Department.

6) The number of times by which the dividend payment is covered by total profits after tax. Wise investors like to see a dividend well covered, since a thinly covered dividend might be cut next year if profits dip. On the other hand, a too heavily covered dividend indicates that cash is available somewhere in the company, and this could attract takeover predators.

7) Yield — gross.

The stock market is not interested in the tax situation of individual shareholders, so it wants to evaluate the shares on the basis of the gross dividend — what the board would have paid out if shareholders were left to pay their own tax.

To convert net dividend to gross on 27 p.c. basic rate, the following calculation applies:

$$\frac{\text{Net dividend in pence x 100}}{73} = \text{gross dividend.}$$

To calculate gross dividend yield, multiply the gross dividend in pence by 100 and divide by the share price. Gross dividend yield is one of the ways in which the stock market values a share. A high dividend yield suggests that the market perceives a high degree of risk to the company's business, either from political or from straightforward commercial factors. A low one means there are hopes of increased payouts in the not too distant future.

8) P/E — or price earnings ratio.
The manner in which the FT calculates company earnings will be outlined shortly. But, for now, the P/E, as this ratio is usually known by the City analysts, is simply the company's share price divided by its earnings per share for the latest twelve-month period. It is the major indicator of the market's view of the company. A high P/E — the share price racing ahead of earnings — shows that the market is confident of the company's prospects. Of course, such confidence can turn out to be misplaced.

P/E ratios were the favoured measuring-stick in the Sixties and early Seventies when the stock market reflected the generally buoyant attitudes of the rest of the British economy. Price/earnings ratios commonly moved above 30 — meaning that the market valued companies at thirty times their latest earnings. The value of P/Es to professional investors has, however, been somewhat reduced by changes in company taxation law which make tax provisions more subjective and less consistent in any particular market sector. The FT calculates P/E ratios on the basis of the stipulated accounting standard, SSAP 15. But some City analysts make assumptions about tax treatment, and this leads to variation in P/E quotations. If your broker's P/E for a company differs from the FT's then it may be his tax assumptions.

Before leaving the London Share Service, note that each Monday, when there is no previous day's session on which to base prices, two important changes are made in the price columns. In place of the high/low for the year, are printed the dates on which dividends are paid, and in the price-change column, is shown the last date on which the shares went ex dividend — the date at which the buyer had no right to the dividend payment.

UK companies are allowed to offset tax due on dividend distributions (Advance Corporation Tax) against their mainstream Corporation Tax. Ability to do so clearly depends on the amount of dividend they choose to pay, as well as on the Corporation Tax for which they are liable. Moreover, companies paying foreign taxes

LONDON SH

INTING—Continued

	Price	Last xd	Div Net	C'vr	Y'ld Gr's	P/E
ng 5p ...	96	29.6	dL2.45	1.2	3.5	(30.1)
)p	191	29.6	t4.0	2.7	2.9	17.7
Red.Pf.	110	—				
l	£22⅜	11.8	Q84c	—	2.3	—
)p	235	9'83	♦—	—	—	—
ttle 5p .	321	15.6	3.9	3.8	1.7	21.9
ations	106	14.9	a2.14	2.0	2.8	24.6
ael)	248	6.4	†2.6	2.4	1.4	40.5
....	572	24.8	†h12.14	2.2	2.9	18.0
'ref£1 ...	116½	23.2	6.3%	—	7.4	—
....	£10½	11.5	G5.75	Φ	0.8	Φ
....	£52⅝	25.8	Q$1.12	—	1.3	—
....	780	23.3	5.5	Φ	1.0	Φ
in) 10p..	83	—	u1.75	2.3	2.9	20.8
S.) 20p .	470	10.8	5.25	4.4	1.5	20.2
n.)	645	1.6	†Q22.2%	4.7	0.8	41.6
ng Servs.	106	23.3	1.8	Φ	2.4	Φ
ition 5p ..	52	—	0.29	4.0	0.8	44.2
. 5p	140	29.6	2.2	2.3	2.2	26.5
tising	204	22.12	2.0	3.7	1.3	27.2
oup 2½p.	79	27.7	1.17	2.1	2.0	19.8
r 10p	265	12.5	8.05	2.4	4.2	13.8
)	546	—	1.5	5.9	0.4	62.0
5p	388	27.7	3.13	4.3	1.1	24.6
10p	873	27.4	†g3.2	4.1	0.5	67.7
20p	325	10.8	Z1.0	—	0.4	69.8
(J.)	334	29.6	6.0	2.3	2.5	21.7
....	575xd	28.9	h6.5	2.3	1.5	38.6
-Lewis10p.	338	13.7	L4.0	Φ	1.6	Φ
ner 5p	275	13.7	2.1	4.6	1.0	28.3

TEXTILES—Cont.

Dividends Paid		Stock	Price	Last xd	Div Net	C'vr	Y'ld Gr's	P
Oct.	May	Corah	117xd	28.9	4.0	0.9	4.7	33
Jan.	July	Courtaulds	532	1.6	9.5	3.2	2.4	14
—		CoxMoore 10p	175	24.8	3.0	2.2	2.3	2
Aug	Nov	Crowther (J.)	216	14.9	†3.5	3.4	2.2	14
Feb.	Sept.	Dawson Intl.	341	13.7	6.9	2.6	2.8	1
Mar	Sept	Drummond Group	160	27.7	h2.47	4.1	2.1	1
Nov.	July	Early's of Witney 10p	150	11.5	1.32	3.6	1.2	2
Jan.	July	Foster (John)	140	1.6	3.5	0.9	3.4	(4
May	Nov.	Gaskell B'loom 20p	270	24.8	†6.0	2.9	3.0	1
July		Glen Abbey	255	16.6	Q30.8%	—	2.8	
—		Haggas (John) 10p	213	9.3	3.0	Φ	1.9	
Apr.	Nov.	Hicking Pentecost	85	2'83	—	—	—	
Jan	Aug	Ill'gworth M. 20p	218	13.7	4.0	Φ	2.5	
Nov.	May	Jerome (Hldgs.)	297	27.4	4.3	3.5	2.0	
July		K'ngsly & F'restr 20p.	77	15.6	3.04	1.3	5.4	
July	Dec	Kynoch (G & G)	340	29.6	3.0	5.2	1.2	
July	Dec	Lamont Hldgs 10p	400	1.6	5.5	3.5	1.9	
Jan.	July	Leeds Grp	360	1.6	†h5.21	3.2	2.0	
Jan	June	Lister	208	24.8	3.0	4.6	2.0	
Sept	Mar	Lowe (Robert H.)	238	24.8	†1.7	6.9	1.0	
Jan.	July	Lyles (S.) 20p	147	11.5	5.75	1.4	5.4	
May	Nov	Mackay Hugh	298xa	28.9	†5.5	2.2	2.5	
—		Munton Bros.	57	18.12	—	—	—	
Feb	July	Palma Group	95	11.5	†2.5	1.9	3.6	
Jan.	June	Parkland 'A'	243	1.6	5.0	2.8	2.8	
Dec	July	Readicut 5p	102½	1.6	2.18	2.7	2.9	
May	Feb.	Richards 10p	100	1.6	†1.9	2.1	2.6	
Mar.	Oct.	SEET 20p	201	14.9	5.3	Φ	3.9	
Jan	Oct	Sekers Int. 10p	165	10.8	2.65	4.7	2.2	
Jan.	May	Sirdar	155	23.3	5.15	1.4	4.7	
Jan	July	Smallshaw (R.) 10p	190	11.5	2.75	4.1	2.0	

have correspondingly less opportunity to offset against UK tax. This creates some uncertainty as to how company earnings should be interpreted. The FT uses what is called the 'net' distribution method in calculating P/E ratios. This implies taking the after tax profits in the company accounts, and adding net dividend cost plus retrentions and minus any unrelievable Advance Corporation Tax.

For dividend cover, the paper uses the 'maximum' distribution method, taxed profits plus the maximum amount of Advance Corporation Tax that could be offset against the tax bill if all profits were paid out as dividend. Unreal, perhaps, but this gives the best indication of the company's ability to pay dividends. And dividends must always be the shareholder's chief concern.

RE SERVICE

FINANCE, LAND—Cont.

Dividends Paid	Stock	Price	Last xd	Div Net	C'vr	Y'ld Gr's
ov July	Nth. Brit. Canadian	483	1.6	7.45	1.0	2.1
	Nth Scotland Inv 10p	34	13.7	0.25	Φ	1.0
ecember	North Sea Assets 50p	51#	11.11	—	—	—
an July	Nthn. American	486	1.6	5.4	0.7	1.5
ec. July	Northern Secs	359	15.6	2.7	1.1	1.0
pril	Pacific Assets Tst 50p	190	23.3	0.77	1.7	0.6
-	Do. Warrants	122	—	—	—	—
-	Paribas French Inv. Ts.	85	—	—	—	—
uly	Personal Assets 12½p	66	15.6	0.5	1.1	1.0
ugust	Plantation Trust	108	15.6	0.25	1.8	0.3
ovember	Precious Metals Tst.	311xd	28.9	0.55	Φ	0.2
—	Primadona	211	—	a2.25	5.1	5.5
ug. Feb.	Raeburn	583	29.6	t16.0	0.9	3.9
March	Rights & Iss. Cap	283	9.3	s0.2	—	—
—	River Merc Grd Prf5p	20½	—	—	—	—
Sept Dec Mar J	Do Inc 50p	121	24.8	K5.5	1.1	6.2
—	River & Mercantile Cap	119	—	—	—	—
Oct Jan Apr Ju	Do. Inc. 12½p	100	29.6	H5.67	—	7.8
—	Do. Warrants 12½p	44	—	—	—	—
July Oct	Do. Stepped Pref. 12½p	93	—	H4.2	—	6.2
Sept. Mar.	River Plate Def.	438	24.8	†9.0	1.0	2.8
April	Robeco (Br.) Fl10	£33¼	30.3	vQ27.2%	1.0	2.5
April	Do. Sub.Sh's Fl1	332	26.3	vQ27.2%	1.0	2.5
December	Rolinco NV Fl10	£32	2.12	vQ14.8%	1.0	1.4
December	....	320	2.12	vQ14.8%	1.0	1.4
Aug Apr	Romney Trust	453	27.7	5.0	0.8	1.5
—	Rorento NV Fl.10	£15⅜	—	—	—	—
Oct. April	St. Andrew Tst.	235	24.8	N3.85	1.1	2.2
Mar Aug	St David's Inv Tst Inc	106xd	28.9	7.1	Φ	9.2
—	Do. Cap	146	—	—	—	—
Dec June	SPLIT Inc. 10p	286	10.11	†19.11	Φ	9.2
—	SPLIT Cap 10p	835	—	—	—	—
—		232	15.6	3.6	Φ	2.1

OIL AND GAS—

Dividends Paid	Stock	Price
—	KCA Drilling 1p	34
—	♥Kenmare Oil Expln	56
—	Kingston Oil & Gas 50	128
—	♥Lennard Oil A$1	6½
June Oct	LASMO	378
Apr Oct	Do. "Ops" 10p	220xd
July Jan	Do. 9⅝pc CmRdPf £1	113
—	✠Lysander Pet. 5p	77
—	♥Magnet Group A 10c	4
—	‡‡Marinex 10p	40#
—	♥Meridian Oil NV	7½
—	♥Monarch Res 10cts	5½
—	✠Monument Oil 5p	23
—	‡‡Moray Firth 50p	15#
—	New London Oil 5p	52
June	Norsk Hydro Kr 25	£23
—	✠Nth Sea & Gen Inv	100
—	‡‡North West Expln.	46
—	♥Ohio Res.	23
May Nov	✠Oilfield Insp. Srvc.	48
—	‡‡Oliver Resources	68
—	Pan Pacific Pet.	10
—	♥Peko Oil	68
—	‡‡Pennine Res.	25
May Oct	Petrocon 12½p	145
—	♥Petrofina SA	£223
—	✠Petrogen Petroleum	31
—	♥Petroz 10c	4
—	✠Pict. Pet. 5p	74
—	Premier Cons.	71
—	Ranger Oil‖	32
Sept June	Royal Dutch Fl.10	£8
Oct May	♥Santos A0.25c	30
—	✠Sapphire Pet 50p	70

FT Unit Trust Information Service

The FT carries three pages of unit trust prices every day, which, like the London share prices, include valuable information for unit trustholders and for those seeking out investments in this sector. They are divided into Authorised Unit Trusts, Insurance trusts, Offshore and Overseas trusts, Money Market Funds and Money Market Bank Accounts.

Unit trust lists are made up of groups of trusts — or families as they are often called — operated under the same management. At the top of each group are the management address and telephone number. The advantage of having a range of trusts in the same family is that unit-holders can swap from one trust to another with usually minimal cost. The chief point to bear in mind is that all the information on these trusts is supplied to the newspaper by the trust managements every day, by telephone, telex or a similar electronic link. Any calculation involved is carried out by the trust management. The second point is that although these prices may resemble share prices, they are different in one significant aspect: there is no open market in the unit trusts, so the prices are calculated by the fund managers on the basis of a daily valuation of the fund's portfolio at stock market quoted prices.

To understand the unit trust price lists, turn to the beginning of the list (see opposite). Only here will you see the column headings which apply to the next several pages. After the name of the fund, is printed the bid price, at which the manager will buy your units, and the offer price at which he will sell. The next column carries the change in price on the day, and the final column the gross yield.

UNIT TRUST INFORMATIO

JTHORISED NIT TRUSTS

ey Unit Tst. Mngrs. (a)
oldenhurst Rd, Bournemouth — 0345 717373

	Bid Price	Offer Price	+ or −	Yield Gross
Income				
ican Income	38.2	40.8	(z)	6.42
& Fixed Int.	116.3	125.0	(z)	9.60
Inc Equity	107.3	114.7xd	(z)	4.80
dwide Bond	185.2	198.0xd	(z)	4.90
tal Growth				
rican Growth	120.8	129.1	(z)	1.80
n Pacific	52.9	56.5	(z)	1.73
ts & Earnings Tst	125.5	134.2xd	(z)	1.75
tal Reserve	76.4	76.9	(z)	1.31
modity & Energy	89.8	96.0	(z)	0.00
opean Capital	62.5	66.8	(z)	1.12
eral	133.6	142.8	(z)	3.15
an	75.5	80.7xd	(z)	0.00
stertrust	64.8	69.2	(z)	4.29
Growth Acc Units	169.0	180.7	(z)	1.35
Growth Dist	115.9	123.9xd	(z)	1.82
. Emerging Co"s	34.6	37.0xd	(z)	0.00
ome & Growth	213.0	227.8xd	(z)	3.38
ical Growth	36.9	39.4	(z)	3.17

trust Management Ltd
Queens Terrace, Aberdeen AB9 1QJ — 0224 633070

	Bid Price	Offer Price	+ or −	Yield Gross
trust UK Growth Fd	27.6	29.3xd	−0.3	2.85
trust Nth Am Inc (z)	21.4	22.8xd	+0.2	3.86
trust World Gth Fd	34.2	36.4xd	+0.5	1.02
trust Extra Inc Fd	34.9	37.1	......	6.20

Etna Unit Trusts Ltd (a)(b)(c)
01 St John St, London EC1V 4QE — 01-837 6494

	Bid Price	Offer Price	+ or −	Yield Gross
uropean Growth	100.3	106.8	+2.2	1.19
xempt	332.9	354.9xd	+0.6	5.37
Accum Units)	799.0	851.8	+1.4	5.37
ar Eastern	170.7	182.4	+1.9	0.10
Accum. Units)	184.6	197.2	+2.1	0.10
in & Property	72.1	76.4	−0.3	2.84
Accum. Units)	115.6	122.5	−0.4	2.84
igh Yield	64.8	68.6xd	+0.1	5.47
Accum. Units)	150.4	159.3	+0.3	5.47
berian Growth	50.0	50.0	......	–
Income	267.6	283.5	+0.2	5.02
(Accum Units)	867.2	918.6	+0.9	5.02
Intl Earnings	161.0	170.6	–	3.20
(Accum. Units)	239.2	253.4	–	3.20
International Growth	79.3	84.4	+0.5	0.24
(Accum. Units)	83.2	88.6	+0.6	0.24
Japan Growth (Acc)	125.3	133.7	+2.1	0.20
Nth American Growth	108.3	115.8	+0.9	2.62
(Accum Units)	126.2	135.0	+1.2	2.62
Preference	122.6	129.9xd	+0.2	9.65
(Accum Units)	355.6	376.7	+0.7	9.65
Smaller Cos.	252.0	266.9	+0.8	1.80
(Accum Units)	342.9	363.2	+1.1	1.80
Smaller Cos. Div.	80.5	85.3	+0.1	4.49
(Accum Units)	97.3	103.1	+0.2	4.49
	117.2	124.2xd	+0.9	1.62

Burrage Unit Trust Mngmnt Ltd
117 Fenchurch St, London EC3M 5AL. — 01-480 7216

	Bid Price	Offer Price	+ or −	Yield Gross
Short Dtd Gilt & FI	51.0	51.2	......	1.47

CCL Unit Trusts Limited
74, Shepherds Bush Green, Ldn, W12 85D — 01-740 7070

	Bid Price	Offer Price	+ or −	Yield Gross
UK General Trust	39.6	42.3	......	–
Global Trust	34.1	36.5	......	–

CS Fund Managers Limited
125 High Holborn, London WC1V 6PY — 01-242 1148

	Bid Price	Offer Price	+ or −	Yield Gross
CS America Fd	37.7	40.1	+0.3	1.26
CS International Fund	40.4	43.0xd	–	2.64
CS Japan Fund	90.5	96.3	+1.3	0.53
CS Portfolio Inv. Fd.	55.2	58.7xd	+0.6	3.40

Canada Life Unit Trust Mngrs. Ltd
2-6 High St, Potters Bar, Herts — 0707 5112

	Bid Price	Offer Price	+ or −	Yield Gross
Can. Gen. Dist.	113.7	119.7	−0.7	2.7
Do. Gen. Accum	182.8	192.5	−1.2	2.7
Do. Income Dist.	81.5	85.8xd	−0.3	5.1
Do. Inc. Accum.	175.8	185.0	−0.8	5.1
Gilt & Fxd. Int. Trust	39.4	41.5	−0.1	0.0

Cannon Fund Managers Ltd
1 Olympic Way, Wembley, HA9 0NB
01-902 8876. — Dealing: 0800 2826

	Bid Price	Offer Price	+ or −	Yield Gross
Growth	28.5	30.9	+0.7	2.
Income	35.7	38.7	+0.4	4.
Far East	22.6	24.5	+0.3	0.
North American	23.5	25.4	+0.6	0.
Global	37.6	40.7	+0.7	0.
European	37.1	40.2	+1.2	1.
Japan	67.4	72.9xd	+0.4	0.
Intl Currency Bond	45.6	48.3	+0.1	6.

Capel (James) Mngt. Ltd
PO Box 551, 6, Bevis Marks, EC3A — 01-621 0

	Bid Price	Offer Price	+ or −	Yield Gross
Capital	348.2	370.5	−1.4	1
Income	310.0	329.8	......	4
North American (z)	204.6	217.7	+3.9	2

Capital House Unit Trust Mngrs
Capital House, Festival Square, Edinburgh.
031-228 4477 Dealing 0800 833561

	Bid Price	Offer Price	+ or −	Yield Gross
European Growth Tst(z)	17.9	19.0	+0.3	
Income & Growth Tst	17.4	18.5	−0.1	
Intnl Growth Tst(z)	17.7	18.8	+0.3	
Japan Growth Tst(z)	18.4	19.5	+0.4	
N. Amer Growth Tst(z)	17.8	18.9	+0.2	
UK Growth Tst	17.0	18.0	–	

Cent. Bd. of Fin. of Church of England‡‡
2 Fore Street, London EC2Y 5AQ — 01-588

	Bid Price	Offer Price	+ or −	Yield Gross
Inv Fund Oct 31		437.50		......
Fxd Int Secs Oct 31		145.20		......
Dep Fd Oct 31		100.00		......

Charinco/Charishare‡‡
33 King William Street, EC4R 9AS — 01-638

	Bid Price	Offer Price	+ or −	Yield Gross
Charinco Inc Nov 18		174.5		......
Charinco Acc Nov 18		601.5		......
Charishare Inc Nov 18		112.4		......
Charishare Acc Nov 18		114.6		......

Charities Official Invest. Fund‡‡
2 Fore Street, London EC2Y 5AQ — 01-588

LONDON STOCK EXCHANGE

Account Dealing Dates			
*First Dealings	Option Declarations	Last Dealings	Account Day
Oct 26	Nov 5	Nov 6	Nov 16
Nov 9	Nov 19	Nov 20	Nov 30
Nov 23	Dec 3	Dec 4	Dec 14

*New time dealings may take place from 9.00am two business days earlier.

Equities and bonds respond to concerted European moves to lower interest rates

INDICATIONS OF a concerted response by European countries to the US accord on reducing the Federal budget deficit strengthened the recovery in UK equity markets yesterday.

Interest rate reductions by the major countries of the European Monetary System (EMS), together with a call from Mr Nigel Lawson, UK Chancellor of the Exchequer, for co-ordinated policies and currency stabilisation by leading industrial nations, strengthened confidence that global economic tensions will be resolved.

Meanwhile, favourable views of the domestic economy were encouraged by the latest UK trade figures, which helped shares extend early gains.

Trading volume in equities picked up from its recent dismal levels, and a gain of more than 30 FT-SE points was consolidated at the close with the help of a firmer dollar and an early upswing on Wall Street. But London seemed unwilling to follow the New York market's early enthusiasm.

The final reading on the FT-SE 100 Index showed a net gain of 31.4 to 1689.1. The market opened quietly firm and chalked up most of its gain in the first half of the session.

Chartists noted that the market jibbed as it approached FT-SE 1700 — yesterday's peak was 1694.4. Some analysts, having identified a new market trading range of 1500 — 1700, are advising selling if the market pierces the top end of the band.

Hopes that UK base rates may follow the other European rates downwards were encouraged by the UK trade figures for October, with a $282m deficit on current account received favourably in the City.

However, the equity market, taking its cue from the London money markets, sensed that there will be no official pressure on domestic rates just yet. Interest rate sensitive sectors, including building stocks, remained subdued.

The clinching factor for UK rate policy may be the level of the pound against the German mark, suggested John Sams of Chase Manhattan's London office. While the pound remains comfortably short of DM 3.00, the UK authorities may choose to leave domestic rates alone.

The best gains came in those blue chip stocks which suffered most in the market shakeout. **Glaxo**, **ICI** and **Pisons** all moved up sharply in moderate trading. There was strong demand again for **Consolidated Goldfields**, as well as for **Vaal Reefs** and the other leading gold producers.

The improvement in the US dollar together with the cuts in European interest rates, brought a brighter tone in the Gilt-edged market and prices turned higher after a dull start.

By the end of the day, gains ranged to ⅝ or so at the longer end, with the mediums also in good form. There was not much retail interest, however, and it was left to the trading houses to provide the running.

Index-linked issues added a further ½ point or so, as the exhaustion of the longer dated tap stock bore witness to the demand for stock.

BPB Industries, the UK-based building materials producer, suffered a major setback, the share price dipping by some 25 pence to 248p following a Financial Times report of increasing competition in the UK plasterboard market. Already facing rivalry from the recently-established Redland-CSR joint venture, which has set its sights on achieving 30 per cent of the UK plasterboard market, BPB were dealt a further blow by news that Knauf, West Germany's biggest plasterboard manufacturer, is looking to set up a UK operation.

BPB is set to announce its mid-term profits tomorrow; brokers Wood Mackenzie expect profits of some £90m against the previous year half-year figure of £69.3m.

Allied-Lyons were temporarily blown off course by the decision to acquire the outstanding 49 per cent in its Canadian subsidiary, Hiram Walker-Gooderham. Immediately after the announcement the shares dipped to 330p as concern arose over the intended issue of Preference shares, convertible into ordinary at specified future dates, but a closer assessment of the complex cash and shares transaction brought a strong recovery to 342p, for a gain of 4 on the session.

When purchasing last year the 51 per cent stake in Hiram Walker, Allied-Lyons was granted an option to buy the remaining share capital. But the timing of the move caught the market by surprise yesterday. Allied-Lyons said the deal had been achieved with the co-operation of Olympia & York which, through its 88 per cent owned subsidiary GW Utilities, will retain a long-term interest in the UK group.

Clearing bank shares remained quietly firm, unworried by the suggestion that base rates may have to fall soon. Interest rates are no longer so dominating for bank profits, which now depend more on lending margins in a flexible loan market, and also on the increased importance of non-interest income.

Midland moved up sharply at first and retained the best gain of the day to close 8 up at 378p. **Barclays**, brushing off the trading outlook at BZW, its securities arm, edged higher. **Royal Bank of Scotland**, with results due on December 3, held steady, with some analysts suggesting that the Bank's tolerance of the Hongkong and Shanghai deal increases the chances of a bid for Royal Bank.

Among merchant banks, **Hambros** jumped 8 to 234p on news of a 46 per cent rise in interim profits, which benefited from its lack of exposure to securities marketmaking.

With the City still nervous over the implications for market trading firms of the setback in global securities markets, attention will focus today on the interim profits statement from **S.G. Warburg**, one of the big league in both UK equities and Gilts.

Wayne Gerry of Kleinwort Grieveson Securities comments that while Warburg's profit figures are expected to be very good, "everything prior to the now infamous crash of October '87 and the BP underwriting" is irrelevant to appraising investment banking operations.

The Building sector remained a relative backwater, sentiment not helped by news the BPB Industries may face increased competition in the plasterboard market and thoughts that a further base rate cut may still be some way off. The leaders did little more than mark time in very thin trading. **Blue Circle** settled a few pence cheaper at 338p, but **Tarmac** were a shade firmer at 219p and **Rugby** hardened to 210p. **Redland**, half-year figures due tomorrow, were static at 369p, but **Magnet** attracted good support in front of today's interim results and spurted 9 to 172p. **Vibroplant** were also in demand ahead of imminent figures and gained 65 to 555p in a restricted market.

Major dollar earner **ICI** staged a useful rally - the share price recently fell below £10 - and the close was ⅜ higher on the day at £10½. **Wardle Storeys**, still responding to good figures, rose 15 more to 525p while **Anchor Chemical**, sharply higher on Monday following the acquisition of a major stake and subsequent bid approach from Air Products and Chemicals, gained a further 28 to 603p as Anchor announced that had received further approaches. USM-quoted **Delmar** added a penny to 52p following the interim statement. **Amersham International** were 19 higher at 373p.

A circular from securities house Wood Mackenzie recommending a trio of stocks — **Burton, Dixons** and **Ratners**, gave added impetus to the Store sector. **Burton** moved steadily higher to close 6 up at 248p. **Dixons** put on 8 to 234p and **Ratners** gained a similar amount to 258p. **Next** were a few pence better at 265p, while **Coats Viyella** put on 13 to 265p. Elsewhere, **Alexon** attracted support ahead of next Monday's interim statement and closed 15 higher at 300p.

MK Electric soared 141p to 555p on the announcement of a 550p per share cash offer, which values the company at £260.5m, from RTZ. The latter, via market purchases yesterday, was able to increase its holding in MK to around 22 per cent. Prior to the announcement of its offer, RTZ purchased 14.6 per cent of the MK equity at 550p.

British Telecom attracted good support ahead of today's half-year figures and rose 7 to 232p and **GEC** firmed 4 to 174p. **Plessey** were also in demand and gained 12 to 146p, while **Thorn EMI**, currently favoured by Kleinwort Grieveson, put on 22 more to 548p. Thorn EMI is expected to announce the sale of its stake in Inmos in the near future after interest from four companies. **STC** made fresh progress to close 8 higher at 204p and **Racal Electronics** firmed 6 to 236p. **Ferranti** were 4 dearer at 81p and **Amstrad** 5 better at 118p.

News of Carclo Engineering's stake in Bridon sparked support for other potential takeover targets within the sector with **Birmid** adding 5 to 202p and **Delta** rising 13 to 210p. **Braithwaite** firmed 8 to 208p. **Powerscreen**, interim results due today, added 3 more to 123p.

Food Retailers enjoyed early support and prices made reasonable headway before settling a shade below the best in places. **ASDA-MFI** touched 169p prior to closing 4 dearer at 168p, but **J. Sainsbury**, after initial progress to 238p, eased back to close 4 cheaper on balance at 230p. **Argyll**, interim results due next Wednesday closed 2 cheaper at 186p, after 192p, while **Kwik Save** softened a couple of pence to 282p awaiting today's preliminary figures. Manufacturers attracted selective buying interest and **Hillsdown** were noteworthy for a gain of 8 at 256p. Old takeover favourite **Fitch Lovell** were again to the fore and put on 9 more at 277p, while **Bernard Matthews** picked up 5 at 114p.

Grand Metropolitan featured the Hotel sector, the shares rising steeply to close 11 higher at 405p on more favourable currency influences - the company has heavy US exposure - and also in response to a strong recommendation from Morgan Grenfell Securities; MGS consider the shares underrated and oversold. **Trusthouse Forte** eased a couple of pence to 204p in the absence of any worthwhile buying interest. THF has acquired Portuguese aircraft catering firm Mourao Don Costa Campos for and undisclosed sum.

International issues were again at the forefront of the advance among miscellaneous Industrials. **Glaxo** advanced steadily to close ⅜ higher at £11, while **Beecham** put on 15 to 453p for a two-day rise of 25½. **Fisons** gained 20 to 260p and **Reckitt and Colman** 7 to 714p, while **BTR** improved 4 to 266p. **Hanson Trust** added a penny to 131p on a turnover of some 6.2m shares. **Pilkington** continued to attract buyers ahead of the Japanese presentation and rose 7 more to 220p and **BET** firmed 12 to 228p following comment on the results. **Boots** attracted support at 230p, up 10.

Bridon were outstanding among secondary issues, the shares jumping 21 to 126p, after 128p, on confirmation that Carclo Engineering had acquired a 5 per cent stake in the company. Bridon, a long-standing takeover favourite, traded as high as 195p prior to the market collapse of a few weeks ago. **BAA** shed 8 to 100p on details of half-year profits much in line with market estimates. **Powell Duffryn's** preliminary profits exceeded market estimates, but the price slipped 5 to 315p. Good annual results boosted **Cosalt** 18 to 110p. **Erskine House** were a shade dearer at 189p.

Advertising Agencies featured **WPP**, up 30 at 390p after news that the $260m credit facility, arranged at the time of the bid for US agency JWT, had been replaced by a medium-term package at a substantially lower cost. Dollar considerations helped **Saatchi & Saatchi** rise 25 to 385p but record annual results were unable to move **TMD Advertising**, which closed unchanged at 186p.

Peachey, sharply higher on Monday as vague bid rumours resurfaced, enjoyed another speculative run yesterday and at one stage touched 365p before profit-taking prompted a late reaction which left the share price only 5 higher on balance at 345p. **Land Securities** were a quietly firm market and improved 5 to 445p prior to closing unchanged at 440p. **MEPC** improved to 433p before settling 5 off at 425p; the latter's annual results are due today and the market expects profits of around £80m for the full-year. **Slough Estates** were supported and rose 9 to 239p and **Mountleigh** revived with a gain of 5 at 145p. Buyers returned for **Helical Bar**, up a further 11 at 178p and **Property Partnerships** spurted 50 to 300p in a restricted market in belated response to the interim figures and confident statement. **Chase Property** firmed 5 to 220p following the interim figures.

Courtaulds attracted support in front of today's interim statement and closed 9 higher at 352p; half-year profits are expected to come out within the £95 to £100m band, although one optimistic analyst is reportedly going for £106m pre-tax. BZW are forecasting £98m. **Readicut** produced good interim figures yesterday, but the shares failed to respond and the price finished just a shade dearer at 78p; the board expect a satisfactory full-year outcome. **Tootal** were supported at 105p, up 8 and **John Crowther** firmed 5 to 110p. Speculative counter **Palma** gained 8 to 68p.

International stock **BAT Industries** moved up 9 to 448p among tobaccos. **Rothmans International**, interim results due tomorrow firmed 8 to 381p.

Oil shares were restrained by the apparent weakness in oil prices, which left traders free to concentrate on "special situations" as Philip Lambert of Kleinwort Grieveson commented. A bright feature was **Enterprise Oil**, which gained ground as the market wondered whether LASMO will return for more shares, after paying 230p for a further 2½ pc stake recently - or even whether LASMO itself will become a bid target of RTZ.

Among the leaders, switching out of **British Petroleum** and into **Shell** continued. The Kuwait Investment Office purchase of **BP "New"** shares masked the wish of institutions to lighten holdings in BP - but only temporarily. UK funds still believe that BP rates a one point yield premium over Shell because the latter is more vulnerable to crude price risk.

Investors turned to Overseas Traders on thoughts that if the equity market generally was attempting to establish a base then the sector was relatively inexpensive. **Lonrho** were additionally pushed higher by the stronger price for bullion and ended 12 up at 222p.

Traded option contracts totalled 26,131 comprising 17,558 calls and 8,573 puts. The **FTSE** contract attracted 487 calls and 497 puts. **Plessey** calls were active at 3,620 contracts with puts at 500. **Thorn EMI** registered 2,105 calls and just 5 puts. **Hanson Trust** calls totalled 606 and puts 1,546.

FINANCIAL TIMES STOCK INDICES

	Nov. 24	Nov. 23	Nov. 20	Nov. 19	Nov. 18	Year Ago	1987 High	1987 Low	Since Compilation High	Since Compilation Low
Government Secs	90.45	90.61	91.03	90.89	90.70	81.11	93.32 (8/5)	83.73 (19/10)	127.4 (9/1/35)	49.18 (3/1/75)
Fixed Interest	95.73	95.91	95.64	95.28	95.64	88.29	99.12 (15/6)	90.23 (2/1)	105.4 (28/11/47)	50.53 (3/1/75)
Ordinary ♦	1335.2	1309.4	1285.7	1289.9	1309.5	1270.4	1926.2 (16/7)	1232.0 (9/11)	1926.2 (16/7/87)	49.4 (26/6/40)
Gold Mines	312.3	293.0	287.2	296.9	285.5	295.2	497.5 (4/8)	261.6 (6/11)	734.7 (15/2/83)	43.5 (26/10/71)
Ord. Div. Yield	4.64	4.73	4.82	4.80	4.73	4.48				
Earnings Yld. % (full)	11.47	11.71	11.95	11.86	11.70	10.36				
P/E Ratio (net)(*)	10.66	10.43	10.25	10.30	10.45	11.81				
SEAQ Bargains (5pm)	24,801	24,205	28,924	22,180	24,702	25,600				
Equity Turnover (£m)	-	674.89	903.81	888.79	1818.04	985.16				
Equity Bargains	-	27,515	30,167	25,130	29,735	37,536				
Shares Traded (ml)	-	349.0	481.4	497.9	646.5	370.5				

S.E. ACTIVITY — Indices	Nov. 23	Nov. 20
Gilt Edged Bargains	121.5	109.7
Equity Bargains	178.3	195.5
Equity Value	1364.1	1826.8
5-Day average		
Gilt Edged Bargains	116.6	115.1
Equity Bargains	185.0	202.2
Equity Value	2166.0	2419.3

♦ Opening	10 a.m.	11 a.m.	Noon	1 p.m.	2 p.m.	3 p.m.	4 p.m.
1308.7	1321.5	1328.3	1327.0	1334.5	1334.7	1337.7	1332.5

Day's High 1339.7 Day's low 1308.7

Basis 100 Govt. Secs 15/10/26, Fixed Int. 1928, Ordinary 1/7/35, Gold Mines 12/9/55, S E Activity 1974. * Nil=10.51.

LONDON REPORT AND LATEST SHARE INDEX: TEL. 01-246 8026

NEW HIGHS AND LOWS FOR 1987

NEW HIGHS (1).
CHEMICALS (1) Anchor Chemicals
NEW LOWS (53).
AMERICANS (10) CANADIANS (8) BANKS (1) BREWERS (2) CHEMICALS (1) STORES (1) ELECTRICALS (6) ENGINEERING (2) FOODS (2) INDUSTRIALS (8) INSURANCE (1) LEISURE (2) MOTORS (1) PAPERS (1) TRUSTS (6) OILS (1) MINES (3) THIRD MARKET (1).

Traditional Options

- First dealings Oct 5
- Last dealings Oct 16
- Last declarations Jan 7
- For Settlement Jan 18

For rate indications see end of London Share Service

Stocks to attract money for the call included De La Rue, Bristol Channel Ship Repairers, M.Y. Holdings, Burndene Investments, Property Trust, MK Electric Grp, Eagle Trust, Consolidated Goldfields, Blacks Leisure, Dares Estates, Parkdale Holdings, Singer & Freidlander, Control Securities. No "puts" were arranged or "doubles" completed.

TRADING VOLUME IN MAJOR STOCKS

The following is based on trading volume for Alpha securities dealt through the SEAQ system yesterday until 5 pm.

Stock	Volume 000's	Stock	Volume 000's	Stock	Volume 000's
ASDA-MFI	2,100	English China Clays	794	Plessey	13,000
Allied-Lyons	6,800	Enterprise Oil	844	Prudential	1,900
Amstrad	1,900	Fisons	3,400	Racal	3,400
Argyll Group	6,600	Gen. Accident	626	Rank Org.	153
Assoc. Brit. Foods	637	Gen. Elect	4,200	RMC	156
BAA	3,200	Glaxo	2,400	RHM	400
BAT	3,500	Globe Investment	488	Reckitt & Col.	708
BET	2,200	Granada	423	Redland	916
BICC	1,000	Grand Met	3,800	Reed Intl	1,800
BOC	962	GUS A	348	Reuters	745
BPB Inds	2,000	Guardian R.E.	79	RTZ	3,370
BTR	1,800	GKN	626	Rolls-Royce	3,300
Barclays	1,300	Guinness	1,400	Rothmans	203
Bass	486	Hammerson	612	Rowntree	207
Beecham	4,600	Hanson Trust	6,300	Ryl Bank Scotland	649
Blue Arrow	5,100	Hawker Sidd	383	Royal Insurance	1,000
Blue Circle	283	Hillsdown Hldngs	2,000	STC	5,200
Boots	2,350	IMI	347	Saatchi & Saatchi	1,400
Brit. Airways	1,600	ICI	1,600	Sainsbury	3,000
Brit. Aero	806	Jaguar	1,600	Scott & Newcastle	425
Brit. & Comm.	403	Ladbroke	1,500	Sears	1,600
British Gas	11,000	Land Securities	1,100	Sedgwick	634
Britoil	2,850	Laporte	72	Shell Trans	785
BP	5,250	Legal & Gen.	717	Smith & Nephew	4,100
Brit. Telecom	4,800	Lloyds Bank	2,100	Standard Chart	232
Bunzl	324	LASMO	344	Storehouse	1,300
Burmah Oil	1,100	Lonrho	2,100	Sun Alliance	193
Burton	2,200	Lucas	801	T & N	593
Cable & Wire	3,100	MEPC	1,600	TSB	1,000
Cadbury Schwps	2,000	Marks & Spencer	4,900	Tarmac	1,100
Coats Viyella	2,200	Maxwell Comm.	497	Tesco	1,600
Comm. Union	327	Metal Box	350	Thorn EMI	3,400
Cons. Gold	1,300	Midland Bank	2,400	Trafalgar House	1,800
Cookson	730	NatWest Bank	1,800	T'house Forte	1,000
Courtaulds	2,300	Next	539	Ultramar	3,800
Dalgety	615	Northern Foods	543	Unilever	972
Dee Corpn	1,300	Pearson	55	United Biscuits	946
Dixons Group	1,500	Pearl Assurance	497	Wellcome	1,200
		P & O	512	Whitbread A	803
		Pilkington Bros	1,800	Woolworth	1,200

FT-ACTUARIES INDICES

These Indices are the joint compilation of the Financial Times, the Institute of Actuaries and the Faculty of Actuaries

EQUITY GROUPS & SUB-SECTIONS (Figures in parentheses show number of stocks per section)	Tue Nov 24 Index No.	Day's Change %	Est. Earnings Yield% (Max.)	Gross Div. Yield% (Act at 27%)	Est. P/E Ratio (Net)	xd adj. 1987 to date	Mon Nov 23 Index No.	Fri Nov 20 Index No.	Thu Nov 19 Index No.	Year ago (approx) Index No.
1 CAPITAL GOODS (213)	673.07	+1.5	10.47	4.24	12.01	19.71	662.84	647.72	654.09	672.94
2 Building Materials (30)	874.32	+0.2	10.79	4.21	11.59	23.87	872.77	852.77	863.49	827.34
3 Contracting, Construction (33)	1231.42	+0.8	10.12	4.05	13.21	34.54	1221.61	1211.73	1222.60	1138.82
4 Electricals (14)	1886.28	+3.9	9.68	4.93	13.47	64.72	1815.77	1805.31	1808.04	1713.27
5 Electronics (33)	1485.98	+2.8	10.73	3.41	12.20	36.02	1444.17	1391.52	1407.31	1472.48
6 Mechanical Engineering (60)	328.24	+1.8	11.25	4.94	11.19	11.92	322.48	318.92	321.05	373.95
8 Metals and Metal Forming (7)	392.71	+1.0	10.03	4.21	12.14	11.55	388.94	377.47	381.98	339.61
9 Motors (14)	240.89	+0.7	12.62	4.81	9.21	7.36	239.27	236.05	239.07	263.62
10 Other Industrial Materials (22)	1174.47	+1.5	8.89	4.42	13.45	37.40	1157.01	1131.29	1141.76	1196.78
21 CONSUMER GROUP (183)	991.88	+1.8	8.58	3.60	14.83	23.47	974.61	959.10	964.72	921.95
22 Brewers and Distillers (21)	924.94	+1.3	11.00	4.02	11.47	18.46	913.03	894.38	888.61	949.21
25 Food Manufacturing (23)	784.37	+1.8	9.65	4.07	13.40	22.49	770.55	760.65	764.71	718.00
26 Food Retailing (17)	2003.81	+0.1	7.60	2.97	17.36	40.77	2000.85	1977.21	1987.13	1816.14
27 Health and Household Products (10)	1784.19	+3.2	6.48	2.52	18.14	33.67	1728.83	1687.46	1686.61	1482.27
29 Leisure (30)	1054.15	+1.1	7.70	4.35	16.22	29.45	1042.95	1012.57	1034.40	955.30
31 Packaging & Paper (16)	455.30	+1.5	9.16	3.97	14.38	12.53	448.37	443.37	450.03	471.27
32 Publishing & Printing (15)	3161.11	+0.6	6.89	4.62	18.33	97.34	3142.54	3125.91	3129.30	2579.95
34 Stores (35)	829.94	+2.1	9.00	3.63	14.91	20.18	812.56	807.63	817.28	836.02
35 Textiles (16)	588.73	+3.6	10.69	3.93	10.82	15.46	568.45	550.46	566.81	539.68
40 OTHER GROUPS (87)	822.62	+2.2	10.62	4.34	11.72	21.23	805.21	791.41	796.59	786.64
41 Agencies (17)	969.46	+4.2	6.33	2.36	20.75	16.91	930.33	909.28	937.15	0.0
42 Chemicals (21)	992.91	+2.6	10.04	4.71	12.17	33.31	968.08	955.36	966.26	975.26
43 Conglomerates (13)	1090.61	+1.4	9.69	4.33	11.81	22.43	1075.19	1059.04	1064.62	0.0
45 Shipping and Transport (11)	1663.36	-0.3	10.23	4.95	12.82	56.73	1667.92	1640.21	1646.73	1808.12
47 Telephone Networks (2)	888.67	+2.9	11.41	4.55	11.69	18.98	864.02	844.11	846.24	779.98
48 Miscellaneous (23)	1151.34	+1.8	13.04	4.12	9.15	33.80	1130.89	1111.98	1117.52	1187.82
49 INDUSTRIAL GROUP (483)	870.43	+1.8	9.61	3.96	13.11	22.29	854.85	839.81	845.84	831.11
51 Oil & Gas (17)	1617.51	+2.2	10.27	6.08	12.00	65.74	1582.99	1547.15	1583.75	1420.74
59 500 SHARE INDEX (500)	933.75	+1.9	9.71	4.28	12.94	26.04	916.56	904.02	908.99	889.62
61 FINANCIAL GROUP (120)	600.55	+0.9	-	5.19	-	21.37	594.95	588.29	597.48	683.74
62 Banks (8)	613.73	+1.0	21.74	6.34	6.08	25.98	607.57	602.15	607.60	698.19
65 Insurance (Life) (8)	888.59	+0.4	-	5.18	-	32.56	884.73	868.08	885.83	848.68
66 Insurance (Composite) (7)	479.77	+0.4	-	5.74	-	20.16	477.86	474.48	474.07	442.01
67 Insurance (Brokers) (8)	794.01	+3.6	13.99	7.22	9.15	39.63	766.21	756.72	765.74	1246.98
68 Merchant Banks (11)	329.39	+2.1	-	4.27	-	8.77	322.68	320.06	329.51	354.84
69 Property (49)	889.64	+0.8	5.58	3.37	23.10	18.92	882.29	874.39	898.39	797.69
70 Other Financial (29)	371.08	+0.9	9.89	4.34	12.81	11.96	367.78	359.98	368.99	366.79
71 Investment Trusts (88)	787.11	+1.6	-	3.17	-	17.14	774.56	766.24	780.15	835.75
81 Mining Finance (2)	410.64	+7.9	11.07	4.16	10.17	12.77	380.62	364.13	370.56	332.42
91 Overseas Traders (10)	889.78	+3.0	10.22	5.49	11.46	37.00	863.67	838.70	847.43	768.19
99 ALL-SHARE INDEX (720)	844.66	+1.8	-	4.30	-	24.49	829.64	818.26	824.11	806.11

	Index No.	Day's Change	Day's High	Day's Low	Nov 23	Nov 20	Nov 19	Nov 18	Nov 17	Year ago
FT-SE 100 SHARE INDEX ♦	1689.1	+31.4	1694.4	1659.0	1657.7	1633.4	1659.1	1643.7	1660.1	1619.3

FIXED INTEREST

PRICE INDICES	Tue Nov 24	Day's change %	Mon Nov 23	xd adj. today	xd adj. 1987 to date
British Government					
1 5 years	124.22	+0.06	124.15	-	10.03
2 5-15 years	142.25	-0.15	142.46	-	12.14
3 Over 15 years	150.05	-0.43	150.69	-	12.41
4 Irredeemables	166.65	-1.31	168.86	-	13.38
5 All stocks	138.55	-0.14	138.75	-	11.56
Index-Linked					
6 5 years	124.69	-0.11	124.82	-	2.18
7 Over 5 years	116.57	+0.16	116.38	-	2.89
8 All stocks	117.07	+0.14	116.91	-	2.82
9 Debentures & Loans	118.86	-0.95	120.00	-	10.46
10 Preference	85.50	+0.19	85.33	-	6.02

AVERAGE GROSS REDEMPTION YIELDS		Tue Nov 24	Mon Nov 23	Year ago (approx.)
British Government				
1 Low	5 years	8.48	8.49	9.95
2 Coupons	15 years	9.16	9.12	10.69
3	25 years	9.08	9.03	10.70
4 Medium	5 years	9.10	9.12	11.43
5 Coupons	15 years	9.37	9.31	11.07
6	25 years	9.30	9.19	10.69
7 High	5 years	9.15	9.16	11.52
8 Coupons	15 years	9.49	9.44	11.26
9	25 years	9.30	9.22	10.76
10 Irredeemables†		8.91	8.88	10.42
Index-Linked				
11 Inflation rate 5%	5yrs	2.99	2.95	3.63
12 Inflation rate 5%	Over 5 yrs	3.89	3.89	3.82
13 Inflation rate 10%	5 yrs	2.86	2.81	2.15
14 Inflation rate 10%	Over 5 yrs	3.94	3.95	3.65
15 Debs &	5 years	10.73	10.56	11.94
16 Loans	15 years	10.66	10.51	11.84
17	25 years	10.66	10.51	11.84
18 Preference†		10.61	10.63	11.80

♦Opening index 1659.0; 10 am 1673.0; 11 am 1681.4; Noon 1680.2; 1 pm 1689.0; 2 pm 1689.7; 3 pm 1692.5; 3.30 pm 1691.7; 4 pm 1685.7

† Flat yield. Highs and lows record, base dates, values and constituent changes are published in Saturday issues. A new list of constituents is available from the Publishers, The Financial Times, Bracken House, Cannon Street, London EC4P 4BY, price 15p, by post 32p.

NAME CHANGES: APV Baker is now APV.

LONDON TRADED OPTIONS

Option		Calls Jan.	Calls Apr.	Calls Jul.	Puts Jan.	Puts Apr.	Puts Jul.
Allied Lyons (*343)	300	55	67	78	13	17	22
	330	34	45	60	23	30	35
	360	18	28	40	37	45	50
Brit. Airways (*143)	130	25	33	38	10	14	18
	140	19	27	32	14	18	22
	160	9	17	23	24	28	33
Brit. & Comm. (*328)	300	43	65	75	20	30	45
	330	28	45	58	40	45	60
	360	15	25	45	60	75	80
B.P. (*254)	240	27	37	42	9	18	25
	260	15	25	35	20	25	35
	280	-	18	27	-	40	48
Bass (*788)	750	63	95	110	30	50	60
	800	40	62	83	58	73	85
	850	20	45	65	95	105	118
Cable & Wire (*304)	280	47	62	77	20	32	42
	300	33	50	65	32	45	54
	330	20	37	54	54	62	67
	360	12	27	40	72	80	87
Cons. Gold (*798)	700	155	170	185	40	60	85
	750	115	135	155	65	90	105
	800	80	105	130	90	120	140
Courtaulds (*354)	300	72	82	95	10	20	28
	330	47	63	75	20	32	40
	360	33	50	60	38	45	55
Com. Union (*299)	280	42	52	65	15	27	37
	300	32	42	55	25	43	53
	330	17	32	42	40	55	70
	360	10	20	30	67	80	90
British Gas (*132)	120	18	23	28	5	9	13
	130	11	18	22	10	16	19
	135	9	-	-	14	-	-
G.E.C. (*173)	160	25	35	40	8	13	17
	180	11	20	30	17	23	27
	200	6	13	20	32	37	45
G.K.N. (*272)	260	33	45	53	20	33	38
	280	22	35	43	30	45	50
	300	15	25	35	43	57	62
Grand Met. (*412)	360	68	78	90	8	17	25
	390	45	58	73	17	30	40
[illegible]							

Option		Calls Feb.	Calls May	Calls Aug.	Puts Feb.	Puts May	Puts Aug.
LASMO (*228)	200	48	58	65	17	25	33
	220	30	43	53	23	35	42
	240	22	32	42	38	45	52
P. & O. (*495)	450	90	105	-	13	17	-
	460	60	78	103	25	30	37
	500	43	58	75	45	52	65
Pilkington (*220)	180	52	65	-	12	20	-
	200	37	50	60	20	25	30
	220	25	37	45	27	35	40
Plessey (*146)	130	27	35	41	10	14	17
	140	22	30	35	15	20	25
	160	13	20	27	25	32	35
Prudential (*798)	750	95	125	-	40	65	-
	800	65	100	120	65	90	100
	850	45	75	95	105	120	135
Racal (*237)	200	50	58	-	10	11	-
	220	35	45	55	16	22	32
	240	25	35	43	26	32	42
R.T.Z. (*333)	280	75	90	-	22	37	-
	300	55	70	95	33	50	65
	330	35	50	70	50	75	90
	360	22	40	-	70	90	-
Vaal Reefs (*$105)	90	27	32	37	6	11	16
	100	19	24	30	12	16	22
	110	12	18	-	20	24	-

Option		Calls Dec.	Calls Mar.	Calls Jun.	Puts Dec.	Puts Mar.	Puts Jun.
Amstrad (*118)	100	25	32	37	7	13	15
	110	15	25	30	10	15	20
	120	10	20	27	14	20	25
Barclays (*450)	420	42	65	77	14	27	40
	460	17	40	58	33	50	60
	500	8	27	37	60	70	80
Beecham (*451)	420	50	75	90	15	30	43
	460	24	53	70	33	50	60
	500	10	35	55	60	72	85
Boots (*230)	220	20	33	40	13	18	23
	240	10	25	32	25	28	35
	260	4	17	22	40	45	50
[illegible]							

November 24 Total Contracts 26,131 Calls 17,558 Puts 8,573
FT-SE Index Calls 487 Puts 497
*Underlying security price.

RISES AND FALLS YESTERDAY

	Rises	Falls	Same
British Funds	69	35	11
Corporations, Dominion and Foreign Bonds	12	3	38
Industrials	572	271	722
Financial and Properties	234	106	291
Oils	47	21	43
Plantations	0	1	13
Mines	96	15	86
Others	108	60	88
Totals	1,138	512	1,292

LONDON RECENT ISSUES

EQUITIES

Issue Price p	Amount Paid up	Latest Renunc. date	1987 High	1987 Low	Stock	Closing Price p	+ or -	Net Div.	Times Covrd	Gross Yield	P.E. Ratio
-	F.P.	23/10	27	13	Atlantic Assets Wrrnts	13	-1	-	-	-	-
§105	F.P.	6/11	160	71	♦Bacon Homes 10p	73		R2.6	2.9	4.9	9.6
330	120	-	88	75	British Petroleum	80½	+1½	N12.5	1.5	5.9	14.4
§18	F.P.	26/11	27	18	♦Chartsearch 1p	26	+½	R0.44	3.0	2.3	13.1
100	F.P.	-	121	103	♦Co. of Designers 5p	111	+5	R3.0	2.2	3.7	13.4
10	F.P.	11/12	14½	5	EFM Dragon Trust 5p	6½	+1	-	-	-	-
†	F.P.	-	268	235	English & Caledonian Inv.	235		-	-	-	-
74	F.P.	9/12	81	74½	♦Fairway (London)5p	78	+2	R2.5	1.8	4.4	13.8
-	F.P.	-	67	26	First Spanish I.T. Wrrnts	26	-2	-	-	-	-
-	F.P.	-	104	70	Hadeo MacLellan 20p	77	-1	1.9	1.5	3.2	-
†	F.P.	-	152	100	Hard Rock Intl. 2p	137	+4	L1.53	3.3	1.5	24.2
†	F.P.	-	125	97	Do 'A' (Restricted Vtg)2p	102	+2	L1.53	3.3	2.1	17.8
-	F.P.	23/10	23	12	Independent Inv. Wrrnts	14		-	-	-	-
§80	F.P.	-	148	81	ISA Intl. 5p	93		R1.17	4.0	1.7	19.7
§60	F.P.	-	82	43	*Kemp (P.E.) 5p	43		-	-	-	8.1
§70	F.P.	-	103	100	*M.L. Laboratories 1p	103		-	-	-	-
§115	F.P.	-	128	65	♦Marcol 5p	65	-3	L2.3	2.1	4.8	13.8
257	F.P.	-	98	55	Moorgate Inv. Wrrnts	55		-	-	-	-
§100	F.P.	-	108	101	New Guernsey Securities	101		-	-	-	-
$10.50	F.P.	-	$21¼	59	Portugal Fund $0.01	$9¼		-	-	-	-
§110	F.P.	20/11	111	71	Power Corp.Ir.£0.01	71	-1	Q36.9	2.5	4.7	9.6
145	F.P.	-	48	46	*Propeller 1p	46		W	-	-	14.4
§86	F.P.	-	90	65	Record Hldgs. 5p	65		R2.0	3.2	4.2	10.2
250	F.P.	12/12	317	138	♦Stanhope Prop.	140		-	-	-	-
§114	F.P.	-	121	115	♦Sykes Pickavant 10p	118		R5.25	2.0	6.1	11.1
§20	F.P.	21/12	26	20	♦Tabular Exhibitions	23	+1	-	-	-	-
§87	F.P.	9/11	88	58	♦URS Intl. $0.01	58		R4.75	1.9	4.5	11.6
§60	F.P.	-	93	73	♦WSP Hldgs. 5p	73		R1.5	3.0	3.9	17.9
†	F.P.	25/11	30	16	Wilshaw Securities	24	+1	-	-	-	-

FIXED INTEREST STOCKS

Issue Price £	Amount Paid up	Latest Renunc. Date	1987 High	1987 Low	Stock	Closing Price £	+ or -
§	F.P.	-	75p	70p	*Abaticot 5¼pc. Cm.Cv.Rd.Pf.2006	70p	-5
-	-	-	95½	90½	Ambacher(H.)9pc.Cnv.Sub.Ln.1995	92½	
100	£10	21/1	14	10¾	Chester Wtr. Wks. 11¾pc Rd.Db.98/2000	11¾	
100p	F.P.	-	87p	63p	Helical Bar 5¾pc. Cnv.Cum.Red.Pf.2012	63p	-8
-	F.P.	-	101⅝	99¼	N'wide Anglia 10⅞pc 12.9.88	101⅞	
-	F.P.	-	101⅛	99½	Do. 10⅝pc 26.9.88	101	
-	F.P.	-	101⅛	100⅝	Do. 10⅞pc 31.10.88	100⅝	
-	F.P.	-	99⅝	99⅝	Do. 9⅛pc 20.11.88	99⅝	
§	F.P.	-	109½	99½	Next 5⅜pc Cnv. 2003	103½p	+1¾
§100	F.P.	-	115p	113p	Record Hldgs. 10pc Cum. Red. Prf. £1	114p	
100	F.P.	-	95p	73p	♦Shield Grp. 5.84pc Cnv. Cum. Red. Pf.	73p	
-	F.P.	13/11	80p	70p	Utd. Scientific 5½pc Cum. N-V. Pref.	80p	+2

RIGHTS OFFERS

Issue Price p	Amount Paid up	Latest Renunc. Date	1987 High	1987 Low	Stock	Closing Price p	+ or -
80	Nil	30/11	2½pm	¼pm	♦Clypsoam 5p	¼pm	
30	Nil	16/12	13pm	11pm	♦Compsoft Hldgs 5p	11pm	
30	Nil	20/11	¼pm	¼pm	Eagle Trust 5p	¼pm	
45	Nil	30/11	5pm	2½pm	Firmac Agric 5p	5pm	
80	Nil	-	44pm	27pm	Pres. Tours	24pm	+3
260	Nil	27/11	¼pm	¼pm	Securiguard Group 5p	¼pm	

[illegible] ... issued in connection with reorganisation merger or takeover. ‖ Allotment price. ◆ Unlisted securities market. ◆ Official London listing. □ Including warrants subscription. * Third Market.

3 Trading on the Stock Market

The *Financial Times*' indices, and even the lists of share prices, are only the outward symbols of the reality that lies at the heart of the investment business and of much of the FT's coverage — the London Stock Exchange, or the International Stock Exchange as it is now called.

The indices, valuable though they are for quickly pinning down the direction in which the market is travelling on one particular day, or in one particular hour, leave a great deal unsaid about the performance of the great mass of shares and fixed interest issues available for investment.

The FT Ordinary Share Index and the 'Footsie' are based upon a small proportion of the 3,000 or so shares traded in the market. A glance at those lengthy share price lists at the back of the paper will show that, even on a busy day, many shares do not follow the same trend as the major company stocks which make up the Ordinary and Footsie indices. Indeed, many will make no move at all on a day when the indices, and the newspaper headlines, suggest dramatic changes. This is a reminder that the Stock Exchange is still essentially a market-place, notwithstanding the introduction of expensive electronic gadgetry and high-powered research into economic trends. For the reality behind the share prices, readers need the FT's daily report on the UK securities markets.

The London Stock Exchange report, a daily half-page feature, provides the lead into the lists of unit trust and share prices. On the same page is published a range of tabular information all relevant to the day's trading in the markets.

To concentrate, however, on the report itself. As the headline usually spells out, the report is something of a hybrid, in that it covers both the equity and the British Government bond markets. And there is one factor in both market sectors to be borne in mind. British-based investors, be they private individuals or big institutions, are by no means the only active players in the London markets. Virtually all the major US, Far Eastern and European investment houses are active in London now. Some foreign houses are permitted a great deal of independence from their own headquarters back home — some rather less so. Most of them are managing funds drawn from outside the UK, and are sensitive to global movements in interest rates or currencies, as well as to trends in the other major world stock markets. So, do not interpret the title 'London Stock Exchange report' too literally, although the first item in the FT market report is a domestic one, and no less significant for being so. At the top of the first column in the report is a table of Account Dealing Dates for the London Exchange. These apply to the equity market only. Since it would be difficult to keep track of accounts payments in a market involving thousands of private clients, the Exchange operates on a system which requires all participants to settle their dues on the same day. This is the basis of the often quoted 'Stock Exchange Account', which usually last for a fortnight, but is often extended to three weeks to cover a Christmas or holiday period.

The table at the head of the market report shows the date when the account commenced ('First Dealings') and the day it ends ('Last Dealings'). No matter how many times an investor trades within those dates, it is on the last day of the account that the line is drawn in the ledgers of the market firms, and all bargains for that account must be settled. Since it would be impossible to deliver all the money and share certificates at the same moment, there is then a gap of ten days or so before Account Day — or Settlement Day as it is more grimly known — after which non-payers are technically 'in default' and probably in trouble.

Settlement Day can be a day to watch in bad times, because it can sometimes be followed closely by a 'hammering', when a trading firm unable to meet its 'obligations' is struck off the Exchange list. In the new electronic market-place, an electric bell has replaced the gavel which heralded the reading of a default announcement. A major hammering was always serious news for the market because the defaulting firm left debts to other market firms which might or might not be paid in full. So rumours of 'Settlement problems' can affect trading in shares, and the professionals keep an eye on the market calendar. The last batch of significant hammerings in the London market came in the mid-Seventies when the collapse of the secondary banking and property sector caused huge losses in the stock market.

Alarm has been triggered by more recent rumours of Settlement problems which have followed the substantial increase in market turnover since Big Bang in October 1986. The combination of rapid

Account Dealing Dates

*First Dealings	Option Declarations	Last Dealings	Account Day
Oct 26	Nov 5	Nov 6	Nov 16
Nov 9	Nov 19	Nov 20	Nov 30
Nov 23	Dec 3	Dec 4	Dec 14

*New time dealings may take place from 9.00am two business days earlier.

electronic trading in the big blue chip stocks with the rush of small bargains in the newly-privatized issues has presented many smaller firms — and some larger ones — with problems in tracking down bargains and delivering documents. Settlement problems tend to come and go as market fortunes rise and fall. But the FT market report, like many others, often refers to the more mundane effects on market trading of the account system.

The 'professional market', which means the marketmaking firms, brokers to particular companies, or just canny traders who follow particular stocks, will always scan the Account calendar to see if there is 'anything due'. 'Anything' can range from official statistics on, for example, the UK trade balance or money supply, to more specific factors, such as the announcement of profits and dividends by a company in which they hold shares. The big economic numbers can cause a significant movement in the market as a whole, while the implication of the trading results for a company's share price speaks for itself. The opening of a new account often brings mysterious movements in share prices which become much less mysterious after a glance at the FT list of Board-Meetings due (Chapter 5).

The professional traders are sometimes nervous at the beginning of a three-week account. Too many unforeseen developments can occur in three weeks, so share purchases or sales may be postponed. But even the conventional two-week trading account imposes its own rhythm on the markets. As the end of the account approaches, fund managers may find it necessary to shuffle their trading portfolios. Shares which were bought ahead of the annual profits statement from the company may be sold now that the news is out of the way. If a share has done well over the account but does not suit the fund's long-term portfolio, then the manager may take his profits.

More generally, if the market has risen very strongly over the account, then there may be many opportunities to take profits, so the last day may well see shares slipping lower. On the other hand, if prices have fallen heavily, then some professional traders will have sold stock they do not hold, and will be obliged to buy shares before the account ends.

As the FT market-report table indicates, however, the dealings for the new account can begin before the old one formally closes. From 9.00 am on the last two trading days, investors can, by paying a small premium on share prices, deal for the next account — that is to say, without settling until the end of the next account. Moreover, the new account begins, not on Monday morning, but at 3.30 pm on the last day of the 'last dealings' date for the old account.

The FT market report sets out to outline the factors underlying the market trends in the session, and to draw attention to significant share movements. Not every one of the 3,000 or so shares on the UK Exchanges will be quoted every day, nor will every single share change be quoted. Some shares trade only rarely, and many shares will move in line with the market. The aim of the market report is to quote those share changes which have significance for the rest of the market, which reflect specific developments at the company concerned, or changes in the market's views on any specific share.

The opening paragraphs set the scene by relating movements in the equity market to any necessary developments in the Government bond markets, or in the other leading world markets.

The big investment institutions, which are the driving force behind securities markets, are constantly weighing the prospects for share prices in London both against those for Government bonds and also for share prices in New York, Tokyo, and the Continental markets. The FT market report will try to track the view taken by these big investors, both by reporting any advice they may give to their clients, but also by spotting where they are putting their money.

The institutions invest for the medium or long term, and confine their attentions to the blue chip stocks which are easily tradeable in fair times and foul. So, if a big investment house is putting £1m or more into one particular UK stock, then the rest of the market will take heed.

Trading interest in London in foreign stocks will be reported in the FT, although the main market in such a stock will inevitably be in its home country. While the same factors are likely to drive the stock price in London as at home base, investment funds will often spread their investment business over the global trading arena. By doing so they can take a substantial position in a stock on a single day, rather than moving from market to market and watching the share price move up ahead of them.

The market report then picks out major stocks in which there have been significant movement for reasons which may not be generally known outside the market. The stress is thrown on the Stock Exchange Alpha stocks, which largely coincide with the FT-SE 100 Index issues. These shares now represent around three-quarters of daily turnover, and are also the observation window for investors wanting to see what the major institutions are up to.

The report will disclose major deals in these blue chip stocks. Only the big funds have the money to shift million share blocks of Imperial Chemical Industries, Beecham, Glaxo and the like.

Sometimes the increase in business follows a recommendation by a leading brokerage house to its clients. Such information, usually backed by a forecast of profits, may not be available to the market at large until after the broker's clients have completed their business. But following the institutions' footsteps is an old stock market practice. Or a movement in a share price may reflect developments outside the stock market. Perhaps a US company is introducing a rival product; or perhaps a foreign court has ruled unfavourably on a new drug. Such information is quickly communicated to the City's trading rooms these days, and as quickly reflected in share prices.

Takeover bids (Chapter 6) are an obvious factor in moving share prices. The first news of a bid, the acquisition of significant stakes in the victim company, the movement of the shares relative to the bid terms, all these will be reported in the market report. And, of course, no market would be complete without its 'bid rumours', which often precede a formal announcement. This does not mean that stock traders are privy to 'inside' information. A company may be correctly identified as a takeover target by the City analysts because of its underperformance in the stock market, or its problems with its products, or its balance-sheet. It is not usually difficult to suggest a

Traditional Options

- **First dealings Oct 5**
- **Last dealings Oct 16**
- **Last declarations Jan 7**
- **For Settlement Jan 18**

For rate indications see end of London Share Service

Stocks to attract money for the call included **Minerals Oil & Resources,Shares Fund Inc, Burton Group, Sound Diffusion, John Crowther, GRP, Norfolk Cap, Tuskar Res, Rolls-Royce, Whim Creek, Ferranti, Aurora.** No "puts" were arranged or "doubles" completed".

potential bidder, and from then on the analysts will be watching like hawks for what looks like an opportune moment. If the target company's results turn out even worse than expected, or if the aggressor is balked of another prey — either factor can set the rumour mills working overtime. But the FT has to tread the difficult line between encouraging speculation and reporting it.

At the end of the report appear accounts of the day's activity in two of the ancillary markets which can affect trading on the stock market proper.

Traditional Options, the long-established conventional form of share option trading in London, have their own account period, whose dates are shown in the column (see above for an example). Investors can either buy a 'call' option, giving the right to buy the shares at that day's price over the account period, or a 'put', which bestows a similar right to sell. Once created, these options are not tradeable. Traditional Options are used by investors seeking to protect a profit in the underlying share over a strictly limited period.

Traditional Options have in the decade since introduction, rapidly expanded to become a major factor in the underlying share market, as has been the case in the US markets. Trading in options on a specific share has often been the first indication of a change of view towards the shares. For the market as a whole, trading in options on the FT-SE 100 Index can also affect movements in the underlying 100 stocks, sometimes bringing sharp changes in the trend of the index itself.

The market report will refer to the appearance of new companies in the quoted markets and to rights issues by existing companies. The details of these issues are also published daily in tables published on the same page. (See page 12).

LONDON TRADED OPTIONS

Option		CALLS			PUTS		
		Jan.	Apr.	Jul.	Jan.	Apr.	Jul.
Allied Lyons	300	55	67	78	13	17	22
(*343)	330	34	45	60	23	30	35
	360	18	28	40	37	45	50
Brit. Airways	130	25	33	38	10	14	18
(*143)	140	19	27	32	14	18	22
	160	9	17	23	24	28	33
Brit. & Comm.	300	43	65	75	20	30	45
(*328)	330	25	45	55	40	45	60
	360	15	25	45	60	75	80
B.P.	240	27	37	42	9	18	25
(*254)	260	15	25	35	20	25	35
	280	-	18	27	-	40	48
Bass	750	63	95	110	30	50	60
(*788)	800	40	62	83	58	73	85
	850	20	45	65	93	105	118
Cable & Wire	280	47	62	77	20	32	42
(*304)	300	33	50	65	32	40	54
	330	20	37	54	54	62	67
	360	12	27	40	72	80	87
Cons. Gold	700	155	170	185	40	60	85
(*798)	750	115	135	155	65	90	105
	800	80	105	130	90	120	140
Courtaulds	300	72	82	95	10	20	28
(*354)	330	47	63	75	20	32	40
	360	33	50	60	38	45	55
Com. Union	280	42	52	65	15	27	37
(*299)	300	32	42	55	25	43	53
	330	17	32	42	40	55	70
	360	10	20	30	67	80	90
British Gas	120	18	23	28	5	9	13
(*132)	130	11	18	22	10	16	19
	135	9	-	-	14	-	-
G.E.C.	160	25	35	40	8	13	17
(*173)	180	11	20	30	17	23	27
	200	6	13	20	32	37	43
G.K.N.	260	33	45	53	20	33	38
(*272)	280	22	35	43	30	45	50
	300	15	25	35	43	57	62
Grand Met.	360	68	78	90	8	17	25
(*412)	390	45	58	73	17	30	40
	420	27	43	55	30	40	50
I.C.I.	950	130	160	185	35	65	80
(*1038)	1000	95	135	160	53	90	105
	1050	70	105	135	77	115	130
Jaguar	280	45	58	70	18	32	37
(*305)	300	35	50	60	25	42	47
	330	23	37	45	45	58	62
	360	13	28	37	67	77	82
Land Securities	420	50	63	83	20	27	38
(*445)	460	25	48	63	40	50	58
	500	15	35	48	75	82	90
Marks & Spencer	180	22	30	38	14	16	20
(*186)	200	9	22	28	24	28	32
	220	4	14	20	40	44	46
Britoil	180	35	45	53	15	22	28
(*199)	200	25	35	43	25	35	42
	220	17	27	35	35	45	55
Rolls-Royce	110	12	20	25	12	16	19
(*112)	120	9	15	21	18	22	25
	130	6	12	18	25	29	32
Sainsbury	220	27	35	43	10	17	20
(*233)	240	15	25	31	18	25	30
	260	7	15	23	30	33	42
Shell Trans.	950	105	135	162	45	85	100
(*1003)	1000	75	110	138	67	110	125

Option		CALLS			PUTS		
		Feb.	May	Aug.	Feb.	May	Aug.
LASMO	200	48	58	65	17	25	33
(*228)	220	30	43	53	23	35	42
	240	22	32	42	38	45	52
P. & O.	420	90	105	-	13	17	-
(*495)	460	60	78	103	25	30	37
	500	43	58	75	45	52	65
Pilkington	180	52	65	-	12	20	-
(*220)	200	37	50	60	20	25	30
	220	25	37	45	27	35	40
Plessey	130	27	35	41	10	14	17
(*146)	140	22	30	35	15	20	25
	160	13	20	27	25	32	35
Prudential	750	95	125	-	40	65	-
(*798)	800	65	100	120	65	90	100
	850	45	75	95	105	120	135
Racal	200	50	58	-	10	11	-
(*237)	220	35	45	55	16	22	32
	240	25	35	43	26	32	42
R.T.Z.	280	75	90	-	22	37	-
(*333)	300	55	70	95	33	50	65
	330	35	50	70	50	75	90
	360	22	40	-	70	90	-
Vaal Reefs	90	27	32	37	6	11	16
(*$105)	100	19	24	30	12	16	22
	110	12	18	-	20	24	-

Option		Dec.	Mar.	Jun.	Dec.	Mar.	Jun.
Amstrad	100	25	32	37	7	13	15
(*118)	110	15	25	30	10	15	20
	120	10	20	27	14	20	25
Barclays	420	42	65	77	14	27	40
(*450)	460	17	40	55	33	50	60
	500	8	27	37	60	70	80
Beecham	420	50	75	90	15	30	43
(*451)	460	24	53	70	33	50	60
	500	10	35	55	60	72	85
Boots	220	20	33	40	13	18	23
(*230)	240	10	25	32	25	28	35
	260	4	17	22	40	43	50
BTR	240	35	45	52	8	15	22
(*265)	260	22	37	40	13	23	32
	280	11	27	30	25	35	42
Blue Circle	330	28	45	52	17	25	35
(*332)	350	18	-	-	28	-	-
	360	-	28	37	-	42	53
Dixons	220	25	40	48	10	17	22
(*234)	240	12	30	38	20	28	33
	260	5	18	28	35	43	45
Glaxo	1000	120	195	235	25	65	85
(*1096)	1050	90	165	210	45	85	110
	1100	60	140	190	65	110	130
	1150	38	120	165	90	145	155
Hanson	110	23	26	31	1½	5	8
(*131)	120	15	19	25	4	9	13
	130	8	13	20	8	13	18
Lonrho	200	30	38	47	10	17	25
(*223)	220	18	27	38	17	27	35
	236	10	-	-	28	-	-
Midland Bk	360	40	52	65	17	35	45
(*383)	390	20	35	50	30	47	60
	410	6	-	-	40	-	-
Sears	120	18	25	28	7	10	13
(*129)	130	10	18	23	11	16	20
	140	7	12	16	21	24	27

FT UNIT TRUST INFORMATION SERVICE

[illegible]

LONDON SHARE SERVICE

BRITISH FUNDS

1987 High	Low	Stock	Price £	+ or -	Yield Int.	Red.
		"Shorts" (Lives up to Five Years)				
[illegible]	[illegible]	[illegible]	[illegible]	[illegible]	[illegible]	[illegible]
		Five to Fifteen Years				
[illegible]	[illegible]	[illegible]	[illegible]	[illegible]	[illegible]	[illegible]
		Over Fifteen Years				
[illegible]	[illegible]	[illegible]	[illegible]	[illegible]	[illegible]	[illegible]

BRITISH FUNDS — Contd

1987 High	Low	Stock	Price £	+ or -	Yield Int.	Red.
		Undated				
[illegible]	[illegible]	[illegible]	[illegible]	[illegible]	[illegible]	[illegible]
		Index-Linked			(1)	(2)
[illegible]	[illegible]	[illegible]	[illegible]	[illegible]	[illegible]	[illegible]

[illegible]

INT. BANK AND O'SEAS GOVT STERLING ISSUES

[illegible]

CORPORATION LOANS

[illegible]

COMMONWEALTH & AFRICAN LOANS

[illegible]

LOANS

[illegible]

Public Board and Ind.

[illegible]

Financial

[illegible]

FOREIGN BONDS & RAILS

[illegible]

AMERICANS

[illegible]

Continued on next page

[illegible]

Money Market Trust Funds

[illegible]

Money Market Bank Accounts

[illegible]

4 The Government Securities Market

The Government bond — or Gilt-edged — market is often but quite unfairly ignored by the private investor, who is inclined to regard it as a powerful and potentially dangerous arena, inhabited by the big investment funds and patrolled by the Bank of England. Powerful it certainly is — daily business in British Government bonds invariably dwarfs that in the equity market — but its cardinal virtue is its safety: British Governments have always paid their debts, and their interest payments, on the due date.

If you think that Gilts are only for the big institutions, remember that English Literature, from Dickens to Somerset Maugham, was full of characters living comfortably on their income from 'the British Funds', as British Government bonds are still called in the *Financial Times*' prices pages. (See page 38.)

The length and complexity of the FT's list of British Funds indicates why a market in such bonds is necessary in the first place. The Government is a heavy borrower — in 1986 alone it raised £14.35bn in the market — and needs to spread its repayment commitments over a convenient time-scale. As the table shows, it will repay some loans in five years, some in fifteen years and more, and some (undated) loans have no set repayment or redemption date.

When Government borrowing is of such size and complexity, it is inevitable that a 'market' has become necessary. But the principle remains the same. A Government bond is a receipt for a loan to the Government and carries stated terms for repayment, either in terms of redemption dates, interest coupon or both. The FT lists of Government bond prices carry the basic information on trading activity in the market-place. From Tuesday to Saturday, the list shows, reading from the left, the high and low price of the bond for the year, the full name and maturity of the bond, the closing price on the previous day, the change on the day, and then two columns showing the interest yield and the redemption yield on the stock. Each Monday, when there is no previous day's session to report, the left-hand column gives the semi-annual interest payment dates and the price change column is omitted.

Prices: All UK Government bonds are in £100 lots, but price changes are quoted in the market in terms of 1/32 of £1. This is slightly confusing for investors but convenient for the traders because the fraction can easily be transformed into 1/4s, 1/8s, 1/16s or 1/2s of £1. The different names on the bonds — abbreviated to Treas, Exch, Funding etc. — have no significance for our purposes.

Redemption dates: Bonds mature, in other words are redeemed or repaid, in the year quoted, but at the precise date quoted when first issued — excluding the undated issues, of course. The percentage printed before the maturity date is the annual interest date, or 'coupon' on that stock.

A FT weekday list of Government bonds.

LONDON SHARE SERVICE

BRITISH FUNDS

"Shorts" (Lives up to Five Years)

1987 High	1987 Low	Stock	Price £	+ or -	Yield Int.	Yield Red.
99[illegible]	97[illegible]	Treas 7¾pc 1985-88‡‡	99[illegible]	......	7.76	8.29
102¼	99[illegible]	Exch 10½pc '88	100[illegible]xd	-[illegible]	10.42	8.64
101[illegible]	98[illegible]	Treas 9¾pc Cv '88	100[illegible]xd	......	9.70	8.70
98[illegible]	93[illegible]	Transport 3pc '78-88	97[illegible]xd	+[illegible]	3.07	6.84
[illegible]	98[illegible]	Treas. 9½pc '88	100[illegible]	-[illegible]	9.44	8.76
[illegible]	101[illegible]	Treas 11½pc 1989	102[illegible]	-[illegible]	11.18	8.89
[illegible]	97[illegible]	Treas 9½pc Cnv 1989	100[illegible]	-[illegible]	9.42	8.80
[illegible]	89¼	Treas 3pc 1989	95[illegible]xd	+[illegible]	3.14	6.12
[illegible]	99[illegible]	Treas 10½pc 1989	102[illegible]xd	-[illegible]	10.26	8.87
[illegible]	98½	Exch. 10pc 1989	101[illegible]	-[illegible]	9.85	8.96
[illegible]	100[illegible]	Exch 11pc 1989	103[illegible]	-[illegible]	10.64	8.92
[illegible]	89[illegible]	Treas 5pc 1986-89	95[illegible]	-[illegible]	5.23	7.51
[illegible]	99[illegible]	Exch 10¼pcCv '89	104[illegible]xd	-[illegible]	9.81	7.71
[illegible]	104[illegible]	Treas 13pc 1990‡‡	107[illegible]	-[illegible]	12.08	8.93
[illegible]	100[illegible]	Exch 11pc 1990‡‡	103[illegible]	-[illegible]	10.59	8.98
[illegible]	103[illegible]	Exch. 12½pc 1990	107[illegible]	-[illegible]	11.66	8.98
[illegible]	84½	Treas. 3pc 1990	91[illegible]xd	-[illegible]	3.26	6.59
[illegible]	93[illegible]	Treas 8¼pc 1987-90‡‡	99[illegible]xd	+[illegible]	8.33	8.69
[illegible]	97½	Treas. 10pcCv 1990	102[illegible]	-[illegible]	9.75	8.98
[illegible]	81[illegible]	Exch 2½pc 1990	89[illegible]xd	-[illegible]	2.80	6.49
[illegible]	102[illegible]	Treas 11¾pc 1991	107[illegible]	-[illegible]	10.97	9.03
[illegible]	87¼	Funding 5¾pc '87-91‡‡	93[illegible]xd	-[illegible]	6.15	7.97
[illegible]	80¼	Treas. 3pc 1991	88[illegible]xd	-[illegible]	3.38	6.67
[illegible]	98½	Treas 10pc Cv '91 ‡‡	104½	-[illegible]	9.56	8.47
[illegible]	101[illegible]	Exch. 11pc 1991	106[illegible]	-[illegible]	10.34	9.00
[illegible]	91[illegible]	Treas. 8pc 1991	96[illegible]xd	-¼	8.26	8.95
[illegible]	107[illegible]	Treas 12¾pc 1992‡‡	112[illegible]	-[illegible]	11.34	9.06
[illegible]	97[illegible]	Treas 10pc 1992	103[illegible]	-¼	9.69	9.03
[illegible]	90[illegible]	Treas. 8pc 1992 ‡‡	96[illegible]	-¼	8.28	8.92
[illegible]	99½	Treas 10½pc Cv 1992‡‡	105[illegible]xd	-[illegible]	[illegible]	[illegible]

BRITISH

U[illegible]

1987 High	1987 Low	Stock
45[illegible]	39[illegible]	Consols 4pc
41[illegible]	34[illegible]	War Loan 3½pc‡‡
52[illegible]	46½	Conv. 3½pc '61 Aft
34[illegible]	29[illegible]	Treas. 3pc '66 Aft.
29[illegible]	24[illegible]	Consols 2½pc
29[illegible]	24[illegible]	Treas. 2½pc

Index

1987 High	1987 Low	Stock
133[illegible]	125½	Treas. 2pc '88(297.[illegible]
119¼	108[illegible]	Do. 2pc '90(333.9)
101¼	93½	Do. 2pc '92‡‡ (38[illegible]
129[illegible]	119[illegible]	Do. 2pc '96(267.9)
111⅜	96⅝	Do 2½pc '01 (308.[illegible]
110	94⅛	Do. 2½pc '03(310.7
113[illegible]	94[illegible]	Do. 2pc '06(274.1)
108	89[illegible]	Do. 2½pc '09(310.7
113[illegible]	93[illegible]	Do. 2½pc '11(294.1
95[illegible]	76[illegible]	Do. 2½pc '13(351.9
103[illegible]	83⅜	Do. 2½pc '16(322.0
101[illegible]	81¾	Do. 2½pc '20 (327.3
86[illegible]	68[illegible]	Do. 2½pc '24 ‡‡(38[illegible]

Prospective real redemption rate and (2) 5%. (b) Figures in par indexing, ie 8 months prior to is and for August 1987: 102.1
(rebased at 100 January 19

Yields: These are the important entries because this is a market-place and any lender wants to know how much he can expect to get back from the borrower — even if it is the Government.

In fact, Government bonds must compete for investors' cash with a whole range of similar bonds issued by, for example, local authorities, foreign governments or any one of thousands of quoted public companies which want to raise money from the public. Moreover, they must compete with other institutions, like the Post Office or the Building Societies, which try to attract investment by offering competitive yields.

So, yields are the lifeblood of the Government bond market, and the professionals tend to talk about yields rather than prices, because

An FT Monday-morning list of Government bonds.

LONDON SHARE SERVICE

BRITISH FUNDS

Interest Due	Stock	Price £	Last xd	Yield Int.	Yield Red.
	"Shorts" (Lives up to Five Years)				
26 Jul 26 Jan	Treas 7¾pc 1985–88‡‡...	99⅞	19.6	7.76	8.56
10Nov 10May	Exch 10½pc '88..............	100 13/16	5.10	10.42	8.38
14Dec 14Jne	Treas 9¾pc Cv '88...........	100⅝xd	9.11	9.69	8.42
1Jan 1Jul	Transport 3pc '78–88.......	97 23/32xd	01.11	3.07	7.05
25 Apr 25 Oct	Treas. 9½pc '88..............	100 21/32	18.9	9.44	8.64
22 Aug 22 Feb	Treas 11½pc 1989...........	102 23/32	16.7	11.18	8.79
18 Oct 18 Apr	Treas 9½pc Cnv 1989.......	100 23/32	11.9	9.42	8.77
15Nov 15May	Treas 3pc 1989................	95 13/32	9.10	3.14	6.32
14Dec 14Jun	Treas 10½pc 1989...........	102 5/16xd	9.11	10.26	8.79
1Feb 1Aug	Exch.10pc 1989................	101 11/16	25.6	9.84	8.85
29 Mar 29 Sep	Exch 11pc 1989................	103 15/32	24.8	10.64	8.91
15 Apr 15 Oct	Treas 5pc 1986–89.........	95 9/16	8.9	5.22	7.49
15 May 15 Nov	Exch 10¼pcCv '89...........	103 11/32	9.10	9.95	8.47
15 Jul 15 Jan	Treas 13pc 1990‡‡..........	107⅝xd	8.6	12.10	9.00
12 Aug 12 Feb	Exch 11pc 1990‡‡...........	103¾	16.7	10.62	9.07
22 Sep 22 Mar	Exch. 12½pc 1990...........	107 1/16	17.8	11.69	9.06
8 Nov 8 May	Treas. 3pc 1990................	91 15/32	2.10	3.28	6.90
15 Dec 15 Jun	Treas 8¼pc 1987–90‡‡...	99⅛xd	9.11	8.32	8.61
25 Apr 25 Oct	Treas. 10pcCv 1990..........	102 7/16	18.9	9.78	9.07
22 May 22 Nov	Exch 2½pc 1990...............	89 1/16	16.10	2.80	6.58
10 July 10 Jan	Treas 11¾pc 1991...........	107 3/32xd	3.6	10.98	9.08
5Oct 5Apr	Funding 5¾pc '87–91‡‡...	93⅜	1.9	6.14	7.97
13 Nov 13 May	Treas. 3pc 1991................	88 1/16	7.10	3.39	6.86
12Jan 12July	Treas 10pc Cv '91 ‡‡.......	103¾xd	5.6	9.63	8.72
25Apr 25Oct	Exch. 11pc 1991..............	106¼	18.9	10.38	9.11
10Jun 10Dec	Treas. 8pc 1991...............	96⅝	3.11	8.30	9.08
22Jly 22Jan	Treas 12¾pc 1992‡‡........	112	15.6	11.39	9.17
21Aug 21Feb	Treas 10pc 1992...............	102⅞	15.7	9.73	9.16
13Oct 13Apr	Treas. 8pc 1992 ‡‡..........	96 3/16	11.6	8.32	9.09

BRITISH

Interest Due	Stoc
1Feb 1Aug	Consols 4pc.....
1Jun 1Dec	War Loan 3½p
1Apr 1Oct	Conv. 3½pc '61
5Apr 5Oct	Treas. 3pc '66
5Ja Ap Jly O	Consols 2½pc..
1Apr 1Oct	Treas. 2½pc....

In

30 Sep 30 Mar	Treas. 2pc '88(
25 Jul 25 Jan	Do. 2pc '90(3
23Sep 23Mar	Do. 2pc '92‡‡
16Mar 16Sep	Do. 2pc '96(2
24Mar 24Sep	Do 2½pc '01
20Nov 20May	Do. 2½pc '03
19Jan 19Jly	Do. 2pc '06(2
20Nov 20May	Do. 2½pc '09
23Feb 23Aug	Do. 2½pc '11
16Feb 16Aug	Do. 2½pc '13
26Jan 26Jly	Do. 2½pc '16
16Oct 16Apr	Do. 2½pc '20
17Jan 17July	Do. 2½pc '24

Prospective real redempti and (2) 5%. (b) Figures indexing, ie 8 months pric for November1987: 103.4 (rebased at 100 Jan

prices tell you nothing about the income you can expect from your Gilt-edged investment.

1) Interest Yields: Often called the 'flat' or 'running' yield, this just tells the investor what percentage return he will get if he buys the bond at the market quoted price. Mathematically, it is obtained simply by dividing the coupon by the price.

2) Redemption Yields: This is the one the professionals watch. It measures the total return on the Gilt if it is held until the maturity date, including the stream of dividend income which is taxable and also the capital gain expected if the price rises towards maturity — which is tax-free. More about tax later, but for the moment, bear in mind that the FT, like other newspapers, quotes Gilt yields gross — so the investor has a tax question to consider.

As can be seen from the FT prices table, there is a definite profile to Government debt. But it is, generally speaking, a long-term debt market, since the Government handles its short-term needs by means of the money markets and tax revenues.

Thus, of the Government's total borrowing of £11.2bn in the Gilt-edged market in 1985-86, only £1.1bn came at the 'short' end of the market, where maturities are within five years. The bulk, £7.25bn, was in bonds with more than fifteen years to run to maturity.

The shorts respond quickly to trends in the day-to-day money markets and, in particular, to views on whether bank base rates will change. Longer-dated Gilts, by definition, are looking a long way ahead and are therefore prey to inflation worries.

Soaring inflation rates in Britain and elsewhere during the Seventies severely reduced the attractions of investment in Government bonds — or in any other form of fixed interest security. But Gilts have returned to favour as inflation has fallen and real interest rates remain high.

The Government moved to counter nervousness over inflation in the Gilt-edged market by the introduction in 1982 of 'index-linked Gilts', which are quoted in the FT (see page 41). These issues carry yields and redemption values which are adjusted for inflation: both are adjusted semi-annually to match the Retail Prices Index.

Daily price movements in Gilt-edged prices look small when printed in fractions in the newspapers, and leave the reader little the

BRITISH FUNDS – Contd

Yield Int.	Yield Red.
7.76	8.29
10.42	8.64
9.70	8.70
3.07	6.84
9.44	8.76
11.18	8.89
9.42	8.80
3.14	6.12
10.26	8.87
9.85	8.96
10.64	8.92
5.23	7.51
9.81	7.71
12.08	8.93
10.59	8.98
11.66	8.98
3.26	6.59
8.33	8.69
9.75	8.98
2.80	6.49
10.97	9.03
6.15	7.97
3.38	6.67
9.56	8.47
10.34	9.00
8.26	8.95
11.34	9.06
9.69	9.03
8.28	8.92

1987 High	1987 Low	Stock	Price £	+ or –	Yield Int.	Yield Red.
		Undated				
45 5/8	39 11/16	Consols 4pc	43 11/32	–1/8	9.23	–
41 7/16	34 11/16	War Loan 3½pc‡‡	39xd	–3/8	8.91	–
52 7/16	46½	Conv. 3½pc '61 Aft	50 1/2	–5/16	6.81	–
34 1/2	29 1/2	Treas. 3pc '66 Aft	32 7/32	–11/32	8.89	–
29 5/16	24 15/16	Consols 2½pc	27 7/16	–11/32	9.19	–
29 5/16	24 15/32	Treas. 2½pc	27 7/16	–11/32	9.08	–
		Index-Linked			(1)	(2)
133 1/16	125½	Treas. 2pc '88(297.1)	133 1/16xd	....	–	–
119¼	108 3/4	Do. 2pc '90(333.9)	117 3/4	–3/8	0.55	1.89
101¼	93½	Do. 2pc '92‡‡ (385.8)	99 5/8	–1/4	1.89	2.59
129 1/2	119 1/16	Do. 2pc '96(267.9)	128 1/2	–5/16	3.35	3.71
111 3/8	96 5/8	Do 2½pc '01 (308.8)	108 1/2	....	3.64	3.92
110	94 1/8	Do. 2½pc '03(310.7)	106 1/32xd	–1/2	3.70	3.93
113 7/32	94 1/2	Do. 2pc '06(274.1)	107 1/32	–1/2	3.75	3.95
108	89 5/16	Do. 2½pc '09(310.7)	100 7/8xd	–1/2	3.75	3.94
113 1/2	93 5/16	Do. 2½pc '11(294.1)	105	–1/8	3.74	3.92
95 1/16	76 1/2	Do. 2½pc '13(351.9)	87 3/8	–5/8	3.73	3.85
103 1/2	83 3/8	Do. 2½pc '16(322.0)	94 3/4	–5/8	3.69	3.81
101 1/2	81 3/4	Do. 2½pc '20 (327.3)	93 1/16	–9/32	3.63	3.72
86 1/2	68 5/16	Do. 2½pc '24 ‡‡(385.3)	79	–5/32	3.48	3.64

Prospective real redemption rate on projected inflation of (1) 10% and (2) 5%. (b) Figures in paretheses show RPI base month for indexing, ie 8 months prior to issue. RPI for January 1987:100.0 and for August 1987: 102.1
(rebased at 100 January 1987 conversion factor 3.945).

1987 High
53
52
50
66
146½
136¼
103½

1987 High
42
40 3/8
18 7/8
19 9/16
30 3/8
35 7/8
25 1/4
12 7/8
22½
65½
24 5/8
25
98p
10 1/8
34 3/8

wiser. To understand them, it is necessary to move closer to the market.

The FT reports on the daily trading activity in Government bonds in the opening paragraphs of the London Stock Exchange which appears just before the stock market prices pages. On Monday mornings, a more thorough analysis of the bond market is carried, which draws attention to any important economic developments expected during the week, and rounds up the City's view of the outlook for Government bonds.

These reports make constant references to Government economic policies, to official statistics published by the British Treasury and also to the Bank of England — and sometimes lump all three bodies together under the cryptic heading of 'the authorities'. In fact, much of the analysis of the Gilt-edged market by both the press and the City brokerage houses consists of trying to read the minds of 'the authorities'. This is inevitable because of the special nature of the market. The Government, through its agents at the Treasury and the Bank, needs an orderly bond market where investors will be willing to buy its debt paper. And since it is the only supplier of new stock, it cannot help influencing prices by its very presence, or absence. To some extent, the Bank of England has to 'manage' the Gilt-edged market, so that the Government can achieve its funding programme without mishap. To this end, the Bank intervenes regularly, but not daily, in the market, buying or selling stock either to balance its own portfolio or to smooth out market movements and open the way for a new issue of stock. It is these actions by the 'authorities' that the FT reports will pick up and place into the context of the trends in the market, often quoting the reaction of the City houses to the new development.

The Bank's methods of operation have been modified by the substantial re-structuring of the Gilt-edged market as part of the Big Bang realignment of the entire UK securities market. The new system of trading Gilts, introduced in October 1986, has a number of characteristics involving fundamental change in market operations.

Marketmakers: There are now around 25 trading firms making markets in UK Government bonds on a regular basis, compared with, effectively, two or three pre-Big Bang. In other words, the market is much more competitive.

Turnover: Comparisons with pre-Big Bang are bedevilled by the growth of inter-marketmaker business, but daily turnover has soared from around £1bn in the old market to around £4.8bn in mid-1987. Against this background, the Bank has spelled out its general approach to operations in the primary market.

Primary market: This is the sale by the authorities of new stocks or large tranches of existing stocks. The old and trusted methods have been retained, and one significant new one added.

1) By Auction: This, the newcomer, was based loosely on the system long operated in the US bond markets, and had its first outing on 13 May 1987, when £1bn of Treasury 8 p.c. 1992 stock was auctioned. The auction went successfully and is certain to become a permanent feature.

For the investor, the significance of the auction system is that, since the Bank sets no minimum price, yet expects to sell the entire issue, it is left to the market to demonstrate its views on interest rate trends. So the investor gets a sudden, and valuable, snapshot of City and foreign views on the economic outlook as seen from the stock market. Since the Bank sanctioned the introduction of a 'grey' or pre-issue market in the period between the announcement and the auction itself, the market's view is kept up-to-date.

As the auction system takes hold, the largest market firms, both UK and foreign, are expected to bid on an increasingly aggressive scale, implying some exciting times ahead.

2) Sales by tender: Market firms are invited to tender, with the Bank setting a minimum price which is normally at or slightly above market levels for a similar stock. The Bank allots stock at the lowest price accepted, and any stock left over is used as a 'tap' stock.

'Tap' stocks, marked with a blob in the FT lists, are available to the Bank to sell to the marketmakers whenever it wants. By the price at which it offers to trade the taps, the Bank can try to influence the market.

114 3/16	103 5/16	Treas 13pc 1990‡‡	104 5/8	−1/8	12.43	11.19	5
108 1/8	97 1/8	Exch 11pc 1990‡‡	99 1/2	.....	11.06	11.19	1
113 1/8	101 13/16	Exch. 12 1/2pc 1990	103 5/8	−1/8	12.06	11.19	3
89 3/4	79 5/8	Treas. 3pc 1990	83 1/4xd	.....	3.60	8.61	1
100 5/16	89 1/8	Treas 8 1/4pc 1987-90‡‡	93	−1/8	8.87	10.58	3
106 1/16	93	Treas. 10pcCv 1990	96 3/8xd	−1/16	10.38	11.15	2
86 3/16	76 1/2	Exch 2 1/2pc 1990	80 3/16 xd	+1/16	3.12	8.35	2
112 3/16	99 7/16	Treas 11 3/4pc 1991	101 3/4	.....	11.55	11.18	5
94 1/4	83 1/[illegible]	Funding 5 3/4pc '87-91‡‡	86 15/16	−5/16	6.61	9.38	2
86 1/8	79 5/16	Treas. 3pc 1991●	79 5/8xd	−1/32	3.77	8.51	2
E96 1/4	—	*Tr 10pcCv'91(£40pd)●*	E96 1/4	.....	10.39	11.04	11
110 5/8	96 [illegible]	Exch. 11pc 1991	99 1/2xd	.....	11.06	11.17	1
		Five to Fifteen Years					3
118 3/4	103 5/8	Treas 12 3/4pc 1992‡‡	106 1/16	+1/16	12.02	11.16	314
107 5/8	92 5/16	Treas 10pc 1992	95 3/16	−1/8	10.51	11.20	4
109 3/4	94 3/16	Treas 10 1/2pc Cv 1992‡‡	97 7/32xd	−3/32	10.80	11.20	1
117 1/4	101 9/16	Exch. 12 1/4pc '92	104 1/16	+1/16	11.77	11.26	1
123 1/4	106 7/8	Exch 13 1/2pc 1992	109 1/8	.....	12.37	11.33	4
108	94	Treas 10pc 1993‡‡	95 1/16	−1/16	10.52	11.09	2
120 7/8	103 1/2	Treas 12 1/2pc 1993‡‡	106	+1/8	11.79	11.19	2
92	78 1/2	Funding 6pc 1993‡‡	84 1/8	−1/8	7.13	9.16	2

Bullet point (●) indicates Tap stocks.

3) 'Tranchettes' of existing stocks: The Bank sells relatively small blocks of stocks from time to time as a means of keeping the trading market running smoothly and keeping its own portfolio balanced. Tranchette sales are not usually regarded as indications of the Bank's policy, or as signals to the market-place.

Primary market operations are all part of the Government's funding programme, and that is why the Gilt-edged market is always interested in the latest estimates of Public Sector Borrowing Requirement. If the market knows, or fears, that the authorities still need to make substantial funding through the market within the next few months, then it will start guessing at what yield levels the funding must be sold. If there seems no threat of funding, then there will be less pressure on existing yields in the market.

These are the market operations, and signals, for which the market reporters of the FT will be looking. But there is one point which involves endless confusion for the newcomer to Gilts. Since it is easier to measure price changes in Gilts, market reporters usually write in terms of them. But for any deeper evaluation of the market, it is still yields that count. On the front page of the paper, the FT-Actuaries yield on 25-year issues is shown.

gh'

ans for the NHS. a cost of using to obtain medical aff, particularly in ties, in order to its open.

al reason, not returns but now e apparent, was capital and reve- talling and run- tion/information ms.

n said that "at m, the shortfall trict level must The situation ediate response to ensure that re maintained. funding of the mpletely unac-

elay'

ave got to stop naking them- se proposition

Bank to offer £1bn gilts

By Simon Holberton

THE Bank of England yesterday suprised the gilt-edged market by saying it would offer £1bn of convertible gilts for sale by tender on Wednesday.

Prices on long-dated gilts, which have been weak in the past days, fell further on the announcement and closed more than 1½ points lower to yield 9.86.

The Bank, which has been under no serious funding pressure, is thought to have judged that this was the best time to issue stock given that opportunities to do so would be limited over Christmas and New Year.

Mr John Shepperd of Warburg Securities said: "It is the most popular stock they could have offered under the circumstances, but the market is very weak."

The offer is of £1bn of 8 per cent convertible Treasury 1990, convertible on four six-monthly intervals from July 16 1988 into 8½ per cent Treasury Loan 2007.

Tokyo to refuse quotation for Reuter

BY IAN ROGER IN TOKYO AND RAYMOND SNODDY IN LONDON

The Tokyo Stock Exchange is expected to refuse any application from Reuter Holdings, the UK-based news and financial information group for a share listing in Tokyo.

The problem is being caused by Reuters A shares held by founder shareholders each of which carry four votes.

Mr Michael Cooling, Reuter's manager of corporate affairs, said yesterday:" We have realised since July there was a potential problem. But we have no intention of changing our share structure. We will continue our negotiations with the Tokyo Stock Exchange."

The company says the privileged A shares are designed to protect Reuter's independence and integrity.

Reuters wanted to list its class B shares, each of which carries one vote. These are the shares which are traded on the London Stock Exchange and on Nasdaq in the U.S.

The Tokyo Stock Exchange opposes privileged share classes and so, according to newspaper reports in Tokyo, it proposes to refuse permission for the listing of Reuter B shares.

In April Reuter shareholders approved changes to the group's articles of association in preparation for a formal application for a listing .

Instead a formal application has yet to be made and negotiations are still continuing with the Tokyo Stock Exchange.

Walker & Staff falls

A lack of project business and reduced margins on contract sales resulted in interim pre-tax profits for Walker & Staff Holdings, valve and pipework distributor, falling from £147,000 to £128,000. Turnover for the six months to end-September rose to £3.06m, against £2.67m.

Tax took £44,000 (£51,000) for earnings per 5p share of 3.36p (4.48p). Full year results are expected to be less than last time.

Traffic rise helps BAA to £136m

BY LYNTON McLAIN

BAA, formerly British Airports Authority and privatised in a stock market flotation in July, increased historic cost pre-tax profits by 26 per cent, after interest charges of £3m, to £136m for the six months to the end-September 1987.

The interim dividend is set at 3p per share. The board expects to recommend the payment of a final dividend which will result in a total of not less than 7.25p per share for the year.

Revenue for the first half was £307m, compared with £262m last time.

In the offer for sale prospectus, BAA reported strong traffic growth in the first two months of the financial year. This continued for the remainder of the period to the end of September, and resulted in a rise of 15.7 per cent in the volume of traffic.

Sir Norman Payne, chairman, said terrorist activity and the Chernobyl incident affected some markets last year. "A better assessment of the underlying growth trend can be established by comparing the passenger figures for 1987 with those for 1985, which was a more normal year," he said.

"This gives a compound growth over the last two years of 8.4 per cent per annum for the first six months of the financial year."

The company's airports handled 36.4m passengers in the first six months of the current financial year - a rise of 5m on the comparable period last year.

Traffic at the south east of England airports, Heathrow, Gatwick and Stansted, rose by 16.7 per cent, while traffic at Glasgow, Prestwick and Edinburgh grew by 11.1 per cent.

Domestic traffic rose by 10 per cent; European scheduled traffic by 15 per cent and traffic on the north Atlantic markets by 24 per cent; traffic in charter markets rose by 18 per cent, with long haul markets, other than those to and from America, up by 10 per cent.

The number of aircraft movements, rose from 338,000 to 362,000, a seven per cent increase. Cargo tonnage rose by 10 per cent to a record 410,000 tonnes.

Sir Norman Payne: aircraft movements rose by 7 per cent

BAA joined the Stock Exchange with 2.2m shareholders on July 28. The shares opened at 140p for the £1 partly paid offer. "After nearly four months the figure is approximately 1.3m shareholders," Sir Norman said.

Over the next five years, the company plans to spend over £850m on capital developments. "We have already taken advantage of private sector opportunities to arrange sufficient financing for this development programme," Sir Norman said.

See Lex

Acquisitions help lift Erskine 83% to £3.5m

WITH THE help of acquisitions **Erskine House Group,** office equipment supplier, reported interim pre-tax profits up by 83 per cent. Mr Brian McGillivray, chairman and chief executive, said a strong performance was expected in the second half.

Turnover for the six months to the end of September 1987 rose from £33m to £45.96m and pre-tax profits were £3.5m (£1.91m).

Earnings per share were 8.3p, against 6p, a rise of 38 per cent. The interim dividend has been raised to 1.6p (1.2p).

Mr McGillivray said that excellent growth from the main UK office equipment businesses and outstanding contributions from the new acquisitions in both the UK and the US had been behind the result.

He added that confidence among the sales staff was high and profit improvement plans should result in better margins.

The sale of furniture distribution, part of Erskine Business Machines, which resulted in an extraordinary debit of £278,000, allowed the overhead structure to be rationalised. The benefits of that would be seen in the second half.

Zeno, the first US acquisition, made progress, the chairman said, but management of its main Dallas activity had to be strengthened. Better performance is expected.

The tax charge was £1.12m (£567,000) and minorities took £1,000 (£3,000).

Trading profits boost Chase to £9.5m midway

BY PAUL CHEESERIGHT, PROPERTY CORRESPONDENT

Chase Property, the successor of Wingate Property Investments, which a year ago took over the Property Holding and Investment Trust, yesterday announced a 60 per cent increase in its interim pre-tax profits.

It is paying a half year dividend of 1.25p, more than double that paid by Wingate at this time last year.

Disclosure of the profits increase helped to hold the shares firm and they climbed from their overnight price of 215p in a thin market.

Pre-tax profits for the six months to September were £9.5m compared with £5.9m, restated to include the PHIT results, for the same period of 1986. Earnings per share were 8.9p against 7.2p for the first half of the 1986-87 year and 16.1p for the whole year.

The company, controlled by Chase Corporation of New Zealand, bases its assets on the PHIT and Wingate portfolios but this year has branched out into trading and development.

Rental income rose to £5.66m from £5.04m in the 1986-87 first half and profits on the sale of investments were £2.13m against £1.96m. But there is also a new stream of earnings - £3.22m of property development profits.

Chase announced that Mr Sidney Bookman is stepping down as chairman. He will be succeeded by Mr Patrick Garner, the deputy chairman. Mr Bookman was the second chairman of Chase out of the ranks of PHIT. Mr Garner represents the new wave of management.

Shareholders are to be asked to give the board authority to make market purchases of its own shares.

● comment

Chase promised more aggressive management of the PHIT and Wingate portfolios and this has come through now in two sets of figures. Full year profits will depend crucially on the ability to dispose of £90m of property now on the market - a high proportion of the total portfolio valued at £243m last March. Pre-tax profits of around £20m for 1986-87 look likely, giving earnings per share of 18.2p and a prospective p/e of 12.08. Next year benefits from the expanding development programme should start to flow through. The following year is the tricky one - when City and West End developments become available at a time when the supply-demand balance could have evened out.

Market gets rights issues fillip

BY CLAY HARRIS

Henry Ansbacher Holdings, the merchant banking group, and **Compsoft Holdings,** the USM-quoted software house, gave the London market some relief yesterday by reporting that their rights issues had been heavily subscribed.

More typical of the current trend was the response to the **TR Energy** and **Turriff Corporation** rights issues, taken up respectively on behalf of 1 per cent and 1.2 per cent of shares. Both cash calls were underwritten.

Ansbacher said that 82.26 per cent of its £69m issue of ordinary shares and convertible loan stock had been taken up, mostly by controlling shareholders Pargesa Holding and Groupe Bruxelles Lambert and their associates. Through underwriting arrangements, their total stake has risen to 76.8 per cent.

Compsoft's £1.52m issue, of which 97.9 per cent was subscribed, was launched as part of a management buy-in

Powell Duffryn at £11.5m halfway

THE SEASONAL bias in **Powell Duffryn's** activities and a stronger price of oil were evident in yesterday's interim figures. Group trading profit before exceptional items was at the same level as the strong first half performance in the year before, although its composition changed considerably.

Profit before tax for the first six months of the year was 9.6 per cent higher at £11.54m, compared with £10.53m in the corresponding period last year. This was on turnover of £312.94m, 4.4 per cent higher than last year.

Mr David Hubbard, chairman, said that last year's interim profits reflected unusually favourable trading conditions, when oil prices were low. This year, however, higher and more stable oil prices during the summer months, coupled with increased producer output, have impacted sales volumes and margins in fuel distribution. Trading profit for the division was down from £5.8m to £3.4m at the half year, on turnover down from £169.3m to £162.4m.

Trading profits were also down for the bulk liquid storage division from £1.9m to £1.6m, on turnover down from £12.8m to £12.6m.

Within the engineering division, where trading profits increased from £2.7m to £4.8m, Hamworthy's sales have risen by one third while sales margins have improved from 7 per cent to 10 per cent. This reflects first contributions from recent acquisitions.

Earnings per share were up 13 per cent to 11.4p (10.1p) and the interim dividend increased by 10.5 per cent to 5.25p.

The chairman explained that the preponderance of the group's distribution and storage profits were made in the winter months. "It is our intention to go on building the business as in the past, particularly by investing in fuel distribution," he said. The remainder of the year is expected to be satisfactory, he added.

●comment

Powell Duffryn cannot win for trying. Although a decline in fuel distribution profits was widely expected - the extraordinarily favourable conditions in the first six months of last year, when low prices gave oil a competitive edge on coal, were scarcely expected to recur - the shares fell 5p to 315p on an otherwise strong day in the market. Pleading mercy because of the cyclical nature of many of the group's activities (fuel distribution, shipping and construction) did not seem to carry much weight either. But the performance in specialist engineering activities should continue to strengthen as recent acquisitions increase their contribution, and assuming even a reasonably miserable British winter, full year pre-tax profits should reach £31m. Despite such an uninspiring spread of businesses, a prospective p/e of just over 10 does not look too demanding. And with Ron Brierley in the wings with a holding of nearly 3 per cent, excitement could yet come to PD.

Non-banking side boosts Hambros to £36.6m halfway

A 46 PER CENT improvement in pre-tax profits, from £25.13m to £36.63m was announced by **Hambros,** financial services and estate agency group, for the six months ended September 30.

While its banking profits showed a 30 per cent increase to £19.66m against £15.17m the non-banking side surged 54 per cent from £14.21m to £21.92m.

To reduce disparity between payments the interim dividend is stepped up to 3p (2.4p) per 20p share. A total of 8.2p was paid for the year to March 31 when profits reached £60.77m.

All the group's banking companies lifted profits. In the UK corporate finance income was below the high level of the first half last year, but that had been outweighed, directors said, by improved results from other divisions. The overseas companies all continued to make good progress.

In its non-banking activities results from insurance broking fell from £3.94m to £1.67m, while stockbroking suffered a £613,000 loss compared with profits of £870,000. Those loses were in line with the rest of the market following the 'Big Bang', Mr Christophe Sporborg, chairman and chief executive of the non-banking side, said. Provisions have been made against losses on the group's underwriting and other positions as a result of the recent stock market fall.

However, profits of £10.72m (£3.23m) from Hambro Countrywide, the UK's largest estate agency, 60 per cent owned by Hambros, and from other activities, more than compensated, directors said. Its property businesses contributed an increased £687,000 (£330,000).

Investment gains rose from £2.66m to £6.61m and income from investments showed a rise from £571,000 to £950,000. Diamond operations last time added £626,000 and profits from other activities improved from £509,000 to 856,000. Central finance and overhead costs for the six months took £4.94m (£4.26m). After tax of £12.3m (£8.02m) and minorities of £3.35m (£1.54m) attributable profits came out 35 per cent ahead at £20.98m (£15.57m) for earnings of 13.5p (12p) per share.

Since the end of the period Hambros has strengthened its network of European collaboration, the directors reported. Banco de Bilbao has acquired a strategic holding of 9.5m shares and made a 15-year £25m subordinated loan to the group.

An agreement has also been signed with Bayerische Vereinsbank, and the group recently created jointly-owned fund management companies with both Sanpaolo Bank and Banco de Bilbao to market internationally invested unit trusts in Italy and Spain. Hambros expects to announce tie-ups with a Dutch and a French financial institution shortly.

At home, Hambro Countrywide directors forecast profits of at least £25m for 1987. That company plans to establish a life insurance company in association with Guardian Royal Exchange, beginning operations in the summer of 1988.

● comment

The impact of lower corporate finance income at home was cushioned by the impressive growth of the non merchant banking earnings. Two exceptions, however, were insurance broking, where the reduction of Hambros's stake in Fielding and problems at CE Heath took their toll, and stockbroking, where Hambros' 30 per cent stake in Strauss Turnbull exposed it to the expensive costs of transacting and settling small private client bargains. Hambros is unlikely to reveal a similar gain in investment income at the year end because of the stock market crash. But the estate agency business should be relatively immune from the City's problems, as the majority of customers live outside London, spend less on houses and have no difficulty finding a mortgage. Hambros should report about £76m for the year, which values the shares on a fair prospective p/e of eight at 228p.

Sound Diffusion holders insist on board changes

BY PHILIP COGGAN

THE DISSIDENT institutional shareholders in **Sound Diffusion,** electrical equipment leasing group, who successfully called last week for the resignation of Mr Paul Stonor, the company's chairman, are insisting on the further board changes they requested.

Throgmorton Trust, Allied Dunbar and Fidelity, the three institutions involved, still want Mr Anthony Cross, the finance director, to resign. They wish to appoint two new directors, Mr David Macdonald, the former director general of the Takeover Panel and Mr Francis Howard the former finance director of Charter Consolidated.

The institutions, which hold 11.7 per cent of Sound Diffusion's equity, added that they "do not consider it in the best interest of shareholders" for the current board to enter into further takeover discussions.

Ibstock buys again

BY MIKE SMITH

Ibstock Johnsen, brick and pulp manufacturer, yesterday made its second acquisition in two days when it agreed to buy Price & Pierce, a marketer of forest products, for $13m (£7.3m) in cash.

Price, which is being bought from Sears, Roebuck and Co, will become the third leg in Ibstock's fibres division. It joins Eucalyptus Pulp Mills, which is becoming a full subsidiary following a £60.5m deal announced on Monday, and fellow forest products sales agency Johnsen, Jorgensen and Wettre.

Mr Ian Maclellan, Ibstock finance director, said this week's acquisitions built up fibres into a meaningful and sensible division and the main thrust of future expansion would be in building materials.

Price, which sells woodpulp, timber, paper and board around the world, has its head office in London and employs 520 people.

In the nine months to September 30, it made pre-tax profits of £1.1m on sales of £87m.

Banner raises TSG holding

Banner Industries, US supplier of aircraft parts and industrial products, has increased its stake in **Transcontinental Services Group,** London-quoted investment business, to about 15 per cent.

Transcontinental, registered in the Netherlands Antilles and managed from New York, specialises in risk arbitrage and medium-term investment. It was taken by surprise by the latest purchases and said it was asking for more complete information.

Banner said yesterday that it had held shares in Transcontinental for about a year, but had raised the stake above 5 per cent only in the past month.

DIVIDENDS ANNOUNCED

	Current payment	Date of payment	Corresponding div	Total for year	Total last year
Alphameric ...int	1†	Feb15	0.75	-	2.5
Anglo Irish Bank ...fin	0.1†‡	-	2.24	3.2	3.2
BAA ...int	3	Jan 27	-	-	-
Cosalt ...fin	3	Jan 27	2.25	4.5	3.5
James Cropper ...int	0.68	Jan 15	0.55*	-	1.63*
Chase Property ...int	1.25	Jan 31	0.61⚘	-	3.25⚘
Erskine House ...int	1.6†	Jan 12	1.2	-	4
Hambros ...int	3♦	Jan 11	2.4	-	8.2
Monks Inv. Tst. ...int	1.2	-	1.1	-	2.8
North Amer Tr ...fin	4	-	4	5.4	5.4
Powell Duffryn ...int	5.25	Jan 5	4.75	-	16.5
Readicut Int. ...int	0.38†	Jan 12	0.25	-	2.18
TMD Advertising §.fin	2.4	Feb 23	2	2.4	2

Dividends shown pence per share net except where otherwise stated. *Equivalent after allowing for scrip issue. †On capital increased by rights and/or acquisition issues. §USM stock. ♦Unquoted stock. ▼Third market. ⚘As Wingate Property Investments.♦To reduce disparity. ‡Irish currency

Lisa Wood on Allied-Lyons' expansion in world markets

Tidying-up a North American pearl

Since finalising its £445m purchase last December of 51 per cent of Hiram Walker, the Canadian spirits business, Allied-Lyons has been at pains to point out that the acquisition was a pearl. At a stroke, the deal lifted its largely UK-based wine and spirits business into the fourth largest player worldwide with major brands including Ballantines, Kahlua and Courvoisier.

Yesterday it put its money where its mouth is by announcing the proposed £572m purchase of the remaining 49 per cent from GW Utilities, some 88 per cent of which is owned by Olympia & York.

The deal includes £370m of convertible preference shares which, when converted in the 1990s will give GW Utilities a 10 per cent stake in Allied-Lyons. The City had feared that Allied might make a rights issue to fund such an acquisition.

British drinks companies, with major exposure to the large US market, have not exactly been flavour of the month since the October stock market crash. Guinness and Grand Metropolitan, have had their shares marked down by the market because of dollar exposure.

However, Allied's latest move, despite the strong exposure to the US and whisky brands, was fairly well received by the City for a variety of reasons, not least that it would afford the company greater opportunity to rationalise its Allied Vintners and the Hiram Walker drinks operations at a time of intense struggle among the major players for a competitive edge in world markets.

Allied - in what was perceived by City sceptics at the time to constitute an attempt to thwart a take-over bid from Elders IXL - agreed to buy the Hiram Walker wines and spirits division in April 1986 for $1.2bn.

However Hiram Walker was subsequently taken over by Gulf Canada, a subsidiary of Olympia & York, the Canadian real estate and resource company controlled by the Reichmann Brothers. Gulf Canada immediately began legal proceedings to block the Allied acquisition.

Lengthy litigation was resolved with Allied taking a controlling 51 per cent in Hiram Walker spirits with the business being run as a joint venture. However, a complicated "put and call" arrangement was made which gave the Reichmann Brothers the right to sell their stake and Allied the right to buy. Both would have been exercisable next year.

While Allied and the Reichmann Brothers have both said that they were good partners,

Sir Derrick Holden-Brown chairman of Allied-Lyons

the Reichmannn Brothers like control of their businesses and Allied was prevented from fully integrating the operation with its own.

In addition, while Allied took the whole of Hiram Walker's operations into its pre-tax profits, paying GW Utilities after tax, it could not take the cash flow of what is a strong cash generating business. Hiram Walker, for the six months ended August 31st 1987 contributed sales of £388.1m and a pre-tax profit of £57.6m.

Since taking the majority interest Allied has put a senior management team into Canada and some rationalisation of management structure has been effected.

Consideration has been concentrated on how best to exploit the two groups' strengths with Allied Vintners major markets being in the UK and Europe and Hiram Walker in the large, but difficult, US and Canadian markets together with a small but expanding presence in the Far East.

Allied-Lyons, like its major competitors, intends to be a significant player in the global market where power is being concentrated in fewer hands.

It is a high risk strategy where it will be competing against the likes of Guinness and IDV, the Grand Metropolitan subsidiary. Both these two groups in the last few months have shown strong aggression towards the market place.

Allied-Lyons, which has recently launched a new corporate advertising campaign which could be seen as a bit on defensive, now has the opportunity to show whether or not it has the management in place to compete in the world drinks market.

5 UK Company Results

The *Financial Times* has a long-established position (as a newspaper of record) in the field of UK corporate affairs. It aims to track the trading fortunes of Britain's public companies, reporting not only the financial information disclosed under UK Company Law but also the flow of secondary information regarding labour disputes, management changes and new product developments. Moreover, it seeks, both in the Lex Column and on those pages devoted to company affairs, to comment widely on developments in specific enterprises and in industry and business at large.

The principal thrust of the paper's coverage of company affairs goes, inevitably, into the reporting of the profits — or losses — which directors of public companies are required to disclose at stated intervals. This chapter concentrates on this aspect of the paper's coverage of business reporting. Chapter 6 looks at the way in which the FT reports the corporate takeover arena, where some acquisition bids may be agreed peacefully between the boardrooms concerned, but some are fought out bitterly over several months, with both sides seeking to capture the support of the shareholders and the City institutions.

Company affairs do not usually divide themselves up as neatly as these two chapters suggest. Takeover bids are, or should be, a part of the overall strategy of the predator company, while the target company will often have been identified as such by the stock market — or, to be more precise, by the analysts at the major City brokerage houses. A company's prospects may be changed radically by the signing of a large export order, or by an unexpected setback with a new product. Consequently, the FT's coverage of corporate matters is not restricted to the pages headed 'UK Company News'. The daily London Stock Exchange report draws investors' attention to the City's reaction to trading or bid developments. The Management page endeavours, by interviewing senior executives, to ferret out the deeper factors behind a company's success or failure. The UK News pages report on relationships between Britain's major companies and their workforces, and customers. Technical developments, important

14

MANAGEMENT: Marketing and Advertising

Financial Times Thursday November 19 1987

SELLING HOLIDAYS

Has Thomson precipitated another price war?

David Churchill queries the UK group's switch in market strategy

After the crash

A bullish view of bear markets

Feona McEwan on the advertising industry's general reaction to recent turmoil

sales contracts, new appointments to the board, also reported in the appropriate pages of the newspaper, must also be recognized as important contributions to the comprehensive picture of corporate Britain that the FT aims to produce for its readers.

But it is the UK Company News pages which carry the major area of corporate reporting. UK companies are required under Company Law to publish once a year a full report and accounts, to be followed by an annual meeting of shareholders. But this legal requirement is no more than the minimum reporting standard for major companies. Under UK Stock Exchange regulations, listed companies must send half yearly, or interim, trading statements to the Exchange, which immediately publishes them both inside the Exchange and also to the news-media. In fact, most interim reports are now sent simultaneously to the Stock Exchange and the teleprinter newsagencies.

Opposite are two examples of FT reports on trading results from British companies quoted on the UK Stock Exchange. In the first example (Amari) the report is clearly split into two parts. The first eight paragraphs contain the facts and figures, while the second part contains the writer's comments on the results. Note that the comment is designated as such, and separated quite firmly from the factual reporting. This principle is followed throughout the FT's corporate reporting pages.

Amari rises by 11% to £3.9m

FOLLOWING the falls of last year, profits at **Amari** were up 11 per cent in the first six months of 1987 with a pre-tax figure of £3.86m against £3.47m. The result was achieved on turnover up from £83.48m to £120.23m, boosted by a number of acquisitions during the past 12 months.

Mr Michael Ward Thomas, chairman, said that as the year progressed industry prices and demand were becoming firmer and the company was benefiting from the investment programme of last year.

In recent weeks Suter has built up a stake of more than 17 per cent in the metals and plastics stockholding distribution and processing group.

Earnings per share were lower at 6p (7.1p). The interim payment is increased from 3p to 3.1p.

The chairman added that the reorganisation of the plastics division had been successful and it was set to achieve record sales and profits for the year.

There had been a pleasing improvement for the US activities following the end of the initial acquisition programme, he added, and that provided a sound base for growth and significant earnings next year.

In the UK the acquisitions completed by Aalco and the engineering developments of Leavlite were now achieving expected profits.

The net interest charge increased to £934,000 (£444,000), tax took £1.45m (£1.43m) and there were minorities of £101,000 (£98,000). Dividends absorbed £982,000 (£873,000) to leave retained profit of £901,000 (£1.2m).

● comment

Amari may be heading for record profits and turnover but shareholders should not get too carried away. Even the most optimistic forecasts put earnings per share for this year at less than those achieved in 1985. The company is clearly doing the right things by moving further into higher value added areas like stainless steel tubing where growth of about 30 per cent is being achieved and be decreasing its dependence on aluminium. There are also benefits to come from rising prices and from the diversification into the US, which is so far still making losses. None of this, however, justifies the p/e of 17½ implied by profits forecasts for this year of £7.5m. Investors hoping to make a killing if a takeover is launched for the company should reflect that Suter, the only company with a declared stake, is not known for paying over the odds.

British Telecom rings up 11.8% growth to £561m

BY TERRY DODSWORTH, INDUSTRIAL EDITOR

STRONG growth in telephone call volume and a comparatively low rate of cost increase combined to produce an 11.8 per cent jump in pre-tax profits to £561m at **British Telecom** in the first quarter.

The figfures, which were published yesterday against a background of increasing criticism of the quality of BT's services, were accompanied by the announcement of a slowdown in the rate of job cuts in the company. BT conceded that this change in the job reduction programme had been made partly in response to these attacks on its services, but said that the group was nevertheless managing to hold down the rate of cost increases by other means.

As a result, total operating costs were up by 5.7 per cent over the corresponding part of last year, while staff costs rose by 5.3 per cent to £814m. This rate of increase compared with a 7.1 per cent rise in turnover to £2.41bn from £2.25bn in 1986.

BT refused to put firm figures on the decision to trim back its staff reduction programme, but said that numbers in its mainstream business had fallen by only 400 people in the last quarter against a total of 4,800 in the 1986/87 financial year, and 800 in the same period of 1986. Maintaining a larger workforce than originally planned, it added, would also help with its ambitious modernisation programme, while meeting the growth in demand for telephone services in London and other urban areas.

The pre-tax profits, which were in line with City expectations, compared with £502m in 1986; operating profits rose by 10.5 per cent from £573m to £633m. Earnings per share jumped more sharply, rising by 14 per cent from 5.1p to 5.8p.

The growth in activity from the group's main businesses was broadly in line with the levels achieved over the past two years, when BT's volumes have benefited from increasing economic activity. Rental income increased by 8.6 per cent to £812m, with the number of business exchange lines increasing by 4.1 per cent and residential by 2.2 per cent. Demand in London, where growth has been fuelled by rapid expansion in the City, was once again particularly high, with private circuit lines increasing by 40 per cent.

Telephone call income increase by 8.3 per cent overall to £1.28bn. Underlying traffic volume, after excluding price increases, was particularly strong in the inland call sector, where turnover increased by 8 per cent against 7 per cent last year, while international call traffic rose by 11 per cent, the same as in 1986.

On the equipment supply side, however, sales were below last year's levels, due to increasing competition, a sluggish overall market in private exchanges, and the aftermath of the industrial action in the winter.

See Lex

The opening sentence sets the interim results from the company in the context of its recent trading history, drawing attention to significant factors such as acquisitions within the past twelve months, which may affect the figures. But, after reporting the profits and turnover figures, the writer reminds investors of the factor which could influence the shares more than the results: another company is known to have built up a 17 per cent stake in the shares.

Thus, there are two points to watch in assessing the shares — a good set of interim results, and the hint of a takeover. The comment draws the two strands together.

The rise in profits in the first half of the year is put in the context of the range of forecasts by City analysts for profits for the full twelve months. Then the writer turns to the share price, pointing out that a high price/earnings ratio (see Chapter 2) seems to reflect the market's hopes for a takeover bid for the company than the outlook for profits. In the final sentence comes the warning that takeover optimism may have been overdone.

In the case of British Telecommunications, the trading results have to be read against a much wider context of public and political

DIVIDENDS ANNOUNCED

	Current payment	Date of payment	Corres - ponding div	Total for year	Total last year
Alphameric ....int	1†	Feb15	0.75	-	2.5
Anglo Irish Bank ...fin	0.1†‡	-	2.24	3.2	3.2
BAA ....int	3	Jan 27	-	-	-
Cosalt ....fin	3	Jan 27	2.25	4.5	3.5
James Cropper ......int	0.68	Jan 15	0.56*	-	1.63*
Chase Property .....int	1.25	Jan 31	0.61✱	-	3.25✱
Erskine House ....int	1.6†	Jan 12	1.2	-	4
Hambros ....int	3♣	Jan 11	2.4	-	8.2
Monks Inv. Tst. .....int	1.2	-	1.1	-	2.8
North Amer Tr ......fin	4	-	4	5.4	5.4
Powell Duffryn .....int	5.25	Jan 5	4.75	-	16.5
Readicut Int. ....int	0.38†	Jan 12	0.25	-	2.18
TMD Advertisng §.fin	2.4	Feb 23	2	2.4	2

Dividends shown pence per share net except where otherwise stated. *Equivalent after allowing for scrip issue. †On capital increased by rights and/or acquisition issues. §USM stock. ♠Unquoted stock. ♥Third market. ✱As Wingate Property Investments.♣To reduce disparity. ‡Irish currency.

interest. In fact, the results are not far away from City estimates and thus unlikely to be the major factor behind the share price. Comment on a company of this size and importance is reserved for the Lex Column, of which more will be said later. The Company News pages' outline of BT's trading figures, while maintaining the distinction between fact and comment, supplies the background context to the corporation's plans for the labour force.

In addition to reporting and possibly commenting on the day's major company results, the FT publishes a daily dividend table (see page 50), showing dividend payments announced to the Stock Exchange in the previous day's session. Dividends are usually quoted net of tax, and the table compares the payment with the corresponding dividend in the previous year. In the case of interim payments, the table gives the total for the previous full financial year. The notes to the table draw attention to adjustments for scrip and rights issues.

On Monday mornings, the Company News pages carry a table showing dividend statements due, together with the details of the corresponding announcement made a year before. Monday's

PENDING DIVIDENDS

Dates when some of the more important company dividend statements may be expected in the next few weeks are given in the following table. The dates shown are those of last year's announcements except when the forthcoming board meetings (indicated thus *) have been officially notified. Dividends to be declared will not necessarily be at the amounts in the column headed "Announcement last year."

	Date	Announcement last year
AB Foods	Nov 3	Interim 2.2
* Abbey Life	Oct 14	Interim 2.5
Bejam	Oct 15	Final 2.25
* Brent Walker	Oct 9	Interim 3.5
Ferguson Ind.	Oct 23	Interim 3.1
* Glaxo	Oct 12	Final 10.0
Hammerson	Oct 22	Interim 2.0
Harris Q'Way	Oct 30	Interim 1.75
* Hawker Siddeley	Oct 21	Interim 5.0
London and Northern	Oct 23	Interim 2.1
Marks and Spencer	Oct 28	Interim 1.4
Rosehaugh	Nov 6	Final 1.0
* UEI	Oct 14	Interim 2.1
Wolseley	Oct 28	Final 8.0

ed Tile sales at £4.4m continued the growth seen in the sec- **The single final divided is 0.6p (0.55p).**

BOARD MEETINGS

The following companies have notified dates of board meetings to the Stock Exchange. Such meetings are usually held for the purpose of considering dividends. Official indications are not available as to whether the dividends are interims or finals and the sub-divisions shown below are based mainly on last year's timetables.

TODAY

Interims- J. Billam, British Island Airways, Capero Industries, Delyn Packaging, Farnell Electronics, Albert Fisher, Fleming Japanese Investment Trust, Hunting Petroleum Services, Kingsley & Forester, London Atlantic Investment Trust, Musterlin, River & Mercantile Geared Capital and Income Trusts. Scottish Mortgage & Trust, Smaller Companies International Trust, TDS Circuits

Finals- Bejam, Britannia Security.

FUTURE DATES

Interims-	
Boot (Henry)	Oct 20
New Ireland Assurance	Oct 19
Stormgard	Oct 28
WA Holdings	Oct 22
Finals-	
GR Holdings	Oct 19
Inter City Holdings	Oct 26
Leisure Investments	Oct 20
Manganese Bronze Holdings	Oct 22
Pict Petroleum	Nov 2
Really Useful	Oct 27
Union Carbide	Oct 28

newspaper also carries a list of other board meetings planned for the future but only disclosed to the Stock Exchange during the previous week.

Takeover deals are dealt with more fully in the next chapter, but the FT also reports widely on the relatively small acquisitions which lie outside the domain of publicly-quoted companies but often indicate aggressive growth by major companies expanding into new fields. For example, it may seem insignificant for British Petroleum to buy a shampoo manufacturer based in Bradford, but the oil monarch paid £3m to add Crestol to its detergents division. Such deals can be important indicators of the direction of corporate strategies.

Changes in boardroom personnel also have an important role to play in corporate policies. The FT recognizes this by publishing daily an Appointments column, reporting senior posts, mostly at director level.

To build up a full picture of the performance and prospects of a major public company, means following the FT Company News pages over a long period. But the combination of the bi-annual profits statements, annual reports and accounts, and feature comment aims to present the reader with a comprehensive portrait of a company which could never be created merely by adding up the profits figures alone.

Appointments

Managing director at Granada Group

ꝜRANADA GROUP has
pointed **Mr Derek Lewis** as
oup managing director from
nuary 1. He is financial direc-
and chairman of the services
business division. The chair-
n, **Mr Alex Bernstein**, will
tinue as a full-time executive
h Mr Lewis assuming respon-
lity for the line management
the group. Other appoint-
ts follow from this newly-
ted position. From the same
Mr Desmond James, a
ctor and company secretary,
also be appointed director of
orate services, with responsi-
es that include company
tarial, legal, property and
ed activities. **Mr Graham**
ace, head of finance and
ning, will be appointed
or of corporate finance,
complete responsibility for
roup's financial and plan-
functions. **Mr Conor**
e will be joining from
sey and Co as chairman of
vices to business division,
ling Mr Lewis.

★

errick Sims has been
ted chief executive of
AC'S building materials
. He is assistant manag-
ctor of the quarry prod-
vision. He succeeds **Mr**
Pearce who is returning
personal business inter-

troller of NEXT.

★

Mr Douglas Smith has been appointed finance director of JULIANA'S HOLDINGS from January 1. He replaces **Mr Nicholas Irens** who is leaving to become finance director of First Leisure.

★

ROPNER has appointed **Mr Robert J. Sale** as a non-executive director from December 1. He was deputy chief general manager of Barclays Bank.

★

Mr Peter Simon has been appointed a director of Bermuda-based C.T.S., and will divide his time between London and North America. He recently retired as deputy group chief executive of Legal and General Group.

★

Mr John O. Conlan has been appointed group managing director of FIRST LEISURE CORPORATION. He has been a director since the company's formation in 1983. **Mr Nicholas J. Irens** will join as finance director on January 1. He is finance director of Julianas Holdings. **Mr James P.G. Naylor** resigns as joint managing director from December 31, but will retain an association with the company.

★

BRITISH ...

RTZ launches £206.5m cash bid for MK Electrics Group

BY DAVID WALLER

RTZ, THE mining, energy and industrial conglomerate formerly known as Rio Tinto-Zinc, yesterday launched a cash-only bid for MK Electrics Group, valuing the electrical accessories and doorbell manufacturer at £206.5m.

After a board meeting and lengthy talks with Kleinwort Benson, its financial advisers, MK said last night that the offer was inadequate and urged its shareholders to take no action. However, it agreed to meet RTZ to discuss its proposals.

RTZ, whose financial advisers are Morgan Grenfell, yesterday acquired 22 per cent of MK's equity in the market after two firms of stockbrokers conducted a "dawn raid." The move provided further evidence that UK companies believe the stock market has stabilised after five weeks of turmoil.

RTZ argued that MK, the largest supplier of electrical wiring ... plastic conduit and ... UK construction ... the ... iary which also serves the construction industry.

Last night, MK said the bid undervalued its potential, both in the immediate and longer term, and that it could see no advantage to its business arising from the proposals.

As the market opened yesterday, Hoare Govett and Barclays de Zoete Wedd, the stockbrokers acting for RTZ, moved swiftly to buy up MK's shares at the offer price of 550p, 33 per cent above Monday's close. By mid-morning, they had acquired 15 per cent of MK's shares on RTZ's behalf and by the end of the day, spoke for 22 per cent of the company's equity.

Although best-known for its mining activities, the most important source of RTZ's profits is its industrial division, which generated about 60 per cent of the group's attributable profits of £245m in 1986. In its last annual report, RTZ highlighted its desire to expand in this sector by making selective acquisitions. ... annual sales of more ... ided equally ... orth America, Pillar generates a... ter of the company's total... its. It makes and sells a ra... products supplied to the bu... trade, including Everest ... glazing and Catnic steel ... RTZ argues that MK will c... ment Pillar's existing a... and diversification overs... be accelerated with ac... RTZ's resources.

MK has had a lacklust... record over the last four ... it has struggled to re... dependence on Middle ... kets. It has found it di... increase its sizable sha... markets.

However, analysts ... upturn in the present ... predict pre-tax profits ... against £19.6m last ye...

MK's shares closed a... night, 5p above RTZ'... 141p above Monday's ... still below the ... achieved before t... crash. Shares in R... intends to finance ... tion out of its own ... gained 23p to 338p.

Details, Pa...
Lex, Back ...

Allied-Lyons in £572m Hiram Walker purchase

BY LISA WOOD

ALLIED-LYONS, the British-based drinks and food group, is to spend £572m buying out the 49 per cent stake it does not already own in Hiram Walker, the Canadian drinks business, from an offshoot of Olympia & York, a Canadian real estate and resources company.

The deal is made up of £202m in cash and £370m in preference convertible shares, which when converted will give GW Utilities - 88 per cent owned by Olympia & York - a 10 per cent stake in Allied-Lyons.

The move is in line with the British group's aim of becoming a significant force in the international drinks business. Hiram Walker brands include Tia Maria, Courvoisier brandy and Ballantines whisky.

Hiram Walker brands have strong exposure in Canada and the large but difficult US market as well as growing sales in the Far East. Allied's own wine and spirits sales are concentrated in the UK and Europe.

Allied-Lyons sought to buy Hiram Walker's spirits business early in 1986. At the time, the British group was fighting a takeover bid by Elders IXL and the move was seen by some in the City as a poison pill.

The Canadian company, however, was meanwhile taken over by Gulf Canada, a subsidiary of Olympia & York and Gulf Can-

Continued on Back Page
Background, Page 24
Lex, Back Page

6 Takeover Bids

The development of the aggressive takeover bid has provided the City with most of its excitement over the past three decades. Takeover strategies have been refined by the rulings of regulatory or quasi-regulatory bodies, and by new tactics, including 'Dawn Raids' explained later. If London follows Wall Street's lead, then we could be in for a host of new game plans, both defensive and offensive.

In reporting takeover stories, the FT and the rest of the business press face a dual responsibility. On the one hand, bids are exciting stories which are now usually extended over a period of time. On the other, there are definite moments when shareholders, be they long-term investors or would-be speculators, face difficult choices which merit cool and careful consideration.

At the dramatic highspots of the bid situation — the day when the predator makes its first move, or the day the victim escapes — the story will probably appear on the front or the back page of the newspaper. But there will be many days in between when the shareholder is showered with advice from both predator and potential victim, not to mention their respective stockbrokers, merchant banks and public relations companies. The FT's Company News pages and its Lex Column then come into play. The facts must be carefully rounded up, for the City Takeover Panel, the Monopolies and Mergers Commission and the Council for the Securities Industry have all laid down ground rules for the takeover battlefield.

Takeover battles rarely arrive completely out of the blue. The company analysts at the big securities houses are expected to know which companies in their sector of interest are likely to be either predators or victims. Sometimes the predator will admit that it is on the lookout for likely acquisitions. Occasionally, it will even go so far as to raise cash in the market for the admitted purpose of pursuing an acquisition policy. The prospective victim may select itself in an almost equally brazen fashion. A series of poor trading figures, an expensive and disastrous failure to break into a new market, a failure to follow its rivals into new technologies — these, and similiar misfortunes, can push the share price below the average for the sector and start market whispers that the company is a target.

The first hint of a bid may come from the stock market, where 'unusual activity' in the shares may indicate that someone — not necessarily a potential bidder — is building up a stake. To counter the danger of secret stakebuilding, UK legislation and the City Panel on Takeovers and Mergers stipulate that:-

1) Any single investor acquiring 5 per cent of any company's share capital must declare it publicly.
2) Any investor acquiring more than 30 per cent of a company voting equity must make a public offer for the rest.

So, unusual activity in a company's shares in the market-place while a clear sign that the company is regarded as a potential bid target, is unlikely to flush out the eventual bidder. Such activity is more likely to be the task of the takeover arbitrageurs — specialists who take stakes in prospective bid targets with a view to selling the shares on to the bidder when he shows his hand.

The announcement by an investor of the acquisition of a 5 per cent stake in a company's equity will be reported by the FT, either on its Company News pages or on the front page of the newspaper, depending on the implications of the move. Clearly, the acquisition of a 5 per cent stake in a major company, a household name but one believed to be in difficulties, rings the alarm more loudly than, say, a similar acquisition in a company with a tiny market capitalization and shareholder base.

Once it is known that strategic equity stakes have been acquired, then the investment community — and the FT — will be watching for any further development. This may not happen. The 5 per cent stakeholder may be a genuine investor, content to stay with his investment. If no bid arrives, then the arbitrageur may have little option but to hold on to his shares. But any further investment news will be reported in the FT, which will draw attention to the previous stake purchases.

Another form of takeover move, or more accurately, partial takeover move, to burst on an unsuspecting stock market in the Eighties has been the Dawn Raid.

Dawn Raids have become more rare since the rules were changed, but any resurgence of the ploy would find its place on the front pages of the FT and other financial newspapers.

The Raids were originally a plan to acquire stakes already held in the target company, and then quickly boost them by active, but briefly prolonged, bidding in the market-place. The Takeover Panel, seeking to slow the process of stakebuilding, has ruled that a predator acquiring a near 15 per cent stake may only purchase a further 10 per cent over a rolling seven-day period. If such a predator wants more than a further 15 per cent — potentially breaking the 30 per cent barrier — then it must make a tender offer to all shareholders, accepting shares on a pro-rata basis.

Dawn Raids apart, however, the next move of significance may be a full takeover bid for the company which has already been put in the market's sights by the disclosure of stake building. Usually, the bidder will make a preliminary statement, spelling out the terms of his offer, before proceeding to post formal offer documents. His preliminary statement will explain whether the bid is:

1) In cash.
2) In exchange of shares.
3) A mixture of shares and cash, or a choice between them.
4) An offer in convertible or fixed interest securities.

These details set a price on the shares of the target company, and the first reaction will come from the stock market.

The target shares may move up to just under the bid price, indicating that the stock market believes that the bid will go through on the terms stated — the price stays below the bid because accepting shareholders will not receive their money until completion of the deal. But the shares may move well above the bid price if the market believes that there are other bidders lurking in the wings, or that some of the known stakeholders may hold out for better terms. In this case, the hunt is on as the City analysts set to work to value the target company, so as to predict the price at which the equity will be taken out.

The move towards the formal offer document is the next important step. The City Takeover Panel insists that takeover offer documents are prepared with integrity. Specifically, it requires that:

1) Profit forecasts and asset valuations must be confirmed by accounting experts.

2) Adequate backing must be disclosed for any cash terms.

This is important information, whether the bid goes through or not. The bidding company is disclosing significant details of its profits outlook and background financing which will remain a factor in the share price whatever the outcome of the takeover contest.

This is why the FT reports fully on takeover documentation which at first glance may seem of only temporary significance.

The issue of the formal offer document should open the way to the bid battle proper. But before considering what this may entail, there are some other possibilities to watch for.

From the time a bid is launched, the entire enterprise can be referred to the UK Monopolies and Mergers Commission on the grounds that it reduces competition in the business area concerned. The snag is that the Commission has six months in which to report, and a great deal can happen in that time. The stock market may fall, the predator may see a better bid opportunity, or interest rates may rise, undermining his financing plans. Prospective bidders often withdraw their bids on the appearance of the Monopolies Commission. Indeed, some make their bid conditional on the absence of any referral to the Commission.

A prospective bidder may withdraw for other reasons. This has happened when a bidder, caught on the hop by rumours in the market, has felt obliged to rush out a statement expressing interest in making a bid, but without announcing terms. After taking a closer look at the target, the prospective bidder has been known to drop out, leaving some burnt fingers in the stock market.

Takeover documents will state the closing date for the offer, and the bidder may try to panic shareholders into accepting quickly.

Shareholders should postpone replying to the bid offer, and keep their eyes on the stock market reports and newspapers of the financial press to see if another bid is brewing. The key sign will be the performance of the shares in the stock market. If the shares stay well above the bid terms, then the omens are good. The stock market is well supplied with professional arbitrageurs who will 'take a position' in a bid stock and are unlikely to lose their nerve until the end of the day. But the shareholder should not allow his view to be completely dominated by the financial pages. He should consider such points as the following:

1) Has the target company been well run by its existing management?
2) What is the bidder's financial record? If you propose to take the bidder's shares/loan stock, then his future becomes yours.
3) What will happen if the bid collapses? Was the target company looking weak before the offer? Is it a poor business anyway, and would you be better off out of it?

These are the kind of questions that the FT Company News pages will be trying to answer. In some cases, the answer will have been indicated in an interview with the company management long before the bid surfaced. But in other cases, the spotlight may not have been switched on until the bidder arrived. Remember that in a buoyant stock market, any company's shares will be enlivened by a takeover move.

All these questions may come into focus as the bid nears its formal closure date. But there is still no need for hasty action. Most bidders declare a 'minimum acceptance level', and will make their offer 'unconditional' once that level is reached. This means that even if you miss the closure date, your shares will probably be accepted. If the bid is accepted by holders of 90 per cent of the equity, then the bidder can buy out the rest on the same bid terms. So, the private shareholder usually has little to lose by holding out to the end, just in case a new offer appears on the table.

The breadth of corporate reporting in the FT helps to place in context the takeover bids which suddenly spring to the front page. Remember that takeover bids, no matter how dramatically they emerge, are never made on the spur of the moment. Growth by acquisition is a perfectly acceptable corporate strategy. The key is to identify companies which pursue such strategies successfully over a lengthy period, and to search out the companies which become their targets.

Chemical New York stays in red in third quarter

BY ANATOLE KALETSKY IN NEW YORK

CHEMICAL NEW YORK, the fourth largest US bank group which includes Chemical Bank and Texas Commerce Bancshares, lost $66.4m or $1.12 a share after tax in the third quarter.

The loss, which compared with a net profit of $99.1m or $1.87 a share a year earlier, resulted mainly from a charge of $135m associated with the restructuring and staff cuts at Chemical Bank announced in September.

The holding company's loss also included a $13.5m third-quarter net deficit from Texas Commerce, the leading bank in Houston, which Chemical acquired in May this year. The troubled Texas bank was not included in the 10 per cent staff cutbacks and consolidation of operations announced by Chemical in September because it was already operating "under a strict austerity programme," the parent company said.

Apart from special charges, Chemical's results were adversely affected by higher non-interest expenses - which were up 18 per cent on an underlying basis - and gains from the sale of investment securities which were $47.1m lower than in the previous year.

Against this, the bank had 23 per cent better profits from its foreign exchange operations, 28 per cent higher fee income from its "core" trust and banking services and provisions for loan losses which were $17m smaller than in the year-earlier period.

For the first nine months of 1986, Chemical has lost a total of $1.08bn or $20.88 a share, after taking a $1.1bn charge for Third World loan losses in the second quarter. The total loss at the Texas Commmerce subsidiary since the May 1 merger date has been $93.1m, including a provision of $80m for LDC loans.

●Bank of New York, the medium-sized Wall Street bank which is attempting to take over Irving Bank, one of its closest rivals, earned $45.2m or $1.22 a share in the third quarter, 18 per cent up on the $37.9m or $1.12 reported last year.

The gain was due to growth of around 30 per cent in both fee income and loans outstanding. The bank also reaffirmed its commitment to pursue the takeover, which is being contested by Irving.

Continental Illinois 46% ahead

BY OUR NEW YORK STAFF

CONTINENTAL ILLINOIS, the big Chicago bank which has been operating under federal government supervision since its near-collapse three years ago, reported a 46 per cent jump in net income to $60.1m or 24 cents a share, compared with $41.1m or 15 cents in the third quarter of 1986. The bank's total assets at the end of last month were $31.5bn, compared with $28.5bn a year earlier.

Continental said that sharp declines in investment portfolio gains and interest collections from Brazil and Ecuador were more than offset by gains from venture capital interests and lower loan loss provisions.

It transferred $203m of poor quality loans to the Federal Deposit Insurance Corporation during the quarter, bringing to $1.5bn the total loans assumed by the FDIC.

●Marine Midland Banks, the New York-based affiliate of Hong Kong and Shanghai Banking Corporation, achieved a 39 per cent improvement in net profits, to $49.3m or $2.47 a share, in the third quarter, on total assets of $25.1bn, compared with $35.4m or $1.75, on assets of $23.5bn a year ago.

Gencor output hit by strike

BY JIM JONES IN JOHANNESBURG

EFFECTS of the three-week stoppage by black miners in August varied considerably on the mines managed by Gencor, the first of the South African mining groups to report September-quarter results for strike-hit mines.

Most of the mines managed to maintain gold recovery grades by milling ore from surface stockpiles, but they nevertheless suffered drops in the tonnages of ore processed.

From a production standpoint, Kinross was the worst affected of the group's mines.

Its black workforce is particularly militant following one of the country's most severe mine disasters, and this year's strike cut mill throughput by more than 20 per cent to 426,000 tonnes in the September quarter, from 535,500 tonnes in the June period.

The gold recovery grade dropped to 5.9 grams per tonne from 6.1g/t.

Neighbouring Winkelhaak suffered a 14.4 per cent cut in mill throughput but maintained its recovery grade at 5.4g/t.

Lower throughputs led to some substantial percentage increases in the unit costs of mining and processing each tonne of ore, even though the strikers were not paid for three weeks.

Black miners' wage increases have added about 5 per cent to total operating costs and the increases given to white workers have added a slightly lower percentage.

The group as a whole suffered a 17 per cent decline in after-tax income to R128.7m ($62.3m). Gold production fell by 8.7 per cent to 21,832kg, from 23,730kg.

Paradoxically, Buffelsfontein, the largest of the Gencor group's mines, increased its production rate to 723,000 tonnes in the September quarter from 678,000 tonnes in the June period.

The mine has been affected by ore shortages after failing to find expected reserves in the newly-opened Lucas Block. It is now recovering from this following several quarters of increased development to open new mining areas.

An explosion at St Helena's new shaft has delayed shaft development by about eight months.

GENCOR GOLD QUARTERLY RESULTS

	Gold produced (kg) Sept 87	Jun 87	After-tax profit (Rm) Sept 87	Jun 87	Earnings per share (cents) Sept 87	June 87
Beatrix	3,073	3,236	16.77	29.09	n/a	n/a
Bracken	661	663	3.15	2.38	19.5	13.5
Buffels	4,308	4,369	16.92	12.24	53.5	190.8
Grootvlei	1,015	1,097	2.03	2.64	13.5	17.8
Kinross	2,494	3,262	16.27	20.66	72.4	93.2
Leslie	775	827	2.77	2.58	14.6	13.7
Marievale	198	201	(0.44)	(0.44)	(10.1)	(13.1)
St Helena	2,130	2,342	14.65	18.22	28.5	62.2
Stilfontein	1,830	1,769	6.87	7.94	47.2	48.8
Unisel	1,758	1,924	12.74	12.12	35.6	38.0
West Rand Cons	996	994	1.33	1.85	6.4	24.6
Winkelhaak	2,594	3,046	35.65	29.45	44.9	86.1

Earnings are calculated after capital expenditure and loan repayments. Figures in parentheses are negative.

INI to place cellulose shares

BY TOM BURNS IN MADRID

INSTITUTO NACIONAL de Industria (INI), Spain's public sector holding company, is to place 38 per cent of the equity of Ence, its profitable cellulose company, on the Madrid stock exchange during the first two weeks of January.

The Ence share offering follows a successful stock market operation last year involving Gesa, a state-owned energy company in the Balearic islands, which was heavily oversubscribed, brought in 54,000 new shareholders and reduced INI's stake in Gesa from 94 per cent to 56 per cent.

The decision to float part of Ence's equity, which will bring INI's equity in the company down to 54 per cent, is part of a general step-by-step strategy to reproduce the success of the Gesa flotation in selected INI companies.

Ence produces some 500,000 tons of cellulose paste annually at its plants in Huelva, southern Spain, and in Pontevedra, in the north-west, and exports around 60 per cent of its output. Executives said they expected to raise Ence's revenue this year from Pta32.5bn ($270m) last year to Pta39.7bn and to earn pre-tax profits of some Pta6bn.

INI's share offerings in selected companies falls short of a privatisation programme, as the state holding company will, according to the present strategy, in all cases retain control of the companies.

The main guideline of the equity programme is to introduce what INI executives call "market discipline" into the public companies.

Among the INI companies shortlisted to follow the Gesa and Ence path are Iberia Airlines, which has announced a strong return to profitability, and Endesa, the electrical utility which is the holding company's chief profit earner.

Steep fall at American Airlines parent

BY OUR NEW YORK STAFF

AMR, PARENT of American Airlines yesterday revealed that its strong growth in revenues is still not working through to profit with a sharp fall in third quarter earnings to $87.1m or $1.41 a share.

AMR, which operates the second largest US airline, described as "disappointing" results in the September quarter which showed a 27.7 per cent increase in revenues to $1.98bn but a 28 per cent drop in net income.

American has been expanding its network aggressively but has run into heavy interest and other costs and has had difficulty sustaining fare increases.

Mr Robert Crandall, chairman and chief executive, said: "We are disappointed with our third-quarter financial results. We must and will lower costs further in the months ahead." In the nine months to September, AMR reported earnings of $199.2m or $3.30 a share, against $272.56m or $4.47 in the comparable 1986 period. Revenues were $5.32bn, against $4.52bn.

PepsiCo heads for record results

By Our Financial Staff

PEPSICO, the world's second largest soft drinks producer, is well on the way to another record year, despite a slackening in profits growth.

Net earnings for the third quarter increased by 25 per cent from $151.7m or 58 cents a share to $189.9m or 72 cents, on sales up 26.7 per cent from $2.32bn to $2.94bn.

This brings net earnings at the nine-month stage to $447.8m or $1.70 a share, an increase of 31 per cent on last year's corresponding $341.2m or $1.31. Nine-month sales improved by 31.9 per cent, to $8.02bn from $6.08bn.

The latest figures include losses from discontinued operations of nil against $1.1m in the quarter and $1.3m against $3.6m in the nine months. The latest nine-month returns also include a loss of $11.5m on the disposal of discontinued operations.

PepsiCo Inc said it expects earnings per share for the full year from continuing operations to be up more than 25 per cent. The company posted operating income of $1.22bn or $1.75 a share on continuing operations in 1986.

Semiconductor sector lifts Motorola

By Louise Kehoe in San Francisco

MOTOROLA, the US electronics manufacturer, has reported a strong rise in sales and earnings, boosted by sharply higher profits in the semiconductor sector.

Earnings in the third quarter rose to $70m, or 54 cents a share, from $31m, or 24 cents, in the same period last year. Sales increased from $1.4bn to $1.7bn.

For the nine-month period, earnings were $206m, or $1.60 a share, up from $131m, or $1.04, in the same period a year ago. Sales increased to $4.9bn from $4.3bn.

The company said semiconductor sales rose by 23 per cent in the quarter, with sharply higher profits and record demand for microprocessors, the chips used to build personal computers and computer workstations.

Apple beats expectations

by Our San Francisco Correspondent

APPLE COMPUTER, the US personal computer manufacturer,has reported stronger than expected earnings and sales for the fourth quarter.

Sales rose 54 per cent to $786.4m while earnings were well above analysts predictions at $71.7m or 54 cents a share, an increase of 116 per cent on the $32.9m or 25 cents registered in the same period last year.

For the full year, Apple's sales rose by 40 per cent to $2.66bn from $1.90bn in fiscal 1986. Net earnings for fiscal 1987 were $217m or $1.65 a share, a 41 per cent advance on the $154m or $1.20 (adjusted for a two-for-one stock split) recorded in fiscal 1986.

Mr John Sculley, chairman and chief executive, said: "Our new products are shipping in record numbers." This year Apple launched new versions of both of its key products, the Macintosh business personal computer and the Apple II for home and school use.

"Fiscal year 1987 has been a year of record achievement for Apple Computer,"added MrSculley."We successfully introduced many new products throughout the year. They have been well accepted, particularly in the business market. We have now completed the repositioning of Apple andenter fiscal year 1988 with strong momentum and a full complement of new products."

Strong records business boosts CBS earnings

BY OUR NEW YORK STAFF

CBS, the rapidly restructuring US media group which is considering an offer of some $2bn for its record business from Sony of Japan, yesterday reported sharply higher profits, with CBS Records contributing most of the gain.

The strong performance of the records division may strengthen the apparent consensus in the CBS boardroom against accepting Sony's bid.

CBS earned $59.9m or $2.31 a share after tax in the third quarter, more than double the net profits of $28.6m or $1.09 last year.

The underlying improvement in the company's businesses was even greater, since barely half of last year's profit came from discontinued operations, particularly the publishing and magazine divisions which CBS has now sold for a total of nearly $1.2bn.

Net income from continuing operations was $58.7m or $2.26 a share in the latest quarter, compared with the $11.3m or 34 cents reported the year before. In the last nine months, net income from continuing operations has been $196.4m or $7.66 a share, 31 per cent up on the $149.9m or $5.97 which the same business earned a year earlier.

However, Mr Laurence Tisch, president, pointed out that the strong increase was "due mainly to the growth of CBS Record profits and to a substantial reduction in interest expense."

Mr Tisch, who is the largest shareholder in CBS through his family-controlled Loews Corporation, is said to oppose the Sony bid for CBS Records, favouring a partial flotation of the business as an independent company instead.

CBS's broadcast group, which accounted for 55 per cent of the $984m revenues in the third quarter, showed an 18 per cent decline in operating profits to $39.4m. In contrast the Records group, which had revenues of $414m, more than doubled its quarterly operating profits from $19.2m to $42.4m.

In the first nine months of the year, profits from the records business advanced from $100.6m to $141m, boosted by sales of compact disks and the unprecedented success of Michael Jackson hits. Meanwhile the broadcast group suffered a 25 per cent profits decline from $233.8m to $215.2m.

Increase in HCA net income

BY OUR NEW YORK STAFF

HOSPITAL CORPORATION of America, the large US health care group which recently sold 104 low-profit hospitals to its employees, has increased its third-quarter net income to $66.5m or 80 cents a share from $53.8m or 65 cents in the corresponding 1986 quarter.

But the results are so distorted by the $1.64bn hospital sale and by charges to account for HCA's wrenching adjustment to its difficult market that comparison between the two quarters is impossible. Sales revenues, which include the contribution of the divested hospitals up to August, were $1.16bn against $1.24bn.

The group puts nine-month net income at $208m or $2.52 a share against $216.7m or $2.57 previously on revenues of $3.76bn against $3.74bn.

HCA, which as industry leader has been badly hit by price controls on the Government's Medicare programme and cost-cutting by insurers, said the third-quarter figures included: a $154m after-tax gain on a hospital sale; a $73m pre-tax charge to recognise uncollectable bills; and a $126m pre-tax write-down of investments and properties.

In addition, HCA is continuing to bear heavy costs from its attempt to write its own health insurance, now a joint venture with the Equitable Life insurance group and known as Equicor. HCA's share in Equicor's third-quarter loss was $12.5m but the company said it remains committed to the business.

Mr Thomas Frist, HCA chairman, said the results "do not fully reflect the benefits of HCA's significant restructuring programme". The hospital sale will permit HCA to buy back about $600m of its own stock under a tender offer which closes on October 22 and pay back some $850m in debt, he said.

If all the transactions had occurred before the beginning of the year, he said HCA would have earned $70m or 99 cents a share in the first nine months of this year after charges.

Digital disappoints with $270m

BY OUR NEW YORK STAFF

DIGITAL EQUIPMENT, the greatly successful US computer company which has become one of the highest-flying stocks on Wall Street, last night reported disappointing results which seem to confirm a gradual flattening in its spectacular growth-curve.

Digital made net profits of $270m, or $2.03 a share, in the three months ended September 26, the first quarter of its financial year.

Although these profits were 48 per cent above the $182.6m reported a year ago, they could prove inadequate to match the market's over-exuberant projections.

As Digital's results were announced late last night, after the close of the New York market, Wall Street will not have an opportunity to render its judgment until this morning.

But one ominous indicator is that the median projection for Digital's earnings in the September quarter was $2.10 per share, according to a recent survey of 17 analysts conducted by Institutional Brokers Estimate System, a service of Wall Street broker Lynch Jones and Ryan.

The company's revenues, at $2.52bn, were 25 per cent up on the quarter a year earlier and only 10 per cent down on the June quarter, which is traditionally the strongest of the year.

Colgate to take $150m charge

By James Buchan in New York

COLGATE-PALMOLIVE, the US household products group which is restructuring its businesses, announced yesterday that it would take a $150m charge to its earnings in the quarter just ended to account for cuts in its corporate staff and the closures of manufacturing plants.

Colgate said that the charge, amounting to $211m before tax and $2.20 a share, would wipe out earnings for the third quarter ended September. In the 1986 September quarter, the group reported net income of $48.05m or 88 cents a share.

But Colgate, which has impressed Wall Street with the vigour of its restructuring since Mr Reuben Mark took over as chief executive in 1984, said that it would partly offset the loss with a gain from the $200m sale of a bandage-making subsidiary. The gain will be booked in the fourth quarter.

"Over the past three years, we have been working to reduce costs and accelerate new products programmes," Mr Mark said yesterday. "Maintaining this momentum is vital."

He said that Colgate would cut some 600 jobs as part of a reorganisation of its corporate headquarters, its US operations and the staff at Kendall, the health care subsidiary which has been hurt by lower hospital spending. The purpose is to support a "decentralised and more entrepreneurial management style."

Sharp gain at Weyerhaeuser

By Our New York Staff

WEYERHAEUSER, a major US forest products company, reported sharply better results, with third-quarter net profits doubling to $128.1m, or 89 cents a share, from $62.3m, or 44 cents a year earlier. Sales rose 30 per cent to $1.82bn from $1.4bn.

In the nine months, its net rose 76 per cent to $317.2m, or $2.27, from $180.6m, or $1.21. Sales rose 24 per cent to $5.21bn from $4.2bn. It increased its quarterly dividend by five cents a share to 37.5 cents.

It attributed the results to continuing improvement in world pulp, paperboard and newsprint markets.

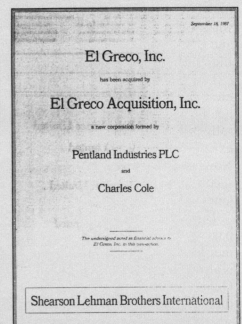

NORTH AMERICAN QUARTERLY RESULTS

AMERICAN PRESIDENT COMPANIES
Shipping

	1987 $	1986 $
Third quarter		
Revenue	45[illegible]m	354.2m
Net income	24.9m	13m
Net per share	1.09	0.55
Nine months		
Revenue	1.34bn	1.03bn
Net income	64.9m	7.8m
Net per share	2.83	0.30

[illegible] DANIELS MIDLAND
[illegible]

	1987 $	1986 $
First quarter		
[illegible]	82.9m	64.9m
Net per share	0.48	0.38

[illegible]INGTON NORTHERN
[illegible]

	1987 $	1986 $
Third quarter		
Revenues	1.78bn	1.69bn
Net income	127m	100.3m
Net per share	1.70	1.25
Nine months		
Revenues	4.91bn	4.65bn
Net income	270.7m	*936.8m
Net per share	3.62	*13.02

*Loss

[illegible] INDUSTRIES
Aerospace, automotive prods

	1987 $	1986 $
Third quarter		
Revenues	384.2m	386.8m
Net income	35.7m	24.5m
Net per share	0.97	0.15
Nine months		
Revenues	1.72bn	1.2bn
Net income	60.2m	73.9m
Net per share	1.71	0.48

DANA
Vehicle parts

	1987 $	1986 $
Third quarter		
Revenues	1bn	889m
Net income	38.1m	12.2m
Net per share	0.86	0.24
Nine months		
Revenues	3.1bn	2.8bn
Net income	11.6m	85.8m
Net per share	2.50	1.64

B F GOODRICH
PVC resins, chemicals

	1987 $	1986 $
Third quarter		
Revenues	564m	574.1m
Net income	42.4m	16.6m
Net per share	1.71	0.70
Nine months		
Revenues	1.6bn	2.06bn
Net income	84.5m	19.7m
Net per share	3.33	0.81

HILTON HOTELS
Hotels

	1987 $	1986 $
Third quarter		
Revenues	198.2m	186.6m
Net income	22.3m	23.7m
Net per share	0.89	0.95
Nine months		
Revenues	623.4m	543.4m
Net income	81.5m	71.7m
Net per share	3.25	2.87

IC INDUSTRIES
Consumer, commercial prods

	1987 $	1986 $
Third quarter		
Revenues	988.9m	860.6m
Op. Net inc	44.2m	11.1m
Net per share	0.39	0.10
Nine months		
Revenues	2.87bn	2.48bn
Op. Net inc	115.7m	57.3m
Net per share	1.02	0.53

MARRIOTT
Hotels

	1987 $	1986 $
Third quarter		
Revenues	1.5bn	1.3bn
Net income	56.7m	49.2m
Net per share	0.42	0.36
Nine months		
Revenues	4.4bn	3.42bn
Net income	161.3m	135.5m
Net per share	1.19	0.99

MORTON THIOKOL
Chemicals, salt, aerospace

	1987 $	1986 $
First		
Revenues	503.9m	449.3m
Net income	40.6m	33.1m
Net per share	0.85	0.70

NCNB
Banking

	1987 $	1986 $
Third quarter		
Net income	43.8m	50m
Net per share	0.52	0.63
Nine months		
Net income	152.1m	152.8m
Net per share	1.87	1.95

RAYTHEON
Defence, aerospace

	1987 $	1986 $
Third quarter		
Revenues	1.96bn	1.71bn
Net income	114.6m	101.5m
Net per share	1.57	1.31
Nine months		
Revenues	5.52bn	5.27bn
Net income	327.2m	293.6m
Net per share	4.44	3.78

SHERWIN-WILLIAMS
Paints

	1987 $	1986 $
Third quarter		
Revenues	512.3m	438.2m
Op.net income	36.4m	29.9m
Op.net per sh.	0.81	0.66
Nine months		
Revenues	1.38bn	1.2bn
Op.net inco	74.2m	62.6m
Op.net per sh.	1.65	1.36

SOUTHEAST BANKING
Banking

	1987 $	1986 $
Third quarter		
Assets	12.6bn	11bn
Net income	29.3m	22.6m
Net per share	0.96	0.77
Nine months		
Net income	10.2m	63.6m
Net per share	0.21	2.22

TELEDYNE
Diversified industrial

	1987 $	1986 $
Third quarter		
Revenues	806m	766.8m
Net income	89.5m	69.3m
Net per share	7.66	5.91
Nine months		
Revenues	2.41bn	2.41bn
Net income	218.4m	191.3m
Net per share	18.67	16.34

TRANSAMERICA
Insurance, financial services

	1987 $	1986 $
Third quarter		
Revenues	1.51bn	1.64bn
Net income	137.8m	107.9m
Net per share	1.76	1.40
Nine months		
Revenues	5.27bn	4.66bn
Net income	354.8m	221.2m
Net per share	4.56	2.85

7 International Company News

It is hardly surprising that the FT has substantially increased its coverage of foreign companies over a decade which has seen Japanese television sets, Italian washing-machines, German motor-cars and Spanish kitchenware all become increasingly commonplace in Britain. The paper now carries the trading results from a large number of overseas companies, selected so as to provide a wide-ranging picture of each major industrial country, but also a permanently running feature film, if you like, of the progress and fortunes of each major world industry.

Some readers will see foreign goods, and the performance of the companies that manufacture them, as welcome suppliers of capital or consumer goods; others as potential rivals for business or even as threats to UK markets or jobs. These reactions often lead straight to the profit and loss accounts of the company concerned and it is these results that the FT aims to cover in a regular and systematic fashion. It would be very difficult, for example, to take any view on the outlook for the British chemicals industry without taking into account what is happening at Monsanto or Dow Chemical in the US, or Bayer and BASF in West Germany, or Asahi Chemicals in Japan, or Air Liquide in France, and so on.

This was always true of the heavy industries but it is becoming increasingly so in the retail and consumer services industries, once neatly divided into their national slots. The development first of self-service stores, then supermarkets and then hypermarkets are all examples of how new retailing ideas have moved around the world. Now, it is the turn of the financial services industry as European securities markets follow the US lead into new forms of consumer lending.

The first place to look for foreign company reports is on the front page of the paper, where they compete for attention on their news merits with reports from British companies. The size of the company is always a major consideration, and the full year's results from General Motors are virtually certain of a place on page one. But there are other criteria. If a foreign company is involved in a bid fight

THE LEX COLUMN

Warburg rides out the storm

S.G. Warburg's first half figures may be of only academic interest, since they were struck before the Great Crash, but a doubling in pre-tax profits to £76.8m and a 17 per cent rise in the interim dividend shows the sorts of returns the group can earn when the financial markets are booming. Indeed, the figures understate the potential since Warburg charged its development spending against profits in the current half, rather than dipping into hidden reserves, and its fixed interest business did not prosper. A dominant position in UK equities, and an impressive performance from Mercury Asset Management which tripled pre-tax profits to £23.9m, provided the bulk of first half growth and gave Warburg the confidence and cash flow to support its ambitious development plans. It stresses these remain intact.

Warburg is unlikely to have made any money yet in the current half year; but at a guess, its losses may be no more than half the size of BZW's. Warburg makes markets in considerably fewer UK equities than BZW and the combination of its Akroyd jobbing team and a broader base of business makes it better placed to withstand the markets' downturn. Its corporate finance business continues to prosper and MAM still has more funds under management than it did a year ago. Barring some cataclysmic event, the group should be able to earn £130m for the full year, putting it on a prospective multiple of around 6½. However, a near one third rise in its workforce in the last 14 months is a reminder that even Warburg may have been a little over-optimistic in its global expansion plans.

FT Index fell 18.6 to 1316.6

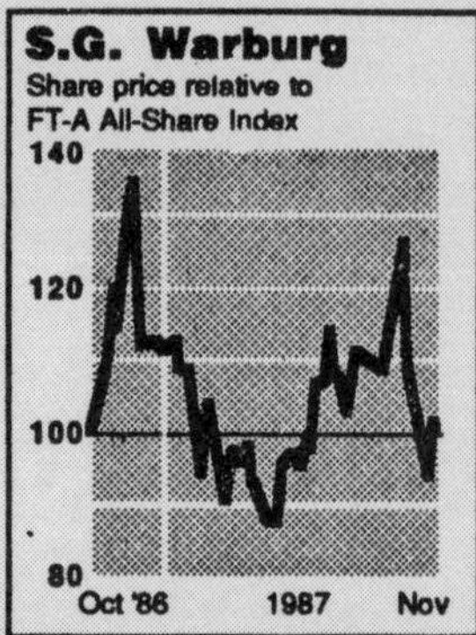

Courtaulds

If Courtaulds were a less self-effacing kind of company, it would surely despair at the 40 per cent fall in its shares over

City forecasts of £230m for the year a little generous, there was no reason for such a harsh reaction. Fibres aside, every division is now doing well, with even industrial paints, the perennial problem area, in better shape.

It would be silly to pretend that Courtaulds is insulated from either the dollar or from recession, but it is not so exposed as to justify a 25 per cent discount to the industrial average. Paradoxically, a mini-recession might be just what its flagging rating needs, as it would put its strength to the test. It might also throw up enough tempting opportunities to wean it from its hitherto unadventurous approach to acquisitions.

Cable and Wireless

The hammering of Cable and Wireless's share price is surely a classic market over-reaction, short of a complete collapse in the dollar. Because the company is still essentially a dollar earner, the interim pre-tax profit rise slipped from 15 per cent to three per cent on translation (with even less favourable terms for

is theoretically worth £3.4bn - nearly £500m more than C and W's London capitalisation. Even allowing for some discount, that is a market anomaly which ought to provide a solid floor to the share price, however flat reported earnings are over the next couple of years. And if the Hong Kong stock market remains too unstable to allow C and W to sell off another five per cent of the subsidiary, the balance sheet can wait. It is true that the company may be a little over-sanguine about the potential slow-down of growth in Hong Kong, in the event of recession, but it would at least be from a stratospheric level.

BAT

Lost once more in labyrinthine nine months' figures from BAT yesterday, the market lopped 24p off the share price to 425p. One reason was uneasiness over the group's post crash decision not to take credit for £41m of smoothed third-quarter investment appreciation on Eagle Star's non-life funds. The issue is complex, especially since BAT says it is sticking to its policy of bringing forward unrealised capital appreciation on Eagle Star's portfolio into the profit-and-loss account. At end-1986, Eagle Star had a solvency margin of a remarkably high 109 per cent, justified according to BAT by the volume of risky liability business in its insurance book. Equity market turmoil had sliced the margin back by late last week, but only to the mid-80s - still ten points clear of General Accident. If the financial strength of composite insurers makes them strong defensive plays, BAT has a recession-proof element here to match its tobacco interests.

Texaco

Mr Holmes a Court's decision to sell half his stake in Texaco to Mr Carl Icahn's TWA, and offer him the right of first refusal on with a company outside its own territory — not necessarily in Britain — then its interested public is consequently larger. If it has been disastrously unsuccessful, or the opposite, with a new product of interest to its rivals throughout the world, then it will lift itself onto the front page of the paper.

In this context, the back page of the *Financial Times* is synonymous with the front, but with the important addition of the Lex Column. The major overseas companies are subjected to the same degree of scrutiny as UK companies have long been treated to in the Lex Column. Lex will often compare the company with its industry rivals in the UK or elsewhere, drawing attention to significant differences in interest rates or stock market ratings in the company's home country with those in other major nations.

However, not all foreign companies are large enough or important enough to rate mention on the front or back page, or in the Lex Column. The bulk of foreign company reporting is to be found inside the paper, on the pages headed International Companies and Finance, or International Capital Markets and Companies. These pages are divided into those carrying company results from North America, those from Continental Europe, and those from the Far East. Since each of these geographical areas contains more than one major industrial country, it has been no easy task to devise criteria to govern the decision of which companies' results must be reported, and which can be left out.

The choice is complicated by the huge growth in cross-border investment in recent years. This has been extended from the conventional form of investment by a company in plant and factories in another country, to the rise in cross-border equity investment following the easing of currency and investment controls in markets around the world. US pension fund managers, for example, who hardly bothered with foreign investment ten years ago, are now encouraged to do so both by Federal Law and by growing pressure to maximize investment returns. In Britain, the removal of exchange rate restrictions has given fund managers and private investors the same opportunities to pursue the best global investment opportunities.

Should the paper report the results only of the biggest companies in each country, or should it take account of whether the shares are listed outside a company's home base, or whether it is a household name, or whether it has factories away from home?

The FT bases its selection of overseas companies qualifying for regular coverage of their trading results on the FT-Actuaries World Index, but with reservations. The reservations are that any foreign company activity involved in a cross-border bid, or any company picked out by the paper's correspondent in the country concerned, will be added to the list.

The FT-World Index, by its very nature, provides a comprehensive picture of corporate events in 2,400 companies in 23 countries. Opposite is printed the list of countries covered in the index, together with the number of companies tracked in each one. The full list of companies included in the FT-World Index comprises just about every prominent name in world industry and thus serves as an excellent basis for the paper's coverage.

FT – ACTUARIE

Jointly compiled by the Financial Times, G
Ltd., in conjunction with the Institu

NATIONAL AND REGIONAL MARKETS Figures in parentheses show number of stocks per grouping	TUESDAY NOVEMBER 17 1			
	US Dollar Index	Day's Change %	Pound Sterling Index	Lo Curr In
Australia (89)	98.92	+2.0	83.12	
Austria (16)	91.44	+1.0	76.83	
Belgium (48)	102.74	−0.1	86.32	
Canada (127)	101.38	−1.2	85.18	
Denmark (38)	108.77	−0.1	91.39	
France (120)	85.56	−1.3	71.89	
West Germany (93)	75.18	−2.7	63.17	
Hong Kong (46)	87.85	−0.7	73.81	
Ireland (14)	103.94	−3.4	87.34	
Italy (94)	77.37	+2.4	65.01	
Japan (457)	134.58	−0.6	113.07	
Malaysia (36)	102.99	−1.2	86.54	
Mexico (14)	159.43	−11.7	133.95	
[illegible]	97.17	−2.6	81.65	
[illegible] (37)	[illegible]	[illegible]	66.75	

FT WORLD INDEX

Australia (89)
Austria (16)
Belgium (48)
Canada (127)
Denmark (38)
France (120)
West Germany (93)
Hong Kong (46)
Ireland (14)
Italy (94)
Japan (457)
Malaysia (36)
Mexico (14)
Netherlands (37)
New Zealand (23)
Norway (24)
Singapore (27)
South Africa (61)
Spain (43)
Sweden (34)
Switzerland (53)
United Kingdom (332)
USA (582)

ORLD INDICES

Sachs & Co., and Wood Mackenzie & Co.
ctuaries and the Faculty of Actuaries

	MONDAY NOVEMBER 16 1987			DOLLAR INDEX		
Gross Div. Yield	US Dollar Index	Pound Sterling Index	Local Currency Index	1987 High	1987 Low	Year ago (approx)
4.26	97.01	82.12	93.91	180.81	85.80	86.68
2.56	90.56	76.66	80.53	102.87	85.53	93.82
5.21	102.80	87.02	91.14	134.89	96.19	92.61
3.19	102.61	86.86	97.89	141.78	98.15	98.72
3.05	108.92	92.19	97.25	124.83	98.18	94.03
3.55	86.69	73.38	78.29	121.82	77.39	93.92
2.86	77.25	65.39	68.37	104.93	68.91	92.88
5.57	88.48	74.90	88.67	158.68	75.82	87.29
4.80	107.65	91.12	97.61	160.22	96.20	89.49
2.66	75.55	63.95	70.36	112.11	72.04	96.52
0.59	135.41	114.62	116.83	161.28	100.00	88.12
3.60	104.29	88.28	100.76	193.64	98.24	100.81
1.02	180.62	152.89	333.25	422.59	99.72	94.02
5.26	99.79	84.47	87.45	131.41	87.70	96.28
4.54	78.40	66.36	67.85	138.99	75.99	92.41
2.79	116.87	98.93	102.20	185.01	96.03	103.59
		[illegible]	93.92	174.28	90.19	101.41
					[illegible]	[illegible]

Unfortunately, this is not the whole story behind foreign company reporting, because companies tend to publish only such information as their own domestic government or Stock Exchanges require, and standards vary considerably.

In the US, companies quoted on the major Exchanges are required to report trading progress every quarter, and to a tight and well-established formula. But reporting requirements are generally more relaxed in other countries, especially in Continental Europe. The FT's policy is to follow the custom of the country — if Ford reports every quarter, then the FT will carry the figures every quarter. This means that at some times in the year, the International Company pages may seem to be full of US companies, simply because it is the end of the quarter and North American companies are pumping out the trading figures.

This wealth — or glut — of results four times a year is a blessing and a curse to readers and journalists, although it pleases the analysts at the big stockbroking firms who draw up careful charts and graphs of the results so that they can try to forecast the next batch.

To satisfy all groups of its readership, the paper puts most of the quarterly figures from smaller US companies into tabular form — see page 67 for an example. During the quarter reporting periods, these tables are carried in alphabetical order, usually at the bottom of the International Company pages reporting on the US. In the early part of the year, some quite large companies may be relegated to tables, since there is limited interest in earnings figures struck only weeks after the annual meeting of shareholders. But as the year progresses and the trend of the company's annual results becomes more clear, the figures need more comment from the FT's correspondents in New York. These extended reports, if not considered worthy of the front or back page of the paper, will be carried on the International Company pages. Where possible, results will be grouped together, so that as Bethlehem Steel discloses its fortunes, they can be measured against those at United States Steel, or Nucor.

By the year-end, the paper expects to be presenting the results, together with pertinent comments from analysts and corporate executives, on all the major sectors of the US industrial and financial industries. The aim is the same where Europe and the Far East are concerned, but there is one important factor involving US reporting. Because of the time difference — New York is several hours behind London — much of the US company news arrives too late for the

NORTH AMERICAN QUARTERLY RESULTS

AMERICAN PRESIDENT COMPANIES
Shipping

	1987	1986
Third quarter	$	$
Revenues	456.8m	354.2m
Net income	24.9m	13m
Net per share	1.09	0.55
Nine months		
Revenues	1.34bn	1.03bn
Net income	64.9m	7.8m
Net per share	2.83	0.30

ARCHER-DANIELS-MIDLAND
Soyabean processing, milling

	1987	1986
First quarter	$	$
Net income	82.9m	64.9m
Net per share	0.48	0.38

BURLINGTON NORTHERN
Railroads, resources

	1987	1986
Third quarter	$	$
Revenues	1.68bn	1.69bn
Net income	127m	100.3m
Net per share	1.70	1.25
Nine month		
Revenues	4.91bn	4.65bn
Net income	270.7m	*936.8m
Net per share	3.62	*13.02

*Loss

COLT INDUSTRIES
Aerospace, automotive prods.

	1987	1986
Third quarter	$	$
Revenues	384.2m	386.8m
Net income	35.7m	24.5m
Net per share	0.97	0.15
Nine months		
Revenues	1.22bn	1.2bn
Net income	60.2m	79.9m
Net per share	1.71	0.48

MARRIOTT
Hotels

	1987	1986
Third quarter	$	$
Revenues	1.5bn	1.3bn
Net income	56.7m	49.2m
Net per share	0.42	0.36
Nine months		
Revenues	4.4bn	3.42bn
Net income	161.3m	135.5m
Net per share	1.19	0.99

MORTON THIOKOL
Chemicals, salt, aerospace

DANA
Vehicle parts

	1987	1986
Third quarter	$	$
Revenues	1bn	889m
Net income	38.1m	12.2m
Net per share	0.86	0.24
Nine months		
Revenues	3.1bn	2.8bn
Net income	11.6m	85.8m
Net per share	2.50	1.64

B.F.GOODRICH
PVC resins, chemicals

	1987	1986
Third quarter	$	$
Revenues	564m	574.1m
Net income	42.4m	16.6m
Net per share	1.71	0.70
Nine months		
Revenues	1.6bn	2.06bn
Net income	84.5m	19.7m
Net per share	3.33	0.81

HILTON HOTELS
Hotels

	1987	1986
Third quarter	$	$
Revenues	198.2m	186.6m
Net income	22.3m	23.7m
Net per share	0.89	0.95
Nine months		
Revenues	623.4m	543.4m
Net income	81.5m	71.7m
Net per share	3.25	2.87

IC INDUSTRIES
Consumer, commercial prods

	1987	1986
Third quarter	$	$
Revenues	988.9m	868.6m
Op. Net inc.	44.2m	11.1m
Net per share	0.39	0.10
Nine months		
Revenues	2.87bn	2.48bn
Op. Net inc.	115.7m	57.3m
Net per share	1.02	0.53

SHERWIN-WILLIAMS
Paints

	1987	1986
Third quarter	$	$
Revenues	512.3m	438.2m
Op.net income	36.4m	29.9m
Op.net per sh.	0.81	0.66
Nine months		
Revenues	1.38bn	1.2bn
Op.net inco	74.2m	62.6m
Op.net per sh.	1.65	1.36

SOUTHEAST BANKING
Banking

FT's first edition. But this late news will simply be added to the paper's second and — if need be — third edition. Moreover, on the day following, the late copy will be repeated in the early editions of the paper, so, whichever edition you read, you will see the full coverage of US company reporting.

Coverage of results and news from companies in Europe and the Far East follows a similar pattern but with reporting requirements lower in many countries, there is more opportunity to report at length, and no need for tabularization of profit figures. Morever, with the world time differential more favourable, there is rarely need to split coverage between editions.

The straightforward reporting of trading results is, however, only part of the business. Readers — be they City analysts, private investors, or the general reader who wants to know what is happening in the world economies, are interested in more than the final trading figures. Does the recent experience of the French coal and steel industry have any lessons for the rest of the world as basic industries contract and workers face redundancy? How are the German motor manufacturers facing up to the problems of US competition? Or, at the simple investment level, which pharmaceutical shares should I be buying — British, German or US? These questions can only be considered over a period, by delving into the background plans of major companies, interviewing the senior executives and taking a look at the factories which produce the goods — and the profits. Moreover, companies may attract attention for many other reasons than their quarterly, half yearly or annual profit figures.

So, throughout the year, the FT correspondents in foreign countries will report on takeover bids involving major companies on their particular patch, or new product developments which may have application for business rivals, as well as the more fundamental examination of a company's operations. Wherever possible, this is done by means of a visit to the company, culminating in an interview with the chief executive officer. Since such men are not easy to pin down, the interview may not happen until many weeks after the results or after the takeover has been completed.

Reporting on bids involving foreign companies inevitably requires more background explanation than when the company is British and familiar to UK readers, who still make up by far the major share of FT readership. More importantly, information on a foreign company may not be easily available to the general public. Does the company

European companies reported in the Financial Times.

INTL. COMPANIES & FINANCE

PWH turns to courts as creditors lose patience

BY PETER BRUCE IN BONN

PHB WESERHUETTE (PWH), the troubled West German materials handling equipment producer, yesterday entered formal judicial composition proceedings after efforts to persuade 58 main creditors to wipe out half the group's borrowings failed.

The company was cast adrift last month by its parent, the Otto Wolff engineering group, after revising estimated losses for this year up to DM130m ($77.3m).

The Wolff group, which was forced to help PWH out after it lost DM128m last year, said it could no longer continue with financial assistance.

PWH has since been trying to persuade its creditors - mainly banks - to waive half its DM335m debt to help it back on to its feet. By yesterday it had become clear that all the creditors would not agree and the company had to turn to the courts.

Hoesch, the big German steel group, has an option to acquire 50 per cent plus one share of PWH for a token DM1. The option lasts until December 28.

If the judicial composition *vergleich* proceedings move quickly, Hoesch could well exercise this option and merge PWH with Orenstein and Koppel, its construction equipment subsidiary.

Some of PWH's creditors had made it clear over the last few weeks that they were angry at the Wolff group's refusal to stand good for the debt. It is obvious the mood among creditors was not completely friendly.

The PWH board said yesterday it hoped the Cologne District Court would be able to put a value on the group - either as a going concern or in terms of break-up value - in order to pay off creditors and avoid total liquidation.

Meanwhile, management said, it was continuing to talk to potential new industrial partners.

Trelleborg in Belgian rubber takeover

By Our Stockholm Staff

TRELLEBORG, the rapidly expanding Swedish industrial products group, has agreed to acquire the rubber division of Pergougnan Benelux, a Belgian investment company.

The size of the deal has not been disclosed, but Trelleborg said it was paying "somewhat more" than BFr450m ($13m), which is the value of the Belgian company's rubber division assets.

The acquisition will give Trelleborg sales in solid resilient tyres - which are used for fork-lift trucks and other heavy vehicles - and a stronger position in the Belgian market.

Mr Fredrik Arp, managing director for Trelleborg Tyres, said: "We will gain a position as a domestic producer in Belgium, where we have produced plastics but not rubber goods before."

Bergougnan Benelux's ... has a turn-

Acquisitions boost Electrolux

BY SARA WEBB IN STOCKHOLM

ELECTROLUX of Sweden, the ... white goods ...

addition, Electrolux had managed to improve earnings and ... in such areas as ...

earnings mainly in the household appliances business area, which accounted for sales of SKr30.4bn in the first nine ...

concerned sell anything in Britain? Does it have a share in the world market? Can the shares be traded outside its own country? All these questions will need to be answered quickly if the bid news is to be put into context.

Paul Betts reports on concern over Ferruzzi's stake in Saint-Louis

French monopoly policy put to test

NEARLY a year after it was set up, the Conseil de la Concurrence, or French monopolies council, is facing its first big international case.

The council has just been asked by Mr Edouard Balladur, the Finance and Economy Minister, to look into the recent acquisition by Ferruzzi, the Italian food and agricultural industry group, of a 13.6 per cent stake in Saint-Louis, France's second largest sugar producer.

The action was taken after Saint-Louis' management expressed concern over unsolicited share buying by Ferruzzi in the French group. The Italian company is controlled by Mr Raul Gardini, who already controls Beghin-Say, France's largest sugar manufacturer.

His move against Saint-Louis, which follows his earlier unsuccessful bid for British Sugar, raises among French authorities questions of industrial concentration since, between them, Beghin-Say and Saint-Louis control about 75 per cent of the French sugar market.

Although Saint-Louis has already acted to protect itself from a hostile bid by consolidating control of the company into the hands of friendly shareholders led by the Worms group, it has also felt the need to refer the issue to the competition council.

The independent council is expected to take two to three months to review the Ferruzzi move. It will then make recommendations to Mr Balladur, who will take the final decision on the issue.

The case will give the council a chance to tackle a complex competitive issue with European, as well as domestic implications.

The council itself was set up last December as part of the French conservative government's new competition bill, designed to remove price controls from most industrial and service sectors while introducing rules to govern cartels and price fixing.

The Government has always been committed to removing price controls for industrial companies, a policy initiated by the previous Socialist administration but accelerated under the present Government.

While lifting price controls and industry and services, the Government has, none the less, retained powers to intervene in a crisis or if prices move out of control without economic justification.

Coupled with the removal of price controls, the Government also decided to hand over the policing of the competition rules to the new independent council, which is comprised of magistrates, lawyers and representatives of business and consumers.

The council has the power to investigate anti-competitive practices, such as price cartels or the abuse of a dominant market position, on its own initiative or at the request of companies or organisations. In these matters, the Finance Minister no longer has any power of veto.

But Mr Balladur has decided to keep in his own hands decisions on mergers and industrial concentrations.

Under the new system, mergers which lead to the creation of a company with a market share of more than 25 per cent or with turnover of more than FFr7bn ($1.23bn) will normally be referred to the council for an opinion. The Ferruzzi share build up in Saint-Louis falls in this category.

However, while the referral of the Ferruzzi move reflects the new French policy on competition in action, it also highlights the peculiarly French characteristics of the system.

For although the administration has sought to adapt the country to the new environment of international competition, it has also ensured that it retains ultimate control over the process. The final decision on the Saint-Louis case will rest firmly with the Finance and Economy Minister.

Financing for British leisure park completed

By Our Euromarkets Staff

A $95m DEBT financing for a huge leisure development in the British Midlands has been completed among a group of international banks led by Security Pacific.

The secured financing for the Wonderworld Theme Park near Corby comprises a $47m fixed-rate 10-year loan from the European Investment Bank, guaranteed by the banks, a $28m five-year revolving credit at 1.5 per cent over London interbank offered rate (Libor), and a $20m working capital loan at 2 per cent over Libor.

A private placement of shares worth $96m, representing some 85 per cent of the company's equity, is being marketed to UK, US, Japanese and Hong Kong institutions.

The placement, whose progress has been hampered by last month's stock market crash, is scheduled for completion some time in January.

Construction work expected to take 39 months, can start at any time. About 4.25m visitors are projected to visit the park, with a site covering 1,250 acres, in its first year.

Zurich referendum called over curbs on registered shares

BY JOHN WICKS IN ZURICH

A REFERENDUM, aimed at protecting shareholders' rights, is to be held in the Zurich Canton to counter restrictions on the negotiability of registered shares.

The motion is being launched by Denner, the discount retail chain, whose proprietor, Mr Karl Schweri, was involved last year in a bid to acquire control of Usego Trimerco, a rival retail group.

His bid was foiled when the company refused to enter into the share register a number of holders of registered shares whom they believed were acting for Mr Schweri.

Managements have refused to enter registered shares in several other important cases in recent months in which Swiss companies have fought off unwelcome takeover attempts.

These include the fending off by Hero, the foods group, of Jacobs-Suchard, the coffee and foods group, and the defeat of an investor consortium by Georg Fischer, the engineering company.

At present, similar measures are being taken by Sulzer Brothers in the face of the purchase of about 35 per cent of its capital by a syndicate headed by Mr Tito Tettamanti, a Lugano lawyer.

The question of registered shares is also to be discussed by the Commission of the States Council, Switzerland's upper house of parliament, next February.

The Denner referendum would limit listings on the Zurich Stock Exchange to those of securities whose transfer to a new holder does not require approval from the issuing company's board.

Denner claims that such approval - as is needed for entry into a share register - represents a curtailment of market activities with a corresponding effect on share prices "and thus the rightful interests of investors."

The referendum, which will need to obtain supporting signatures before it can be put to the ballot, would allow registered shares "only where registration is aimed against foreign control" of a company.

The Zurich Stock Exchange is controlled by the cantonal authorities, which explains the need for the motion both to come before the cantonal council and to be put to a popular vote.

●Total assets of the 71 largest Swiss banks rose 10 per cent in the third quarter from the same period a year ago, in spite of the dollar's marked weakness, **Reuter reports from Zurich.**

The Swiss National Bank reported that assets had risen 9.2 per cent in the year to June 30, though it gave no absolute figures.

Fiduciary deposits administered by the banks continued to decline, dropping 3.7 per cent in the quarter when measured in foreign currencies and 3.5 per cent in Swiss franc terms.

Banks' holdings of securities were up 17.4 per cent, while financial investments as a whole grew 3.4 per cent.

Total credits held by the banks were up 11.5 per cent from the third quarter of 1986, although foreign credits grew faster than domestic loans, reversing a recent trend.

Foreign loans increased 16.5 per cent, while domestic credits grew by 10.3 per cent.

Deposits by the public were 8.9 per cent higher in the quarter.

Spanish banking mergers urged

By Tom Burns in Madrid

MR CARLOS SOLCHAGA, the Spanish Economy Minister, has fuelled speculation over a sweeping reorganisation of the banking sector by calling for further mergers among Spanish banks.

His comments come hard on the heels of Banco de Bilbao's recent and controversial bid to absorb Banco Espanol de Credito (Banesto).

Meanwhile in an apparent response to possible merger overtures, Banco Central, Spain's premier bank in asset terms, yesterday announced a one-for-five shares capital increase which it said would raise capital to pta42bn ($372m).

Central's statement added it would use its reserves for a further capital increase of one-for-10 in the first semester of next year.

Mr Solchaga was quoted yesterday as saying he did not know of any new mergers under discussion. But he added: "We would be happy if there were."

The minister said the Government had been kept fully aware of Bilbao's designs on Banesto and that it "looked favourably" on the proposed absorption.

He added that although it was difficult to predict the impact that Bilbao's bid would have on further moves to integrate the Spanish banking sector, "it is difficult to imagine (integration) stopping at this point."

Mr Solchaga's remarks came as the domestic banking sector was still reeling from the boldness with which Bilbao - Spain's third largest bank in terms of assets - bid at the end of last week for control of the second-ranking Banesto, with a view to creating a new, and clearly dominant, banking group.

Central's capital increase came amid speculation that the bank might shortly be courted, much in the way Banesto is being approached, by a smaller institution. Banking sources said the Bilbao move had sparked talk of a domino effect and prompted speculation on potential pairings among the domestic banks.

At a tense meeting on Monday of the Supreme Banking Council, the sector's watchdog, senior executives of several of Spain's "big seven banks" made it clear they were upset and angered by Bilbao's move.

Mr Epifanio Ridruejo, of Banco Central, was quoted as saying the bank he represented did not "like at all what is happening" while the representative of Banco Popular, the seventh-ranking bank, was quoted as saying the "harmony" that reigned in the sector had "been broken."

In a revealing statement at the meeting, Mr Jose Maria Lopez de Letona, Banesto's managing director, was quoted as saying that Banesto considered itself "prejudiced" by the manner in which Bilbao's bid had been made.

The watchdog council meeting, in spite of the misgivings, did not oppose the merger proposals.

This was due in large measure to the presence at the meeting of Mr Guillermo de la Dehesa, Secretary of State for the Economy, who is reported to have kept the focus of the meeting on the legality of Bilbao's move and to have averted a vote being taken on whether the council approved the proposed merger.

Yesterday, Mr Lopez de Letona and Mr Jose Angel Sanchez Asiain, Bilbao's chairman, began formal negotiations - likely to last into next week - which will define the eventual hostility or friendliness of the bid.

Aegon plans partly-paid bullet bonds

AEGON, the leading Dutch insurance company, plans to issue Fl 100m, 7 per cent, partly-paid bullet bonds due 1998 at an issue price of 101 per cent, Reuter reports from Amsterdam.

Amro bank, which is leading the issue, said this was the first time a partly-paid bond had been issued on the Dutch capital markets.

A first payment of 20 per cent of the issue has to be made on January 4 1988, while the remaining 80 per cent has to be paid on July 4 1989. Subscriptions close on December 1. Coupon date is January 1.

The underwriting syndicate is led by Amro, ABN and Morgan Bank Nederland and consists of NMB Bank, Rabobank, Pierson, Heldring en Pierson, Bank Mees en Hope, Van Haften en Co, Citicorp Investment Bank (The Netherlands), and Swiss Bank Corporation International Holland.

Markets welcome cuts in European interest rates

BY CLARE PEARSON

BOND MARKETS were heartened yesterday by cuts in European short-term interest rates which appeared to give the stamp of approval to last Friday's US budget deficit reduction deal.

The Bundesbank's surprise ¼ point reduction in its securities repurchase rate to 3.25 per cent yesterday morning was swiftly followed by cuts in certain French and Dutch rates.

The cuts raised hopes that leading industrial nations might agree to lower other key rates - notably the West German 3 per cent discount rate - after the $76bn budget package had been passed by Congress, to give greater stability to the dollar.

But immediate price gains in non-dollar bonds were tempered by concerns that lower interest rates were already built into prices, and by the firmer dollar.

Meanwhile, Eurodollar bonds developed a firmer tone although, in the face of a quiet US Treasury bond market, prices were unable to make much headway and closed unchanged to ⅛ point better.

Prices of West German government bonds, which are mostly bought by foreign investors, shed around 20 basis points at the longer maturities yesterday. But shorter-dated bonds closed a touch firmer in response to the lower repurchase rate.

Early gains in D-Mark Eurobonds were pared later as dealers focused on the D-Mark/dollar exchange rate, although shorter-dated bonds still closed around ¼ point firmer on the day.

Commerzbank announced a new DM150m five-year 5⅞ per cent bond for **East Asiatic**, the Danish trading company, priced at par. Dealers said the borrower's name was not very well-known in the market, but the bond's terms looked fair. The bond was quoted at around less 1⅛, to give a yield about 65 basis points higher than comparable domestic bank bonds.

Ecu bonds were firmer during the morning, but then suffered profit-taking to close about only ⅛ point higher. Dealers said one or two new issues could surface

INTERNATIONAL BONDS

this week, although they would have to be for a high-quality name. An Ecu100m three-year bond for **IMI Bank**, launched on Monday, was quoted at less 1⅛ bid, the level of its total fees, but dealers said it was attracting little retail interest.

A DM250m eight-year floating rate note, convertible into a fixed rate bond, for the **Council of Europe**, which was launched on Monday was bid yesterday at 99.90, compared with a par issue price.

Eurosterling bond prices closed unchanged, after an afternoon speech by Mr Nigel Lawson, Chancellor, which indicated he had no immediate plans to follow West Germany in cutting interest rates.

Speculation was rife that a long-awaited bond for **Belgium** might finally be surfacing in the Euroyen market. But, though one syndicate manager said the kingdom had taken firm bids for an issue in a variety of currencies yesterday morning, the bond failed to emerge.

Earlier, dealers were talking about a Y55bn seven-year 5⅛ per cent bond, priced at par - terms which struck them as attractive.

Sanwa International launched a $30m bond for **Flash Four**, a special purpose vehicle, maturing in July 1992, and backed by Japanese ex-warrant bonds. The bond, priced at 100.10, pays 20 basis points over six-month London interbank offered rate (Libor). But during the short, first coupon period, it pays the same margin over 1½ month month Libor.

In Switzerland, prices ended the day a touch firmer in fairly high volume. Dealers said retail deamnd was still strong for high quality issues. A SFr150m bond for **Electricite de France**, launched on Monday, was oversubscribed and quoted in the grey market at levels around its issue price.

A SFr200m dual-tranche issue for the **World Bank** traded for the first time yesterday. The 5 per cent, seven-year portion closed at 101¼, 1¼ points above its issue price, while the 5¼ per cent 10-year tranche closed at 101, compared with a 99¼ issue price.

Oesterreichische Kontrollbank's SFr200m 5 per cent 10-year bond, also trading for the first time, closed ⅛ point below its 100⅜ issue price. The SFr40m 5¼ per cent tranche, due in 1996, of an issue for **City of Copenhagen,** closed its first day's trading at 101, one point above its issue price. The SFr40m 5⅛ per cent 10-year tranche closed at 100⅛, against a par issue price.

Banque Paribas (Suisse) led a SFr41m five-year 4½ per cent bond, priced at 99¾, for **Office Central de Credit Hypothecaire,** guaranteed by Belgium.

NY downturn wipes out early gains

BY JANET BUSH IN NEW YORK

US TREASURY bonds turned down sharply yesterday afternoon, more than wiping out the small gains made on news of modest interest rate reductions in West Germany, France and the Netherlands.

The small reduction in the Bundesbank's securities repurchase rate was regarded as unconvincing by US currency dealers who simply took the opportunity to switch their dollar sales from against the D-Mark to the Japanese yen. The US bond market turned negative as soon as the dollar started to dip again.

The US Treasury's 8.875 per cent 30-year bond closed nearly 1¼ points lower to yield more than 9 per cent.

FT INTERNATIONAL BOND SERVICE

Listed are the latest international bonds for which there is an adequate secondary market.

Closing prices on November 24

US DOLLAR STRAIGHTS	Issued	Bid	Offer	Change on day	Change on week	Yield
Abbey National 7½ 92	200	93¼	93¾	+0¼	+0⅝	9.41
All Nippon Air 9⅝ 97	100	94⅛	94⅝	+0⅛	+0½	10.30
American Brands 8⅞ 92	150	97⅞	98¼	+0⅛	+0½	9.40
A/S Eksportfinans 7⅞ 93	100	92	92½	0	+0¼	9.36
A/S Eksportfinans 7¼ 92	150	93⅞	94¼	-0⅛	+0¼	9.03
Belgium 9¼ 92	400	99⅝	100⅛	-0⅛	+0¼	9.14
British Telecom 7⅜ 96	250	87⅛	87⅝	0	+0½	9.82
British Telecom 8⅞ 94	150	97⅛	97⅝	-0¼	+0⅜	9.40
Canada 9 96	1000	98	98½	+0⅛	+0½	9.30
Canadian Pac 10⅜ 93	100	102½	103⅛	0	+0⅝	10.02
C.C.C.E. 7⅞ 91	113	94	94⅛	0	+0¼	8.96
C.N.C.A. 7¼ 91	150	93⅞	94⅛	+0⅛	+0½	9.11
Coca-Cola Ent 8¼ 90	100	†98¼	98⅝	+0⅛	+0⅛	8.88
Credit Lyonnais 9 91	200	99⅞	100⅜	+0⅛	+0⅜	8.93
Credit National 7⅜ 92	100	94	94½	-0⅛	+0¼	8.99
Credit National 7¾ 91	150	94¼	94⅝	-0⅛	+0⅜	8.92
Denmark 7⅛ 92	500	92¼	92⅝	0	+0¼	9.35
Denmark 8¼ 91	300	97⅞	98¼	+0⅛	+0⅜	8.89
E.E.C. 7 91	100	94⅛	94⅝	-0⅛	+0¼	8.71
E.E.C. 7¼ 93	250	92⅛	92⅝	-0⅛	+0¼	9.12
E.E.C. 8¼ 96	100	92½	93	0	+0½	9.51
E.I.B. 7⅝ 93	100	92⅞	93¼	0	+0⅜	9.18
E.I.B. 9⅜ 97	150	98¼	98¾	0	+0⅜	9.61
Finland 7⅛ 97	200	88⅜	88⅞	-0⅛	+0¼	9.80
Finland 7½ 93	200	92	92½	-0⅛	+0¼	9.28
Ford Motor Cred 11⅜ 90	100	105½	106	+0⅛	+0½	8.40
Gen Elec Credit 10¼ 00	200	102¼	102½	0	+0⅛	9.91
G.M.A.C. 8 89	250	98⅝	99⅛	-0¼	+0¼	8.68
G.M.A.C. 8¼ 89	200	99⅜	99¾	-0¼	+0⅜	8.54
Hoesch 8¼ 97	100	†89	89½	+0½	+1	10.06
Hoesch 7⅜ 92	100	†94⅞	95¼	-0⅛	0	8.79
Hoesch 7⅛ 94	300	†90⅞	91¼	+0⅛	+1	9.83
Liberty Mutual 8½ 96	150	91⅞	92⅜	0	+0½	9.88
L.T.C.B of Japan 8 91	100	96⅛	96⅝	-0¼	+0¼	9.17
L.T.C.B. of Japan 8 97	200	87⅛	87½	+0⅛	+0⅜	10.20
Merced-Benz Cred 8¼ 92	100	98⅛	98⅝	-0¼	+0⅜	8.67
Mitsubishi Fin. 7⅞ 93	100	90⅞	91⅜	+0⅛	+0⅜	9.91
Mutual America 7⅜ 92	100	†93½	94	-0⅛	+0¼	9.52
Norway 7¼ 91	500	94⅞	95⅜	0	+0¼	8.86
Pepsico Inc 7⅜ 93	200	91⅞	92⅜	0	+0⅜	9.29
Prudential Crp. 8⅜ 94	125	96⅛	96⅝	+0⅛	+0⅜	9.49
Qantas Airways 10⅜ 95	140	102⅞	103¼	0	+0⅜	9.76
Rep. of Italy 9 90	1000	100⅞	101⅛	-0¼	+0¼	8.52
Saab Scania 9½ 91	125	100⅞	101⅛	-0⅛	+0¼	9.10
Saskatchewan 10⅜ 92	100	105⅜	105⅞	0	+0⅜	9.08
State Bk S Aust 9¼ 93	100	98½	99	+0⅛	+0⅜	9.55
Swedish Expt Crd 7¼ 91	100	94¼	94⅝	+0⅛	+0⅜	8.92
Swed Exp Cred 10 92	100	103⅞	104¼	0	+0¼	8.86
Sweden 7 91	250	94⅛	94⅝	+0⅛	+0⅜	8.68
Sweden 7 92	250	93⅝	94	0	+0⅜	8.86
Sweden 8⅜ 96	200	94⅞	95¼	-0⅛	+0⅜	9.61
Sweden 8½ 92	200	98¼	98¾	-0⅛	+0½	8.88
Taiyo Finance 7⅜ 94	100	90	90½	0	+0⅜	9.92
Toyota Mtr Cred 7⅛ 92	150	92⅞	93¼	-0⅛	+0¼	9.20
Victorian Rep 11⅜ 92	150	107⅞	108¼	0	+0⅜	9.31
World Bank 7 92	300	†93⅞	94¼	0	+0⅜	8.76
World Bank 9 97	300	96⅛	96½	+0⅛	+0⅜	9.60
Yasuda Trust Fin 8½ 93	100	94¼	94⅝	0	+0⅜	9.80

Average price change... On day 0 on week +0⅜

DEUTSCHE MARK STRAIGHTS	Issued	Bid	Offer	Change on day	Change on week	Yield
Arab Banking 5½ 92	150	97⅞	98⅜	+0⅛	+1	5.97
Avis Fin.SVS 5⅞ 92	100	†100½	101	+0½	+1½	5.66
Bank of Greece 6½ 95	150	97	97⅜	-0⅛	+0⅛	6.95
Bank of Tokyo 5⅜ 93	100	†101½	102	0	+0¼	5.35
Central BK. Turkey 7 92	200	†100½	101	-0¼	0	6.81
Degussa Int. 6⅛ 97	200	96½	97¼	0	+1⅛	6.57
E.I.B. 5½ 98	150	93¼	94	-0¼	+0¼	6.35
E.I.B. 6 97	300	98⅝	99⅛	-0⅛	+0⅞	6.14
E.I.B. 6⅛ 96	300	99⅜	100⅛	+0⅛	+1½	6.16
E.I.B. 6⅛ 97	400	99⅝	100⅛	-0¼	+2	6.15
E.I.B. 6⅞ 95	300	104¼	105	-0⅛	+1¼	6.12
Euro Coal& Steel 5⅞ 97	175	96⅝	97⅜	+0⅛	+1	6.31
Eurofima 6⅛ 96	100	101⅛	101½	0	+1⅛	6.01
Elec De France 5⅞ 97	300	94⅞	95⅜	-0¼	+1⅛	6.42
Hoesch Int'l Fin.7 95	100	99⅝	100⅜	-0½	-1½	7.00
I.A.D.B. 6 97	200	96¼	97	0	+1	6.48
IBJ 5⅞ 92	100	†102	102½	0	+1½	5.34
Japan Finance 5⅞ 97	100	94½	95¼	+0⅛	+1⅛	6.50
Ireland 6½ 97	300	†98	98½	0	0	6.75
Korea Dev BK 6⅝ 93	100	99⅝	100⅜	-0¼	+0⅛	6.61
Malaysia 6¼ 94	150	97½	98	0	+0¼	6.67
Oesterr Kont BK 5⅝ 92	200	†102¼	102¾	0	+1	5.03
Portugal 5⅞ 92	150	99⅜	100⅛	+0¼	+0⅜	5.88
Portugal 6⅝ 95	150	†99¾	100¼	+0¼	+0¼	6.57
Royal Insurance 5½ 92	300	†100½	101	0	+0⅜	5.29
Statoil 6⅛ 97	200	†96½	97	0	+1	6.72
Soc Cent Nuclear 7¼ 95	150	102⅝	103⅜	+0¼	+1¼	6.72
Stinnes 5½ 96	100	94⅛	94⅞	0	+0½	6.35
Tokyo Elec. Power 6 97	300	†95½	96½	+0⅛	+2¼	6.58
World BK. 6⅛ 97	400	100⅛	100½	+0⅛	+1⅛	6.17

Average price change... On day +0 on week +1

SWISS FRANC STRAIGHTS	Issued	Bid	Offer	Change on day	Change on week	Yield
African Dev Bk 5⅜ 96	100	†98	99	+0½	+1½	5.84
Ashland 5 92	150	†95¾	96	0	+0¼	5.41
Bayer W/W 2½ 02	250	†97	97¼	+0⅛	-0⅛	2.74
BBL W/W 2⅞ 97	100	†82	83	+0½	+0¼	5.24
Elec De France 5 07	100	†97½	97⅞	-0⅛	-0⅛	5.19
E.I.B. 4⅞ 97	200	†98	98½	+0⅛	+0½	4.98
E.I.B. 4⅞ 97	200	†97⅞	98⅜	+1¼	+1⅛	4.86
Enso Gutzeit 5 99	100	†98	98½	0	0	5.20
Ireland 5 02	350	†91	91½	0	0	5.91
Newfoundland 5⅛ 02	150	†100¼	101	0	+0⅛	5.06
[illegible] 6 92	75	†96½	97	-1	-1	6.90
Prov of Manitoba 4⅞ 02	200	†99	99⅜	0	0	4.98
Prov. of Quebec 5 03	200	*†97⅝	97⅞	0	+0⅛	5.22
[illegible] Airways 4⅞ 97	110	†93½	94	-0⅛	-0⅛	5.59
SHW Holdings 4⅞ 94	100	†99⅞	102	+0⅛	0	4.77
[illegible]	[illegible]	[illegible]	[illegible]	[illegible]	[illegible]	[illegible]
[illegible]	[illegible]	[illegible]	[illegible]	[illegible]	[illegible]	[illegible]
[illegible]	[illegible]	[illegible]	[illegible]	[illegible]	[illegible]	[illegible]
[illegible]	[illegible]	[illegible]	[illegible]	[illegible]	[illegible]	[illegible]

Average price change... On day [illegible] on week [illegible]

YEN STRAIGHTS	Issued	Bid	Offer	Change on day	Change on week	Yield
Belgium 4⅞ 94	45	96½	96⅞	+0¼	+1½	5.24
E.I.B. 4⅝ 94	40	97¼	97⅝	+0⅛	+1⅝	5.06
Elec. De France 5⅛ 94	20	99⅜	100¼	-0⅛	+1	5.12
Kansai Electric 4⅞ 94	60	96	96⅛	0	+1¼	5.35
Norway 4¼ 92	60	97	97⅜	0	+0⅞	4.98
S.N.C.F. 4⅞ 93	20	98⅜	99⅜	0	+1½	5.08
Sweden 4⅞ 92	50	97¼	97⅞	+0¼	+1⅛	4.99
World Bank 5½ 92	50	102½	102⅞	+0⅛	+1½	4.84

Average price change... On day +0⅛ on week +1⅜

OTHER STRAIGHTS	Issued	Bid	Offer	Change on day	Change on week	Yield
Aegon 5⅞ 91 FL	100	98⅞	99⅜	+0⅛	+0½	6.00
Aegon 8¼ 89 FL	100	103	103½	0	+0¼	6.02
Air Products 6⅞ 91 FL	100	100½	101⅛	+0⅛	0	6.47
Alg. Bk. Ned. 5⅞ 91 FL	100	98½	99⅛	+0⅛	+0⅛	6.12
Alg. Bk. Ned. 7⅞ 89 FL	150	103	103⅝	-0⅛	-0⅛	5.92
Alg. Bk. Ned. 8 89 FL	200	101⅞	102⅜	0	-0⅛	6.12
American Express OC 10 94	40	99⅜	100	+0¼	0	10.06
BP Capital 13⅞ 92 A$	75	†99⅞	100½	0	+0½	13.65
Creditanstalt 14½ 90	60	†99⅛	100	0	+0½	14.14
Denmark 7⅞ 92 ECU	100	†99½	100	+0¼	+0⅜	7.81
DG Fin. Co. 13⅜ 90 A$	50	*†102½	102⅞	0	0	12.57
DG Fin. Co. 14 90 A$	75	*†102	102	0	0	13.00
DG Finance 14⅛ 92 A$	50	*†103½	103½	0	0	13.21
Deutsche Bank 9⅛ 97 £	75	†98⅜	99⅛	+0⅛	-1	10.00
Deutsche Bk.14⅛ 92 A$	100	*†100⅜	100⅜	0	0	14.06
Dresdner Fin.13⅞ 91 A$	100	*†99⅝	99⅝	0	0	13.93
Electrolux 8 89 FL	60	102⅝	103	0	+0⅛	5.93
E.I.B. 8⅝ 93 LF	1000	†102½	103½	0	0	7.88
Euratom 7⅝ 97 ECU	145	†91⅛	92⅛	+0⅛	+2⅛	8.86
Euratom 11½ 88 FL	150	102⅝	103⅛	0	-0¼	0.06
Eurofima 7½ 92 FL	50	103⅜	104	0	0	6.52
Eurofima 17½ 89 Z$	50	†99⅝	100⅛	0	0	17.57
Finland 6 91 FL	100	98⅜	99⅛	+0⅛	+0¼	6.29
Ford Mtr.Cred 13⅞ 91A$	75	†97⅛	97⅝	0	+0½	14.65
G.M.A.C. 9 92 £	50	98⅝	99⅛	+0¼	+1½	9.29
G.M.A.C. 9¼ 92 C$	75	95½	95⅞	+0⅛	+0½	10.49
G.M.A.C Aus.Fin.14 90 A$	50	†99	99½	0	+0½	14.36
Halifax BS 10⅜ 97 £	100	99⅞	100⅛	0	-0⅜	10.36
Honda Mtr. W/W 3⅛ 90 FL	100	104½	106	+0¼	-4⅛	1.55
Hunter Dgas. N.V. 7 91 FL	50	101⅛	101⅝	+0⅛	+0⅛	6.46
Imp Chem Inds 10 03 £	100	97⅜	97⅞	-0⅛	+0¼	10.30
Inv.in Ind.Intl 10 93 £	60	100½	101⅛	+0¼	+0⅜	9.79
Lease Fin. Ned 6 91 FL	50	†97½	98	+0⅛	+0¼	6.66
Leeds B.S 10⅞ 93 £	50	101⅛	101⅝	+0¼	-0¼	9.86
Mort.Bk.Denmark 6 91 FL	150	98⅜	98⅞	+0⅛	-0⅛	6.43
Mtge. Bk. Dn. 6⅞ 91 FL	100	100⅜	101	0	+0⅜	6.52
Nat.Australia 14 92 A$	50	†99⅞	99⅞	0	+0½	0.25
Nat. West.Bk.13⅞ 92 A$	50	†97⅛	97⅞	0	0	13.85
Nationwide BS 10⅞ 93 £	75	100⅜	101⅛	+0¼	-0¼	9.88
New Zealand 7⅞ 93 ECU	200	†97⅛	97⅝	+0⅛	+1⅞	8.37
Oesterr.Ksk 13⅞ 94 A$	75	†98⅞	99⅞	0	+0½	13.82
Prudential Fin.9⅜ 07 £	150	90⅝	91⅛	-0¼	-0⅜	10.46
S.D.R. 7⅜ 95 ECU	90	†96⅞	97⅜	+1¼	+2	8.28
Tsthouse Forte 11⅛ 90£	50	102⅜	102⅞	+0⅛	-0⅛	9.89
Thyssen 7⅜ 90 FL	50	101⅞	102¼	0	0	6.37
Wessanen 6⅞ 90 FL	50	101⅞	102⅜	+0¼	+0⅛	6.01
World Bank 13⅞ 92 A$	100	†97⅜	98⅛	0	+0½	13.93

FLOATING RATE NOTES	Spread	Bid	Offer	C.dte	C.cpn
Alberta 3 93	.0312	99.92	100.02	11/12	7.64
Alliance & Leic Bld 98 £	.08	99.24	99.29	21/01	10.27
Belgium 91	0	100.02	100.12	19/02	7.19
Britannia 5 93 £	0⅛	99.65	99.70	8/01	10.37
Chase Manhattan Corp 91	0¼	99.15	99.40	22/02	7.19
Citicorp 98	†0¼	96.95	97.20	30/11	7.12
Credit Lyonnais 5 00	†0¼	98.31	98.41	13/01	7¼
EEC 3 92 DM	†0	100.14	100.19	22/02	4.31
Halifax BS 5 94	1	99.31	99.36	8/02	8.97
Midland Bank 01 £	1	96.12	96.32	11/02	8.97
Milk Mkt.Brd. 5 93£	0¼	99.37	99.42	10/12	10.37
New Zealand 5 97 £	.07	99.26	99.36	18/02	9.06
New Zealand 5 01	0	98.78	98.88	4/02	7¼
Shearson Lehman Hldg 91	†0¼	98.87	99.37	8/02	7.62
United Kingdom 5 92	0	100.19	100.25	7/01	8.19
Woodside Fin. 5¼ 97	0	98.95	99.06	28/01	7.69
Woolwich 5 95 £	0⅛	99.18	99.23	19/11	8.81

Average price change... On day +0.00 on week +0.05

CONVERTIBLE BONDS	Cnv. date	Cnv. price	Bid	Offer	Chg. day	Prem
Alcoa 6¼ 02	†8/87	62	92	94	0	28.85
Alco Health 6¼ 01	7/86	26.25	71	72½	-0¼	58.54
American Brands 7⅛ 02	9/87	56.1	97	98½	-0¼	33.55
American Can Co. 5½ 02	4/87	66.75	64⅛	66⅛	+1	22.11
Ashikaga Bank 2¼ 02	4/87	963	108⅝	109⅝	+0⅛	2.45
Avon 5 92 DM	12/83	438.6	130⅝	134⅛	0	-1.47
CBS Inc. 5 02	4/87	200	92⅛	93⅛	-0¼	14.15
Chiba Bank 2⅛ 02	†1/87	790.5	174	176	0	7.12
[illegible] 3 00	[illegible]	876	131	132⅛	-0¼	-0.12
Fujitsu 3 99	5/84	1106	187	188⅛	+9⅛	1.40
Gunma Bank 2¼ 02	4/87	880	125	126⅛	-0⅛	-1.28
MCA INC 5½ 02 US$	†9/87	69.62	72½	74½	+0½	42.63
Minolta Camera 2⅛ 94DM	2/84	1004	87¼	88⅛	+0⅛	47.25
Mitsui Trust 2⅜ 01	10/86	1903	125½	127½	+0½	-0.70
News PLC 5⅛ 03 £	†11/87	4.1	101½	103	+0⅜	68.49
Nippon Elec. 2⅛ 00	1/85	1295	287	288	+12⅛	5.05
Oki Elec Ind 3½ 99	10/84	805	176½	178¼	+5⅛	6.23
Omron Tateisi 2⅜ 02	4/87	2310	152½	153¼	+4⅛	4.05
Redland 7⅛ 02 £	†1/87	5.4	94	95	+0¼	23.66
Yokohama Bank of 2⅜ 01	10/86	1019	159	160	0	2.71
W.R. Grace 6¼ 02 US$	9/87	47.12	73¼	74¼	-0½	-27.12

* No information available previous day's price

† Only one market maker supplied a price

Straight Bonds: The yield is the yield to redemption of the mid-price; the amount issued is in millions of currency units except for Yen bonds where it is in billions. Change on week=Change over price a week earlier.

Floating Rate Notes: Denominated in dollars unless otherwise indicated. Coupon shown is minimum. C.dte=Date next coupon becomes effective. Spread=Margin above six-month offered rate (‡three-month; §above mean rate) for US dollars. C.cpn=The current coupon.

Convertible Bonds: Denominated in dollars unless otherwise indicated. Chg. day=Change on day. Cnv. date=First date of conversion into shares. Cnv. price=Nominal amount of bond per share expressed in currency of share at conversion rate fixed at issue. Prem=Percentage premium of the current effective price of acquiring shares via the bond over the most recent price of the shares.

8 The International Capital Markets

The powerful expansion of the international capital markets — the Euromarkets as they are often called — has been the phenomenon of the global financial services industry over the past twenty years. Around $250bn is now raised annually in these markets by means of Eurobonds and bank credits and notes. Investors in Continental Europe have long been active players in the Eurobond markets but the British have been slow to follow, although the lifting of UK Exchange Control restrictions opened the way for them to do so.

A Eurobond issue is a bond issue underwritten and traded by a group of international banks and sold outside the country in whose currency it is denominated. US corporations may borrow in Swiss Francs, Japanese corporations in German marks: both bonds can be traded with investors living in France, Belgium, the UK or elsewhere.

Among the attractions of Eurobonds for some investors are their bearer form and their payment of interest without deduction of any taxes. These features have appealed to private investors in many countries — for some reason, the typical Eurobond investor has been typecast as a Belgian dentist.

The most common form of Eurobonds are:

1) Straights, or bullets. These carry a fixed interest coupon and a fixed maturity date.
2) Floating Rate Notes (FRNs). These have an interest rate tied to an agreed international rate, usually London Inter Bank Offer Rate.
3) Convertibles, which are convertible to ordinary shares on the terms stated.

Eurobonds

Eurobonds started life as the Eurodollar markets, where international borrowers gained access to large funds of dollars which were held in European and other banks outside mainland US. Bonds are now denominated in other currencies as well as US dollars, and this imposes one significant feature on the market: it is highly vulnerable to currency fluctuations.

Bonds are issued in most of the world's major currencies, with the Japanese Yen and the Deutschmark sectors the most popular. A newly-issued bond is sold directly by the borrower to the leading

Markets welcome cuts in European interest rates

BY CLARE PEARSON

BOND MARKETS were heartened yesterday by cuts in European short-term interest rates which appeared to give the stamp of approval to last Friday's US budget deficit reduction deal.

The Bundesbank's surprise ¼ point reduction in its securities repurchase rate to 3.25 per cent yesterday morning was swiftly followed by cuts in certain French and Dutch rates.

The cuts raised hopes that leading industrial nations might agree to lower other key rates - notably the West German 3 per cent discount rate - after the $76bn budget package had been passed by Congress, to give greater stability to the dollar.

But immediate price gains in non-dollar bonds were tempered by concerns that lower interest rates were already built into prices, and by the firmer dollar.

Meanwhile, Eurodollar bonds developed a firmer tone although, in the face of a quiet US Treasury bond market, prices were unable to make much headway and closed unchanged to ⅛ point better.

Prices of West German government bonds, which are mostly bought by foreign investors, shed around 20 basis points at the longer maturities yesterday. But shorter-dated bonds closed a touch firmer in response to the lower repurchase rate.

Early gains in D-Mark Eurobonds were pared later as dealers focused on the D-Mark/dollar exchange rate, although shorter-dated bonds still closed around ¼ point firmer on the day.

Commerzbank announced a new DM150m five-year 5⅞ per cent bond for **East Asiatic,** the Danish trading company, priced at par. Dealers said the borrower's name was not very well-known in the market, but the bond's terms looked fair. The bond was quoted at around less 1⅜, to give a yield about 65 basis points higher than comparable domestic bank bonds.

Ecu bonds were firmer during the morning, but then suffered profit-taking to close about only ⅛ point higher. Dealers said one or two new issues could surface this week, although they would have to be for a high-quality name. An Ecu100m three-year bond for **IMI Bank,** launched on Monday, was quoted at less 1⅜ bid, the level of its total fees, but dealers said it was attracting little retail interest.

INTERNATIONAL BONDS

A DM250m eight-year floating rate note, convertible into a fixed rate bond, for the **Council of Europe**, which was launched on Monday was bid yesterday at 99.90, compared with a par issue price.

Eurosterling bond prices closed unchanged, after an afternoon speech by Mr Nigel Lawson, Chancellor, which indicated he had no immediate plans to follow West Germany in cutting interest rates.

Speculation was rife that a long-awaited bond for **Belgium** might finally be surfacing in the Euroyen market. But, though one syndicate manager said the kingdom had taken firm bids for an issue in a variety of currencies yesterday morning, the bond failed to emerge.

Earlier, dealers were talking about a Y55bn seven-year 5⅛ per cent bond, priced at par - terms which struck them as attractive.

Sanwa International launched a $30m bond for **Flash Four,** a special purpose vehicle, maturing in July 1992, and backed by Japanese ex-warrant bonds. The bond, priced at 100.10, pays 20 basis points over six-month London interbank offered rate (Libor). But during the short, first coupon period, it pays the same margin over 1½ month month Libor.

In Switzerland, prices ended the day a touch firmer in fairly high volume. Dealers said retail deamnd was still strong for high quality issues. A SFr150m bond for **Electricite de France,** launched on Monday, was oversubscribed and quoted in the grey market at levels around its issue price.

A SFr200m dual-tranche issue for the **World Bank** traded for the first time yesterday. The 5 per cent, seven-year portion closed at 101¾, 1¾ points above its issue price, while the 5¼ per cent 10-year tranche closed at 101, compared with a 99¾ issue price.

Oesterreichische Kontrollbank's SFr200m 5 per cent 10-year bond, also trading for the first time, closed ⅛ point below its 100⅜ issue price. The SFr40m 5¼ per cent tranche, due in 1995, of an issue for **City of Copenhagen,** closed its first day's trading at 101, one point above its issue price. The SFr40m 5⅜ per cent 10-year tranche closed at 100¾, against a par issue price.

Banque Paribas (Suisse) led a SFr41m five-year 4½ per cent bond, priced at 99⅞, for **Office Central de Credit Hypothecaire,** guaranteed by Belgium.

member of a group of international banks which have agreed to take the paper into their portfolios. This part of the transaction is called the primary market. But the banks may now choose to sell their newly-acquired bonds to any other international bank or investor prepared to buy — this is the secondary market.

Unlike most domestic markets, the Eurobond secondary market can prove much less liquid than its primary sector. Since the players are the big international houses, their investment attitudes can be changed overnight by a host of factors ranging from currency shifts to changes in government or in investment regulations in their home countries. Thus, although the secondary market in Eurobonds remains the second largest bond market in the world — after the US — it does not follow that every Eurobond is readily tradeable every day at the prices shown in the world's press.

The FT tries in its coverage of this highly specialized international bond market, to allow for the special factors which must be taken into account by the day-to-day reader. New issues (the primary market) will reflect views on the currency involved, on other, similar, issues already in the market, on the attitudes of major investors, and on the yield structure in the sector.

From Tuesday to Friday, the FT's coverage of the Eurobond markets appears on the International Capital Markets and Companies page, which can be found in the back half of the newspaper. It consists of:

1) A report on trading in the Euromarkets on the previous day, under the heading 'International Bonds'.
2) The Eurobond prices table — headed FT International Bond Service.
3) News-stories on any particularly significant international bonds or credits.
4) A report on the previous session's trading in the New York domestic bond market.

The international bonds report (see opposite for an example), is written in London by the FT's Euromarkets staff. London is a major Eurobond market centre and most of the major international banks and their customers are represented in the City. The FT writers in London can also contact — or be contacted by — international banks in New York, Tokyo, and the Continental money centres. They also have ready access to London's foreign-exchange markets, where the currency shifts so significant to Eurobond traders, can be quickly identified. And the Euromarkets staff can draw on the expertise of the FT's foreign correspondents, who can supply the background data on overseas markets or business corporations.

Thus, the daily Eurobond report can draw together the threads of both primary and secondary market activity in the international bond sector. The report opens with the major development in one of the market's major sectors — usually the US dollar, Japanese Yen, or German mark.

This will almost always be a new issue — although there are many sessions when the primary market is quiet. Each new issue will be reported in detail, since such important data may be difficult to find elsewhere. The name of the borrower, the amount raised, the maturity of the bonds and the interest coupon are stated. But then comes the price at which the bond makes its entry into the market-place.

The bond itself will have been arranged over several days, with the pricing left until the moment of issue. Thus the price, the key to the yield, discloses the view of the bank leading the syndicate, usually also named in the report, on the prospects for bonds of a specific currency and maturity on the day when the pricing decision is taken. The report will for this reason then proceed to sketch out the background to the issue, reminding readers of the recent events concerning the currency or the market, hinting at the lead manager's view and also at the likely response from the market itself. Comparisons will be made with other recent similar issues, and with their performance in the secondary market which the new issue must now enter. Reference will also be made to the domestic bond market relative to the currency in which the new bond is denominated. This may give some indication of the yields against which the new Eurobond issuer — and his lead bank — made their pricing decision.

The main body of the daily Eurobond report consists of an analysis of trading activity in the major sectors — the US dollar, the German mark, and so on. In each case, the FT writers attempt to isolate the background factors affecting the trend of the sector. Comments from traders at the major Eurobond houses help explain the reasons behind the sector's activity, or lack of trading interest.

The FT International Bond Service — the list of the day's Eurobond prices — is compiled for the newspaper by a subsidiary of

FT INTERNATIONAL BOND SERVICE

or which there is an adequate secondary market.

Closing prices on November 24

fer	Change on day	week	Yield
93¾	+0¼	+0⅝	9.41
94⅝	+0⅛	+0½	10.30
98¼	+0⅛	+0½	9.40
92½	0	+0⅜	9.36
94¼	−0⅛	+0¼	9.03
00⅛	−0⅛	+0¼	9.14
87⅝	0	+0½	9.82
97⅝	−0⅛	+0⅜	9.40
98½	+0⅛	+0½	9.30
03⅜	0	+0⅝	10.02
94⅜	0	+0¼	8.96
94⅛	+0⅛	+0½	9.11
98¾	+0⅛	+0⅛	8.88
00⅜	+0⅛	+0⅜	8.93
94½	−0⅛	+0¼	8.99
94¾	−0⅛	+0⅛	8.92
92⅝	0	+0¼	9.35
98¼	+0⅛	+0⅜	8.89
94⅝	−0⅛	+0½	8.71
92⅝	−0⅛	+0¼	9.12
93	0	+0½	9.51
93¼	0	+0⅝	9.18
98¾	0	+0⅝	9.61
88⅞	−0⅛	+0¼	9.80
92½	−0⅛	+0¼	9.28
106	+0⅛	+0½	8.40
02½	0	+0⅛	9.91

YEN STRAIGHTS	Issued	Bid	Offer	Change on day	week	Yield
Belgium 4⅝ 94	45	96½	96⅞	+0¼	+1½	5.24
E.I.B 4⅝ 94	40	97¼	97⅝	+0⅛	+1⅝	5.08
Elec. De France 5⅛ 94	20	99¾	100¼	−0⅛	+1	5.12
Kansai Electric 4⅝ 94	60	96	96⅜	0	+1⅝	5.35
Norway 4¼ 92	60	97	97⅜	0	+0⅞	4.98
S.N.C.F. 4⅞ 93	20	98¾	99⅜	0	+1½	5.08
Sweden 4⅜ 92	50	97¼	97⅝	+0¼	+1⅛	4.99
World Bank 5½ 92	50	102½	102⅞	+0¼	+1½	4.84

Average price change... On day +0⅛ on week +1⅜

OTHER STRAIGHTS	Issued	Bid	Offer	Change on day	week	Yield
Aegon 5¾ 91 FL	100	98⅞	99⅜	+0⅛	+0½	6.00
Aegon 8¼ 89 FL	100	103	103½	0	+0¼	6.02
Air Products 6¾ 91 FL	100	100½	101⅛	+0⅛	0	6.47
Alg. Bk. Ned. 5¾ 91 FL	100	98½	99⅛	+0⅛	+0⅜	6.12
Alg. Bk. Ned. 7¾ 89 FL	150	103	103⅝	−0⅛	−0⅛	5.92
Alg. Bk. Ned. 8 89 FL	200	101⅝	102⅜	0	−0⅛	6.12
American Express OC.10 94	40	99⅜	100	+0¼	0	10.06
BP Capital 13¾ 92 A$	75	†99¾	100½	0	+0½	13.65
Creditanstalt 14⅛ 90	60	†99½	100	0	+0½	14.14
Denmark 7¾ 92 ECU	100	†99½	100	+0¼	+0⅜	7.81
DG Fin. Co. 13¾ 90 A$	50	*†102½	102½	0	0	12.57
DG Fin. Co. 14 90 A$	75	*†102	102	0	0	13.00
DG Finance 14⅜ 92 A$	50	*†103½	103½	0	0	13.21
Deutsche Bank 9⅞ 97 £	75	†98⅞	99⅜	+0⅛	−1	10.00
Deutsche Bk.14¼ 92 A$	100	*†100⅜	100⅜	0	0	14.06

DataSteam International which collects its prices from the major marketmakers.

The daily list contains around 200 prices, chosen, once again, so as to match the balance of the market, with the US dollar, German mark, Swiss francs and Yen bonds taking the lion's share. The column headed 'other straights' carries data on bonds denominated in other currencies, including pounds sterling, Dutch florins, Canadian dollars, French francs and Luxembourg francs.

The tables of prices for the 'straights' give the data traditionally quoted in bond market lists. The first column gives the price at which the bond was originally issued in the primary market, and the next two columns quote the prices at which the market will buy (bid) the bonds, and sell (offer) them to investors. Then, after the columns showing the change in price on the day and the week, comes the column quoting the yield available on the bond at the quoted price.

In the case of the Floating Rate Notes, the footnotes explain the

)¾	9.55
)⅛	8.92
)¼	8.86
)⅝	8.68
)⅜	8.86
)⅜	9.61
)½	8.88
)⅜	9.92
)¼	9.20
)⅝	9.31
)⅜	8.76
)⅝	9.60
)⅜	9.80

Nationwide BS 10⅛ 93 £..........	75	100⅝	101⅛	+0¼	−0¼	9.88
New Zealand 7¾ 93 ECU..........	200	†97⅛	97⅝	+0⅛	+1⅞	8.37
Oesters.Ktbk.13⅝ 94 A$..........	75	†98¾	99¼	0	+0½	13.82
Prudential Fin.9⅜ 07 £..........	150	90⅝	91⅛	−0¾	−0⅝	10.48
S.D.R. 7¾ 95 ECU..........	90	†96⅞	97⅜	+1⅛	+2	8.28
Tsthouse Forte 11⅛ 90£..........	50	102⅛	102⅝	+0⅛	−0⅜	9.89
Thyssen 7¼ 90 FL..........	50	101⅞	102½	0	0	6.37
Wessanen 6¾ 90 FL..........	50	101⅝	102⅛	+0¼	+0⅛	6.01
World Bank 13⅜ 92 A$..........	100	†97¾	98¼	0	+0½	13.93

FLOATING RATE NOTES	Spread	Bid	Offer	C.dte	C.cpn
Alberta 3 93..........	.0312	99.92	100.02	11/12	7.64
Alliance & Leic.Bld 94 £..........	.08	99.24	99.29	21/01	10.27
Belgium 91..........	0	100.02	100.12	19/02	7.19
Britannia 5 93 £..........	0⅛	99.65	99.70	8/01	10.37
Chase Manhattan Corp 91..........	0 1/16	99.15	99.40	22/02	7.19
Citicorp 98.	†0¼	96.95	97.20	30/11	7.12
Credit Lyonnais 5 00..........	†0 1/16	98.31	98.41	13/01	7¼
EEC 3 92 DM..........	†0	100.14	100.19	22/02	4.31
Halifax BS £ 94..........	.1	99.31	99.36	8/02	8.97
Midland Bank 01 £..........	.1	96.12	96.32	11/02	8.97
Milk Mkt.Brd. 5 93£..........	0 1/16	99.37	99.42	30/12	10.37
New Zealand 5 97 £..........	.07	99.26	99.36	18/02	9.06
New Zealand 5 01..........	0	98.78	98.88	4/02	7¼
Shearson Lehman Hlds 91..........	†0 1/16	98.87	99.37	8/02	7.62
United Kingdom 5 92..........	0	100.19	100.25	7/01	8.19
Woodside Fin. 5¼ 97..........	0	98.95	99.06	28/01	7.69
Woolwich 5 95 £..........	0⅛	99.18	99.23	19/11	8.81

Average price change... On day +0.00 on week +0.05

...ek	Yield
+1	5.97
1½	5.66
)⅛	6.95
)¼	5.35
0	6.81
1⅛	6.57
)¾	6.35
)⅞	6.14
1⅜	6.16
+2	6.15
1¼	6.12
+1	6.31
1¾	6.01

Floating Rate Notes: Denominated in dollars unless otherwise indicated. Coupon shown is minimum. C.dte=Date next coupon becomes effective. Spread=Margin above six-month offered rate (‡three-month; §above mean rate) for US dollars. C.cpn=The current coupon.

change in the pattern of the columns. The significant column for the investor is the first column, which shows the spread at which the bond was originally issued.

Also quoted are prices for a range of convertible bonds, which carry the right to a switch into the ordinary shares of the borrowing company at the stated date and price.

Eurocredits, which are merely bank credits arranged for a borrower, and have no secondary trading market, are reported as and when announced, subject to the usual newspaper judgements on their news value. The criteria include the size of the credit, the importance of the borrower, and the interest coupon as measured against the rest of the international credit sector.

The daily report on trading in the New York bond market is

8.86
9.29
9.49
9.78
8.52
9.10
7.00
6.48
5.34
6.50
6.75
6.61
6.67
5.03
5.80
6.57
5.29
6.72
6.72
6.35
6.58
6.17

CONVERTIBLE BONDS	Cnv. date	Cnv price	Bid	Offer	Chg. day	Prem
Alcoa 6¼ 02	†8/87	62.	92	94	0	28.85
Alco Health 6¼ 01	7/86	26.25	71	72½	−0¼	58.54
American Brands 7¾ 02	9/87	56.7	97	98½	−0¼	33.55
American Can Co. 5½ 02	4/87	66.75	64¾	66¾	+1	72.11
Ashikaga Bank 2⅛ 02	4/87	967.	108⅜	109⅞	+0⅛	2.45
Asics 5 92 DM	12/83	438.6	138¼	139¾	0	−1.47
CBS. Inc. 5 02	4/87	200.	91¾	93¾	−0¼	14.15
Chiba Bank 2⅜ 02	†1/87	790.5	174	176	0	7.12
Fuji Hvy Inds 3 00	8/85	676.	131	132¾	−0¼	−0.12
Fujitsu 3 99	5/84	1106.	187	188⅜	+9⅛	3.40
Gunma Bank 2⅛ 02	4/87	808.	125	126⅝	−0⅝	−1.28
MCA INC 5½ 02 U$	†9/87	69.62	72½	74½	+0½	42.63
Minolta Camera 2¼ 94DM	2/86	1004.	87¼	88¾	+0¼	47.25
Mitsui trust 2⅜ 01	10/86	1903.	125½	127½	+0½	−0.70
Next PLC 5¾ 03 £	†11/87	4.3	101½	103	+0⅝	68.46
Nippon Elec 2⅞ 00	1/85	1295.	287	288	+12⅝	3.05
Oki Elec Ind 3½ 99	10/84	805.	176½	178¼	+5⅜	6.23
Omron Tateisi 2⅝ 02	4/87	1310.	152⅛	153¼	+4⅝	4.05
Redland 7¼ 02 £	†1/87	5.4	84	85	+0¼	23.66
Yokohama Bank of 2⅜ 01	10/86	1014.	159	160	0	2.71
W.R. Grace 6¼ 02 U$	9/87	42.12	73¼	74¾	−0½	-27.72

* No information available-previous day's price

† Only one market maker supplied a price

Convertible Bonds: Denominated in dollars unless otherwise indicated. Chg. day=Change on day. Cnv date=First date of conversion into shares. Cnv. price=Nominal acount of bond per share expressed incurrency of share at conversion rate fixed at issue. Prem=Percentage premium of the currenteffective price of acquiring shares via the bond over the most recent price of the shares.

Yield
5.84

printed on the same page as the Eurobond market because of its size and significance. The New York bond market is the world's largest, while the US dollar sector dwarfs all the other sectors of the Eurobond market. Because of the time difference, New York's final prices are struck while Europe is sleeping, so that the keen Eurobond dealer wants to see them before starting work in London, Frankfurt, Paris, Zurich and the other Continental centres. The *Financial Times*' US Bond report is almost required reading for the keen Eurobond dealer.

The European or Japanese domestic bond markets are referred to, when necessary, in the text of the daily Eurobond report. The exception is the UK Government bond market which is outlined in the opening paragraphs of the London Stock Market report.

The Monday Morning FT

Monday morning, when there are no overnight markets to report, provides the opportunity to round up the week's trends in the Eurobond markets, as well as to publish some of the other data on which traders and investors feed. On Mondays the FT carries two pages of International Capital Markets.

The first feature to catch the eye of the Monday-morning reader is the substantial expansion of the Eurobond prices column, which becomes the FT/AIBD International Bond Service. The data is supplied by the Association of International Bond Dealers (AIBD), so that this weekly table provides a definitive list of bond prices. The list extends to 500 prices and represents a substantial expansion of the US dollar and Floating Rate Notes sectors, as well as of several other less prominent areas of the Eurobond market.

FT/AIBD INTERNATIONAL BOND

US DOLLAR STRAIGHTS	Issued	Bid price	Chg on week	Yield
ABN Bank 8½ 91	150	97⅜	+⅝	9.37
Aetna Life & Cas 7¾ 16	200	89⅜	−⅛	8.77
AHFC O/S Fin 11¾ 94	100	99⅝	−1⅞	11.80
AIDC 11 89	75	101⅛	−⅛	9.95
Alcoa Australia 11 92	80	100¼	−½	10.92
American Exps 12⅝ 88	150	103⅛	0	9.28
sian Dev Bk 11¾ 93	100	104	0	10.81
ustralia 11¼ 90	100	102⅛	−¾	10.42
ustralia 11¼ 00	100	100¾	−⅜	11.11
ustria Zero 95	100	45¾	+½	10.54
k of Montreal 16¼ 91	150	102⅛	0	15.46
ank of Tokyo 8⅜ 96	100	86	−¼	10.98
ank of Tokyo 11 90	125	102	−¼	9.97
ank of Tokyo 11⅞ 90	100	104½	−⅛	10.14
ank of Tokyo 13⅞ 89	100	106¼	−¼	10.22
rclays Jersey 10⅛ 90	250	100½	0	9.89
rclays Jersey 10⅝ 95	250	98¾	−½	10.85
lgium 7½ 91	250	91⅞	−⅛	10.03
lgium 7¾ 91	300	93⅜	0	10.03
tawest Prop 7¾ 93	150	89¼	−¼	10.34
CE 7¼ 93	100	86¾	−¼	10.46
Nova Scotia 7⅞ 91 SW	150	93⅛	+⅛	10.15
P 8¾ 93	125	92¾	−½	10.54
P 13½ 89	150	106¼	−½	9.91
Capital 9⅝ 93	150	97	−⅛	10.36
Capital 11⅛ 92	150	102½	−⅛	10.34
Col Hydro 10¼ 88	200	100⅜	−⅛	9.69
Col Hydro 11¾ 93	200	105¾	−⅜	10.42
pbell Soup 10½ 95	100	100⅜	−½	10.41
ada 10⅞ 88	500	101⅝	−¼	9.20
ada 11½ 90	500	104	−⅜	9.55
ada Imp Bk 16¾ 91	100	107⅞	[illegible]	[illegible]

Pru Rlty Secs 0 99
Qantas Airways 8⅝ 96
Quebec Prov 13 90
Queensld Gvt 11⅜ 89
Ralston Purina 11¾ 95
Reynolds R. J. 10¼ 93
Richardson-Vicks 11½ 9
Rockwell Int 9⅞ 90
Saskatchewan 7 91
Saskatchewan 8½ 91
Saskatchewan 11⅞ 89
Saskatchewan 15 92
SAS 10⅛ 95
Sears O/S Fin 0 98
Sears O/S Fin 11⅝ 93
Sears Roebuck 10½ 91
Sec Pacific 10½ 88
Shell (Canada) 14⅜ 92
Shell Oil 9½ 90
Standard Oil 10½ 89
St Bk Sth Aust 9¼ 93
State Elec Vict 10 92
Sth Aus Gov Fin 8¾ 93
Sumitomo Fin 11¾ 92
Sweden 7 92
Sweden 8⅛ 94
Sweden 10¼ 92
Swedish Export 8⅝ 91
Swedish Export 11½ 89
Taiyo Kobe 11⅞ 90
Taiyo Kobe 12 90
Tenneco Corp 11½ 89
Tenneco Corp [illegible]

A second table (below) displays the new issues of Eurobonds announced over the past week, quoting the basic data on size, coupon and maturity and also the all-important price and the name of the securities house leading the issue — the 'book runner'.

These two tables provide a comprehensive snapshot of the Eurobond market, enabling investors to measure it against the other international credit markets also covered in the FT Monday-morning International Capital Markets pages. To complete the coverage of statistics, the pages also carry the weekly data on Euromarket turnover, once again supplied by the Association of International Bond Dealers.

Turning from statistics to text, the Monday pages are headed by expanded weekly reports on both the Eurobond market, and also the Euronotes and Credit sector.

NEW INTERNATIONAL BOND ISSUES

Borrowers	Amount m.	Maturity	Av. life years	Coupon %	Price	Book runner	Offer yield %
US DOLLARS							
Keppel Corp§#	75	1997	10	2¾	100	Morgan Grenfell	2.750
Koyo Seiko♣#	60	1992	5	3½	100	Nikko Secs (Europe)	3.500
Taisei Prefab Con.♣#	40	1992	5	3½	100	Nikko Secs (Europe)	3.500
Hazama-Gumi♣#	50	1992	5	3⅜	100	Daiwa Europe	3.375
Asahipen Corp.♣#	30	1992	5	3½	100	Nomura Int.	3.500
Morita Fire Pump Mfg.♣#	25	1992	5	3½	100	Yamaichi Int. (Eur)	3.500
C. Itoh Fuel Co.♣#	50	1992	5	3½	100	Nikko Secs (Europe)	3.500
Taio Paper Mfg. Co.♣#	70	1992	5	3½	100	Yamaichi Int. (Eur)	3.500
Sumitomo Electric Ind.♣#	200	1992	5	3⅛	100	Daiwa Europe	3.125
Sabre VI†(a)♣	72	1992	5	25bp	100.05	Yamaichi Int. (Eur)	-
Canon Inc.♣	300	1992	5	(3⅛)	100	Yamaichi Int. (Eur)	*
Canon Inc.♣	200	1993	6	(3⅞)	100	Nomura Int.	*
Kao Corp.♣	100	1992	5	(3⅛)	100	Nomura Int.	*
Senko Co.♣	40	1992	5	(3½)	100	Daiwa Europe	*
Ryoden Trading Co.♣	30	1992	5	(3½)	100	Daiwa Europe	*
Daishowa Paper Mfg.♣	70	1992	5	(3½)	100	Nikko Secs (Europe)	*
News Int.(c)#	100	1990	3	9	100⅛	Banque Paribas	8.951
Tosoh Corp.♣	200	1992	5	(3¼)	100	Yamaichi Int. (Eur)	*
Fuji Bank§	200	2002	15	(1¾)	100	Fuji Int. Fin.	*
Nippon Paint♣	70	1992	5	(3½)	100	Nikko Secs. (Europe)	*
Ogden Corp.§	75	2002	15	5¾	100	Salomon Bros.	5.750
CANADIAN DOLLARS							
Genelcan‡#	50	1992	5	10½	113¼	Dominion Secs.	7.247
Shell Canada#	100	1992	5	11½	101¼	Wood Gundy	11.160
Credit Lyonnais*	75	1990	3	11⅜	101¼	Credit Lyonnais	10.865
AUSTRALIAN DOLLARS							
Nat. Westminster Bank#	50	1992	5	13⅛	101⅞	County NatWest	12.597
World Bank#	70	1994	7	12¾	101⅝	Banque Paribas	12.390
GMAC Australia#	60	1991	3¼	13	101⅜	Hambros Bank	12.404
SBC Australia#	75	1991	4	12⅝	101¾	SBCI	12.048
D-MARKS							
Minolta Camera Co.§#	200	1997	10	0	100	WestLB	-
Leykam Muerztaler♣#	100	1994	7	6½	125	Deutsche Bank	2.554

INTERNATIONAL CAPITAL MARKETS

EUROCREDITS

Mandate terms to be put under intense scrutiny

WHILE THE Eurobond market's Christmas cocktail parties are predictably shrouded in gloom and not a little fear those attended by bankers in the Euro credit market have a more sprightly air. They are looking back on a good flow of business in 1987 and looking forward to an even healthier outlook for 1988.

The key question, however, is how profitable next year's business will be. A string of corporate borrowers have been tapping the markets for large financings in the past few months. Many have won fine terms and a number of recent deals have been oversubscribed.

But the age-old syndrome is re-emerging: mandates are won with highly competitive bids which, many bankers would feel, produce over-aggressive terms. Despite their feelings, banks pile into the deal because they feel it essential to maintain or establish a relationship with the borrower.

Of course, there is a strong argument that this is just good old competition working to provide the most efficient funding. But, in the past, the effect has been to produce substantial business of questionable profitability for lenders and — more important — on terms unreflective of the credit risk involved.

The progress announced last week by central bankers towards common capital adequacy standards both for on- and off-balance sheet lending will eventually force banks to build in more realistic pricing. One central banker said that a factor spurring the development of the proposed new standards had been "a tendency for the risk/reward ratio to get out of kilter." Competitive pressures, he said, had distorted the ratios between risk and pricing of credit.

It would be unfair to suggest that all recent deals have been too aggressively priced. But the terms of each new mandate will be under intense scrutiny in the market.

Among recent oversubscribed deals are a seven-year credit for **Household Finance** of the US, increased from $500m to $656m, the $600m credit for **American Brands**, reported to be substantially oversubscribed, a $450m loan for **Saatchi and Saatchi**, said to be "appreciably" oversubscribed, a $700m financing for **Volvo** — despite its fine terms, subscriptions to the $350m committed portion so far exceed $500m, and a FFr1.5bn financing for **Agence Havas**, which received FFr2.77bn of commitments.

Meanwhile, the flow of new mandates is slowing ahead of Christmas. The largest is a $600m multi-option facility for **RJR Nabisco**, the US food and tobacco group, being arranged by Bank of America International to replace an expiring $400m facility. Terms of the five-year facility including a 6.25 basis point spread over Libor and a utilisation fee of 6.25 basis points if drawings exceed one-third of the total are the same as before with the exception of the facility fee, which has been cut to 8 from 10 basis points.

Waterford Glass Group of Ireland has mandated Chase Manhattan to arrange a £100m five-year multi-option facility on terms which many bankers viewed as aggressive: a 6.25 basis point facility fee, a 10 basis point margin over Libor, and a 2.5 basis point utilisation fee if more than half drawn. Chase is understood to be seeking participations of £12½m with a 5 basis point front-end fee, though it declined to comment on this. It did say that it had already encountered interest from several banks.

Waterford reported that profits increased from I£9.53m to I£[illegible] in the first half of 198[illegible], helped substantially by its acquisition of Wedgwood in November 1986. Its crystal operations have suffered severely from the falling dollar

commitment fee of 12.5 basis points, and front end fees ranging up to 12.5 basis points.

United Scientific Holdings of the UK mandated Barclays de Zoete Wedd for a £100m multi-option facility including a £50m five-year committed credit. **Great Western Bank**, a US savings bank, is seeking a $200m three-year revolving underwriting facility through Merrill Lynch International with a 10 basis point commitment fee.

In the Eurocommercial paper market, Canada's **Federal Business Development Bank** has a $400m programme arranged by Citicorp, with First Chicago and Swiss Bank Corporation International as additional dealers. **IBC Investments**, a subsidiary of International Signals and Controls, has increased its programme from $50m to $175m and added Merrill Lynch as a dealer alongside Bank of America International and SBCI.

State Bank of Victoria has a $250m programme with SBCI Warburg and Shearson Lehman as dealers. Merrill Lynch is sole dealer for a $100m programme for **Primary Industry Bank** of Australia, a subsidiary of Rural and Industries Bank of Western Australia. **Century Leasing (UK)**, a subsidiary of a Japanese leasing company, has established a $100m programme with the guarantee of Dai-Ichi Kangyo Bank and five dealers.

Alexander Nicoll

INTERNATIONAL BONDS

D-Mark bright spot in

"THERE ISN'T a busy person in the Eurobond market — apart from those looking for a job, of course," said one syndicate manager on Friday afternoon.

His five strong syndicate and new issues trading team, he added, were variously employed playing backgammon, putting on their coats (since the pubs were due to open in an hour), and sleeping.

So much for the cut and thrust of the international capital markets. The Eurobond market has decided to forget it all till the New Year and has settled in for a good long session of pre-Christmas torpor.

In this less than vibrant atmosphere, even last Thursday's news that the US trade deficit stood at a massive $17.63bn in October left the Eurobond sector almost unmoved.

Though in the Eurodollar market prices were marked down broadly in line with US Treasury bonds, very little actual business was done. Unofficially, many dealers had already squared their books and closed down ahead of the Christmas holiday.

As justification for this unwillingness to trade, one dealer said: "It's not surprising people are taking an early break. It's been a simply awful year and it would be a fool's game to open up a position with this amount of confusion about which way the market is going to move."

One thing however is clear. The plunge in the dollar last Thursday underlined the extent to which the trade deficit problem is at the heart of the dollar's weakness. As Nomura economist Mark Cliffe points out: "Even if the US succeeds in cutting the budget deficit, if the trade deficit fails to fall significantly the dollar will remain under downward pressure."

And the US Administration has made it clear that as long as the fear of recession remains it will be disinclined to support the currency by raising interest rates.

As far as the bond market is concerned, its fate will depend not just upon the trade deficit but upon US economic growth. The problem is that at the moment an almost unprecedented degree of uncertainty prevails about what the US economy really looks like in the wake of the stockmarket crash in October.

Recent data has shown that the economy was stronger going into the crash than had previously been supposed and that production has since been buoyant with large increases in employment in October and November.

This has helped take the wind out of the bond market, which rallied strongly in the immediate aftermath of the crash. But the picture is blurred. Last Friday's unchanged November producer prices figure was mildly encouraging for the bond market, suggesting that inflationary pressures are still at bay.

Nomura Research's weekly review of bond markets sets out four possible scenarios for the US deficit and economic growth, and indicates what these would imply for the dollar and the bond market.

● *The trade deficit remains high, economic growth weakens substantially.* This would point to a lower dollar but also possible further weakness in the equity market, triggering cuts in short-term rates, so the fall could gather mon… The long-end of the bonc… might then take fright… prospect of higher inflati…

● *Trade deficit hig… nomic growth strong.* A… combination", in which … end of the market w… highly likely to fall foul … tion fears.

● *Trade deficit and e… growth both fall subst…* This would help the doll… the US authorities migh… to cut interest rates shar…

● *Trade deficit fal… nomic growth strong.* … authorities might be pre… tolerate a rally in the dol… in short-term rates woul… likely, but the stronge… would offset growth… worries in the bond mark…

It was not surprising … that primary market acti…

NEW INTERNATIONAL BOND ISSUES

Borrowers	Amount m.	Maturity	Av. life years	Coupon %	Price	Book runner	Offer yield %
US DOLLARS							
Wings 3 Ltd. (a)‡♦	37.4	1992	5	20bp	100.10	Mitsui Fin Int.	-
New Zealand (c)♦	250	1992	5	9¼	99⅝	Morgan Stanley	9.564
Sanwa Int. Fin.(d)‡♦	100	1993	5	10bp	100.10	Sanwa Int.	-
CANADIAN DOLLARS							
Fed. Business Dev. Bank♦	75	1991	3	10¼	101	McLeod Young Weir	9.849
D-MARKS							
IKB Int. Luxembourg♦	75	1995	7	6	100¼	Industriekreditbank	5.955

Borrowers
FRENCH FRANCS
World Bank♦
DANISH KRONER
East Asiatic Co.♦
LUXEMBOURG FRANCS
EIB**♦
Mitsui Tst Bk (Europe)**
Banque Indosuez**♦

The expanded Eurobond report (headed International Bonds), freed from any need to report day-to-day happenings, concentrates on the highlights of the week, drawing out the deeper factors exposed by the fortunes of selected bond issues. To this end, the report seeks to interview the chieftains of the leading Eurobond houses, and tries to identify the factors which will govern the Euromarkets in the weeks ahead.

The weekly Euronotes and Credits report provides the opportunity for a closer look at these important credit sectors which are difficult to track on a daily basis because they lack a secondary market. The growth of international takeover activity has lifted the international credit sector to public awareness. At the same time, the huge investment now required to finance expansion into the international trading arena has forced business corporations to turn from their domestic credit markets to the international sector, where credits of

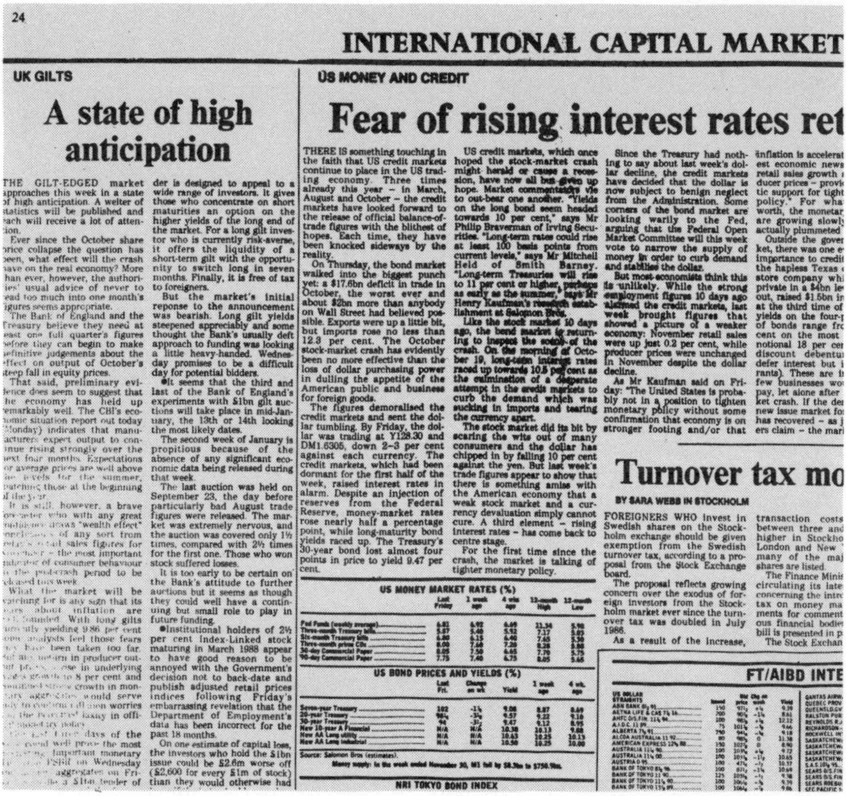

24

INTERNATIONAL CAPITAL MARKET

UK GILTS

A state of high anticipation

THE GILT-EDGED market approaches this week in a state of high anticipation. A welter of statistics will be published and each will receive a lot of attention.

Ever since the October share price collapse the question has been, what effect will the crash have on the real economy? More than ever, however, the authorities' usual advice of never to read too much into one month's figures seems appropriate.

The Bank of England and the Treasury believe they need at least one full quarter's figures before they can begin to make definitive judgements about the effect on output of October's steep fall in equity prices.

That said, preliminary evidence does seem to suggest that the economy has held up remarkably well. The CBI's economic situation report out today (Monday) indicates that manufacturers expect output to continue rising strongly over the next four months. Expectations of average prices are well above the levels for the summer, matching those at the beginning of the year.

It is still, however, a brave forecaster who with any great confidence draws "wealth effect" conclusions of any sort from [illegible] retail sales figures for November – the most important indicator of consumer behaviour in the post-crash period to be released this week.

What the market will be watching for is any sign that its fears about inflation are [illegible] founded. With long gilts currently yielding 9.86 per cent some analysts feel those fears may have been taken too far. But any upturn in producer output prices, a rise in underlying wages growth to 8 per cent and [illegible] growth in monetary aggregates would serve only to confirm [illegible] worries [illegible] the [illegible] laxity in official monetary policy.

[illegible] days of the [illegible] will prove the most [illegible] important monetary [illegible] PSBR on Wednesday [illegible] aggregates on Friday [illegible] a £1bn tender of [illegible]der is designed to appeal to a wide range of investors. It gives those who concentrate on short maturities an option on the higher yields of the long end of the market. For a long gilt investor who is currently risk-averse, it offers the liquidity of a short-term gilt with the opportunity to switch long in seven months. Finally, it is free of tax to foreigners.

But the market's initial reponse to the announcement was bearish. Long gilt yields steepened appreciably and some thought the Bank's usually deft approach to funding was looking a little heavy-handed. Wednesday promises to be a difficult day for potential bidders.

●It seems that the third and last of the Bank of England's experiments with £1bn gilt auctions will take place in mid-January, the 13th or 14th looking the most likely dates.

The second week of January is propitious because of the absence of any significant economic data being released during that week.

The last auction was held on September 23, the day before particularly bad August trade figures were released. The market was extremely nervous, and the auction was covered only 1½ times, compared with 2½ times for the first one. Those who won stock suffered losses.

It is too early to be certain on the Bank's attitude to further auctions but it seems as though they could well have a continuing but small role to play in future funding.

●Institutional holders of 2½ per cent Index-Linked stock maturing in March 1988 appear to have good reason to be annoyed with the Government's decision not to back-date and publish adjusted retail prices indices following Friday's embarrassing revelation that the Department of Employment's data has been incorrect for the past 18 months.

On one estimate of capital loss, the investors who hold the £1bn issue could be £2.6m worse off (£2,600 for every £1m of stock) than they would otherwise had

US MONEY AND CREDIT

Fear of rising interest rates ret

THERE IS something touching in the faith that US credit markets continue to place in the US trading economy. Three times already this year – in March, August and October – the credit markets have looked forward to the release of official balance-of-trade figures with the blithest of hopes. Each time, they have been knocked sideways by the reality.

On Thursday, the bond market walked into the biggest punch yet: a $17.6bn deficit in trade in October, the worst ever and about $2bn more than anybody on Wall Street had believed possible. Exports were up a little bit, but imports rose no less than 12.3 per cent. The October stock-market crash has evidently been no more effective than the loss of dollar purchasing power in dulling the appetite of the American public and business for foreign goods.

The figures demoralised the credit markets and sent the dollar tumbling. By Friday, the dollar was trading at Y128.30 and DM1.6305, down 2–3 per cent against each currency. The credit markets, which had been dormant for the first half of the week, raised interest rates in alarm. Despite an injection of reserves from the Federal Reserve, money-market rates rose nearly half a percentage point, while long-maturity bond yields raced up. The Treasury's 30-year bond lost almost four points in price to yield 9.47 per cent.

US credit markets, which once hoped the stock-market crash might herald or cause a recession, have now all but given up hope. Market commentators vie to out-bear one another. "Yields on the long bond seem headed towards 10 per cent," says Mr Philip Braverman of Irving Securities. "Long-term rates could rise at least 100 basis points from current levels," says Mr Mitchell Held of Smith Barney. "Long-term Treasuries will rise to 11 per cent or higher, perhaps as early as the summer," says Mr Henry Kaufman's research establishment at Salomon Bros.

Like the stock market 10 days ago, the bond market is returning to inspect the scene of the crash. On the morning of October 19, long-term interest rates raced up towards 10.5 per cent as the culmination of a desperate attempt in the credit markets to curb the demand which was sucking in imports and tearing the currency apart.

The stock market did its bit by scaring the wits out of many consumers and the dollar has chipped in by falling 10 per cent against the yen. But last week's trade figures appear to show that there is something amiss with the American economy that a weak stock market and a currency devaluation simply cannot cure. A third element – rising interest rates – has come back to centre stage.

For the first time since the crash, the market is talking of tighter monetary policy.

Since the Treasury had nothing to say about last week's dollar decline, the credit markets have decided that the dollar is now subject to benign neglect from the Administration. Some corners of the bond market are looking warily to the Fed, arguing that the Federal Open Market Committee will this week vote to narrow the supply of money in order to curb demand and stabilise the dollar.

But most economists think this is unlikely. While the strong employment figures 10 days ago alarmed the credit markets, last week brought figures that showed a picture of a weaker economy: November retail sales were up just 0.2 per cent, while producer prices were unchanged in November despite the dollar decline.

As Mr Kaufman said on Friday: "The United States is probably not in a position to tighten monetary policy without some confirmation that economy is on stronger footing and/or that inflation is accelerat[…] est economic news [...] retail sales growth [...] ducer prices – provi[...] tic support for tight[...] policy." For wha[...] worth, the monetar[...] are growing slowly [...] actually plummeted [...]

Outside the gover[...] ket, there was one e[...] importance to credit [...] the hapless Texas [...] store company whi[...] private in a $4bn le[...] out, raised $1.5bn in [...] at the third time of [...] yields on the four-[...] of bonds range fr[...] cent on the most [...] notional 18 per cen[...] discount debentu[...] defer interest but i[...] rants). These are i[...] few businesses wo[...] pay, let alone after [...] ket crash. If the de[...] new issue market fo[...] has recovered – as j[...] ers claim – the mar[...]

US MONEY MARKET RATES (%)

	Last Friday	1 week ago	4 wks ago	12-month High	12-month Low
Fed Funds (weekly average)	6.81	6.92	6.69	11.34	5.90
Three-month Treasury bills	5.87	5.40	5.92	7.17	5.05
Six-month Treasury bills	6.80	6.15	6.40	7.65	5.30
Three-month prime CDs	8.00	7.60	7.20	8.28	5.88
30-day Commercial Paper	8.05	7.50	6.65	7.70	5.75
90-day Commercial Paper	7.75	7.40	6.75	8.05	5.65

US BOND PRICES AND YIELDS (%)

	Last Fri.	Change on wk	Yield	1 week ago	4 wk. ago
Seven-year Treasury	102	-1¼	9.08	8.87	8.69
20-year Treasury	98⅛	-3⅛	9.57	9.22	9.10
30-year Treasury	94	-3½	9.47	9.12	8.95
New 10-year A Financial	N/A	N/A	10.38	10.13	9.88
New AA Long utility	N/A	N/A	10.63	10.25	10.13
New AA Long industrial	N/A	N/A	10.50	10.25	10.00

Source: Salomon Bros (estimates).

Money supply: In the week ended November 30, M1 fell by $8.3bn to $750.9bn.

NRI TOKYO BOND INDEX

Turnover tax mo

BY SARA WEBB IN STOCKHOLM

FOREIGNERS WHO invest in Swedish shares on the Stockholm exchange should be given exemption from the Swedish turnover tax, according to a proposal from the Stock Exchange board.

The proposal reflects growing concern over the exodus of foreign investors from the Stockholm market ever since the turnover tax was doubled in July 1986.

As a result of the increase, transaction costs [...] between three and [...] higher in Stockho[...] London and New [...] many of the maj[...] shares are listed.

The Finance Minis[...] circulating its late[...] concerning the intr[...] tax on money ma[...] ments for comment [...] ous financial bodie[...] bill is presented in p[...]

The Stock Exchan[...]

FT/AIBD INTE

US DOLLAR STRAIGHTS	Issued	Bid price	Chg on week	Yield
ABN BANK 8½ 91	150	97½	+¼	9.39
AETNA LIFE & CAS 7⅛ 16	700	90⅜	-1¼	8.61
AHFC O/S FIN. 11⅛ 94	100	95⅝	+⅛	12.12
A.I.D.C. 11 89	75	101⅞	-⅛	9.46
ALBERTA 7⅝ 91	750	94¼	-⅜	9.18
ALCOA AUSTRALIA 11 92	80	98⅝	0	11.38
AMERICAN EXPRESS 12⅜ 88	150	102⅞	0	8.90
AUSTRALIA 11¼ 90	100	103⅝	+⅛	9.72
AUSTRALIA 11¼ 00	100	103⅛	-1½	10.65
AUSTRIA 0 95	100	47¼	-½	10.37
BANK OF TOKYO 8⅛ 96	100	87½	-1¼	10.69
BANK OF TOKYO 11 90	125	103¼	-½	9.38
BANK OF TOKYO 11⅛ 90	100	106⅛	-⅜	9.39
BANK OF TOKYO 13⅛ 89	100	106⅛	-⅞	9.86

QANTAS AIRW[...]
QUEBEC PROV[...]
QUEENSLD GV[...]
RALSTON PUR[...]
REYNOLDS R.J[...]
RICHARDSON-[...]
ROCKWELL IN[...]
SASKATCHEW[...]
SASKATCHEW[...]
SASKATCHEW[...]
SASKATCHEW[...]
S.A.S. 10⅛ 95[...]
SEARS O/S FIN[...]
SEARS O/S FIN[...]
SEARS ROEBU[...]
SEC PACIFIC 1[...]

$1bn or $3bn are no longer a surprise. While private investors can play no role in the Eurocredit markets, they can still find much food for thought by scanning the reports of major financings by blue chip companies gearing up for expansion or acquisition projects.

Also on the Monday pages appear detailed surveys of the US and British Government bond markets, both of which are major investment forums for the international institutions.

The influence of the US bond markets on other world credit markets can hardly be over-estimated. Investors need to know what The US Federal Reserve Board is saying about prospects for the US economy and interest rates. They need to be warned of Wall Street's views on any US economic data due in the week ahead. And, with the US securities and investment houses now spreading their trading operations around the world, investors want to know how these huge firms have been behaving on their home patch.

To underline the international character of the bond markets, the FT's Monday pages also carry tables showing interest rates and bond yields in the US and in Japan.

Under 'US Money Market Rates', the table quotes the US Federal Funds Rate, the key interest rate by which the US Federal Reserve Board seeks to influence other short-term rates, and selected Treasury bill and commercial paper rates. The next table shows, *inter alia*, the yield on US Government bonds and on best quality

US MONEY MARKET RATES (%)

	Last Friday	1 week ago	4 wks ago	12-month High	12-month Low
Fed Funds (weekly average)	7.77	7.44	6.88	11.34	5.71
Three-month Treasury bills	6.64	6.50	6.38	6.68	5.01
Six-month Treasury bills	6.85	6.87	6.54	6.91	5.06
Three month prime CDs	7.90	7.60	7.20	7.90	5.46
30-day Commercial Paper	7.40	7.30	6.90	7.70	5.65
90-day Commercial Paper	7.75	7.40	7.15	7.75	5.45

US BOND PRICES AND YIELDS (%)

	Last Fri.	Change on wk	Yield	1 week ago	4 wk. ago
Seven-year Treasury	92⅞	-½	9.45	9.35	9.10
20-year Treasury	96¾	+⅛	9.76	9.77	9.54
30-year Treasury	92⅛	-⅛	9.69	9.68	9.46
New 10-year "A Financial	n/a	n/a	10.50	10.35	10.20
New "AA Long utility	n/a	n/a	10.80	10.75	10.60
New "AA Long industrial	n/a	n/a	10.75	10.65	10.50

Source: Salomon Bros (estimates).

Money supply: In the week ended September 21 M1 rose by $5.4bn to $755.8bn.

NRI TOKYO BOND INDEX

December 1983 = 100	17/9/87	Average yield (%)	Last week	12 wks ago	26 wks ago
	PERFORMANCE INDEX				
Overall	132.13	5.75	133.73	137.07	139.11
Government Bonds	131.71	5.51	133.69	138.19	141.11
Municipal Bonds	132.39	6.28	133.14	137.25	139.07
Govt.-guaranteed Bonds	133.23	6.31	134.00	138.06	139.97
Bank Debentures	130.37	5.31	131.96	132.38	133.49
Corporate Bonds	132.78	6.29	134.53	136.40	136.72
Yen-denom. Foreign Bonds	136.78	6.73	138.52	139.77	137.65
Government 10-year†	6.38	–	6.27	4.91	4.62

† Estimated par yield

Source: Nomura Research Institute

commercial loans. The 30-year US Treasury bond is a benchmark for global comparisons.

These US yields can be compared with the returns on the various Tokyo credit instruments shown in the NRI Tokyo Bond Index table. These are the key numbers around which the other world credit markets revolve.

Go-ahead given for bullion association

By Kenneth Gooding

THE FORMATION of the London Bullion Market Association has been given the go-ahead by the UK Department of Trade and Industry.

It is expected that the association will become fully active in January, after the Bank of England completes formalities.

Mr Robert Guy, of the N. M. Rothschild & Sons, merchant bank, chairman of the association's steering committee, said yesterday two main factors had acted as catalysts in its creation:

Rapid growth

• There had been rapid growth in the number of participants in the London gold market. There used to be only five market-makers - the members of the London Gold Fixing - but now there were six others, and more institutions were expected to follow suit.

Excluding the market-makers today there were another 40 or so institutions active in the market on a regular basis.

Bank of England

• The passing of the Financial Services Act. As a result of this the Bank took supervisory responsibility for the wholesale bullion market and needed a formal body with which it could liaise on a regular basis.

Mr Guy said the new association would assume from the London Gold Market and the London Silver Market the responsibility for publishing the Good Delivery List and Acceptable Melters and Assayers.

"We shall certainly review the existing procedures but we will still aim to produce the standard work for the international markets", he said.

Mr Guy pointed out that all association members, whether or not they are market-makers, will have to abide by the Bank's code of conduct.

"We shall have in London the greatest concentration of wholesale market-makers in the world and we will have the benefit of supervision by our central bank - this is not paralleled in any other major financial centre," he said.

First subscribers to the memorandum of association are: N. M. Rothschild & Sons; J. Aron and Company (UK); Mocatta & Goldsmid; Morgan Guaranty Trust of New York; Sharps Pixley; and Rudolf Wolff.

Producer selling blamed for sluggish gold market

BY KENNETH GOODING, MINING CORRESPONDENT

THE PRICE of gold failed to perform as widely expected and rise sharply during recent turmoil in the stock and money markets mainly because gold producers were selling aggressively, two seasoned observers suggested yesterday.

When the metal rose briefly to $490 a troy ounce on October 19 "producers everywhere, including South Africa and the USSR, tried to capitalise on the high price and sold," said Mr Jeffrey Nichols, president of the American Precious Metals Advisors consultancy group.

Mr Robert Guy, a director of merchant banker N. M. Rothschild and Sons, agreed. He told a conference in London organised by Institutional Investor magazine: "The new major gold mining companies have by their trading activities and financing techniques become a major influence on the movement of the gold price.

"Whatever the enthusiasm of some investors, the rise in the gold price above $470 was too good an opportunity for some mining companies to miss."

The mining companies' wish to "lock in profitability" by aggressive forward selling "was compounded by a new inability to tap the equity markets because of the fall in the value of their own shares," Mr Guy added.

Both he and Mr Nichols dismissed as groundless the theory that sales of gold by central banks to prevent the flight to the US dollar becoming even more pronounced was a factor in holding the price down.

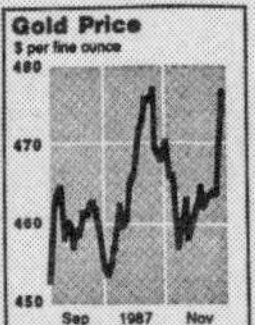

Presenting a generally bullish view of gold, Mr Nichols pointed out that by quitting the market when the price subsided to $460 an ounce, the producers were effectively putting a floor under the price.

He suggested that the impact of producer selling would soon fade away and that the price had some catching up to do after the fall in the value of the US dollar. Gold was $325 an ounce at the end of 1985 and $460 and the end of September this year, a time when there was an almost identical increase in the value of the Japanese Yen and West German Deutschmark against the dollar.

In the past few weeks the Yen and Deutschmark had advanced another 7 to 10 per cent against the dollar and by this comparison the price of gold should be at $495-$500 to keep pace, said Mr Nichols.

Although demand for gold was slightly down this year, supply was sharply lower, he pointed out. Production was likely to be 58m ounces compared with 66m in 1986.

He predicted gold's price would move higher in the next 12 months regardless of the economic or equity climate. "Gold thrives on fear, anxiety and uncertainty - all of which will be present for some time."

Mr Guy supported this view. "As long as doubts persist about the US Administration's capacity to resolve its current economic problems and there remains a vacuum in international monetary policy then gold will continue to attract good long-term investment demand whatever the vagaries of the market on a daily basis."

He gave a warning, however, that "gold's image as a safe haven in periods of currency instability has been damaged. There are scars in the gold market just as there are in the equity market and these may take some time to heal."

Copper price hits record level

By Kenneth Gooding

THE CASH price for Grade A copper reached a record £1,610 a tonne on the London Metal Exchange yesterday morning.

At the same time the price for three months delivery climbed to £1,347, the highest since the peak £1,391 paid in February 1980, traders said.

Fears of shortages of physical copper continued to fuel the price rise and analysts pointed out that there was a widespread belief that supply and demand would not be in balance until the first quarter of 1988.

Demand for copper has outstripped supply for the past four years. LME and Comex (New York Commodity Exchange) stocks fell again last week by a combined 15,210 tonnes and now stand at an extraordinarily low level of 96,553 tonnes compared with 261,000 tonnes at the end of 1986.

Several producers took advantage of the situation and lifted prices yesterday by 5 or 6 cents a lb to between 121 cents and 124 cents for electrolytic copper cathode.

In afternoon trading the Grade A copper cash price eased back a little but closed £40 up from Tuesday's level at £1,581 a tonne while the price for three months delivery continued to improve - to £1,357.50, some £60 ahead of the Tuesday close.

Oils and fats row flares up again at EC Commission

BY TIM DICKSON IN BRUSSELS

THE EUROPEAN Commission's controversial proposal for an oils and fats tax - the subject of bitter argument between member states earlier this year but temporarily sidelined in the last few months by the wider debate on agricultural reform - suddenly flared up again yesterday in Brussels.

Much to the embarrassment of officials, a full meeting of the 17-man Commission was unable to agree last night on the wording of a report on the tax - or so called "stabilisation mechanism" - which will be presented to heads of state at next week's European Community summit.

At issue is not the proposal itself, which is now established Commission policy, but the way in which the results of two new Commission studies on the oils and fats tax idea are conveyed to the member states in Copenhagen.

The whole question of the tax - deliberately kept out of the Commission's proposals for budget stabilisers currently being negotiated by the EC's Farm Ministers in Brussels - is expected to resurface in the context of the overall budget reform package which will dominate the Summit.

The Commission continues to see the measure as a vital part of any political solution to the rapidly rising costs of the oilseeds sector.

The tax would increase sharply the present price of refined vegetable oil and would, according to Commission estimates, raise about Ecu2bn in extra revenue in a full year, which would help pay for the costs of the regime. Moreover, Brussels argues that it is now an even more necessary *quid pro quo* for the tough price penalties which Mediterranean producers in particular would have to suffer under the proposed stabiliser mechanism for this sector.

The measure has aroused fierce opposition, however, both inside and outside the Community, on the grounds that it penalises consumers, breaks a pledge to halt protectionism.

The British, West German, Danish and Dutch Governments succeeded in blocking the tax at the June Summit, but the Commission refused to let the matter rest and agreed to go away and examine in more detail the likely effects of the tax on "third" country imports and the impact on consumption of vegetable oils.

It is understood that all the oil-exporting nations contacted by the Commission for this purpose repeated their firm opposition to the plan, but that an independent study on the internal consumption consequences suggested that there would only be a modest fall in demand.

The issue yesterday was whether these conclusions should simply be presented without comment or whether(as proposed by Mr Frans Andriessen) they should be accompanied by a rehearsal of the arguments in favour of the plan.

UK ministry's forecasting criticised

BY BRIDGET BLOOM

THE UK Ministry of Agriculture has been criticised for not being able properly to calculate the impact on farmers' incomes of changes in the European Community's Common Agricultural Policy.

The influential all-party Public Accounts Committee of the House of Commons says in its latest report that statistical information collected by the ministry only provided historical data.

It says this means officials are unable to judge with any accuracy the effect on farmers of price and other changes negotiated in Brussels within the CAP.

The committee says it is concerned that, at present, information on farm incomes "provides a historical record in relation to past policies rather than a useful basis for forecasting the impact and effect of possible changes in policy."

Fifth Report from the Committee of Public Accounts, 1987-88, The Measurement of Farm Incomes; HMSO; £3.20

Indonesia's upwardly mobile cocoa industry

BY JOHN MURRAY BROWN IN JAKARTA

PAKUI, in Sulawesi, is like any other Indonesian village in many respects. It has no bank, hardly any made-up roads and no telephone or electricity supply. Yet it now boasts the highest per capita income of any rural area throughout Indonesia. The reason is cocoa, a commodity which is spreading like wild fire and could soon turn Indonesia into a major player in the $5bn(£2.79bn) -a-year world cocoa market.

The cocoa bean, first introduced by the Dutch in the 19th century, is replacing palm oil and rubber in many smallholder plots. Its shorter maturation period offers a quick return on investment, enabling the farmer to cover initial development costs with two good harvests.

DROUGHT-related delays have resulted in Indonesian cocoa production lagging about 30 per cent behind last year's level during the early weeks of the season, according to Gill & Duffus, the London merchant. "It is probable, however, that these initial difficulties will be more than made up later in the season," it says in the latest issue of its quarterly Cocoa Market Report.

Gill & Duffus keeps its forecast for Indonesian output in 1987-88 at the 43,000 tonnes level indicated in its last report two months ago. But it cuts its projection for total world production by 12,000 tonnes and raises the consumption forecast by 26,000 tonnes. As a result it has cut its estimate of the 1987-88 production surplus from 115,000 tonnes to 77,000 tonnes (after allowing for loss of weight during processing).

The merchant attributes the lower projected surplus principally to inadequate rainfall in the Bahia growing region of Brazil. This has caused premature pod-ripening and, as a result, a 27,000 tonnes cut in Gill & Duffus's forecast for the country's 1987-88 crop - now put at 398,000 tonnes.

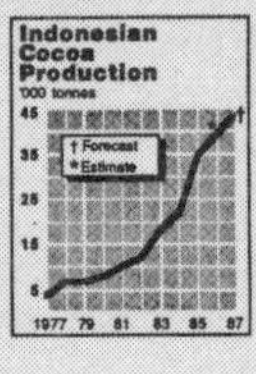

"The name of the game is early yields," says Mr Ibrahim Hasan who, with his father, a former Indonesian Finance Minister, runs Hasfarm, the country's biggest private cocoa plantation company. It has interests in Java, Sumatra, Sulawesi and Kalimantan. Its 12,000 hectare estate in Kalimantan is the world's biggest cocoa plantation.

Today Indonesian output, just 39,000 tonnes last year, lags way behind the main producers - Ivory Coast, Ghana, Brazil and Malaysia. Almost half the plantings - about 30,000 hectares - are made up of immature trees, however, and the Government's joint-marketing association is projecting output at 75,000 tonnes by 1995. With much of the growth coming from non-government estates and smallholders, Jakarta traders believe the figure could be even higher.

The emergence of Indonesia as an important producer of cocoa is sure to have a dramatic effect on the world market, where prices have historically been determined by supply and demand factors in just two geographic areas - West Africa and South America. So increased in production from south-east Asia could help to iron out seasonal price fluctuations.

More worryingly, however, it could also add to the problem of excess supply.

Indonesian production currently has a seven-year lag behind Malaysia, which could very soon be overtaking Ghana in the cocoa export league. But it suffers none of the land and labour constraints of Malaysia, where the prodigious recent growth of production in Sabah state has been largely sustained by immigrant labour from Indonesia.

"Malaysia is very concerned," says Mr Hasan. "We can pull the rug from under their feet at any moment."

That moment is probably some way off, however. For one thing foreign investment is stymied by the Government's refusal to relax land title regulations, which in effect prevent the prospective investor from using his estate as collateral for raising security.

London Sumatra, Harrisons & Crosfield's subsidiary, is one wholly-owned foreign company which has some cocoa estates, but its main interests are in rubber and palm oil.

In Irian Jaya the Commonwealth Development Corporation has a $12m joint-venture investment with the Irian Development Foundation - a 1,000 hectare cocoa plantation, employing about 600 local workers.

The project's isolation - it is only accessible by sea - is in part offset by climatic advantages, says corporation director Mr George Jones. The site tends to enjoy better rainfall patterns than areas like Kalimantan or Sulawesi and is less vulnerable to disease.

Disease continues to be a major concern for cocoa growers in Malaysia. They have been badly hit by both the cocoa moth and vsd - a dieback condition, affecting the water-carrying vessels. To prevent its spread, the Government has been keen to encourage domestic seed production, at the same time banning the import of foreign seeds varieties.

Mr Hasan has been given a licence to produce seeds at a nursery in Kalimantan, delivering them at Rp 30 (about 1p) each to smallholders, and Rp 56 for plantations.

This, however, generates its own problems. The locally-produced seed is widely perceived to be too acidic. "This is not exactly a question of the pH level, more a flavour problem," says Mr Hasan. "It doesn't matter if we sell to [cocoa] butter manufacturers, but if we try to set up direct trade with chocolate producers, then the trouble occurs."

As long as Indonesia remains outside the International Cocoa Organisation, its exporters should in theory be able to increase market share to other non-members, like the US, by avoiding the compulsory $45 a tonne ICCO sales levy. In practice, however, the deficient quality of Indonesian cocoa, which can only be improved by the costly use of additives during processing, tends to reduce that price advantage.

In the short term Indonesia's expansion plans are likely to be affected this year by the prolonged drought, particularly in Kalimantan.

With staggered planting, however, cocoa can promise continuous fruit throughout the year, so the extended dry season should only affect production by at worse 5 per cent to 10 per cent.

A greater worry is kutu loncat, the so-called jumping bug. This affects the shade trees, which are vital for protecting cocoa plants. Mr Hasan is reported to have found a solution to this problem - but if he has, he is not letting on.

Scientists investigate 'wind waggle'

By Maurice Samuelson

A TEAM OF British scientists is investigating why so many trees are being blown down in normal weather conditions.

Even before the destruction of millions of trees by hurricane-force winds last month in southern England, foresters in Scotland were concerned about the loss of hundreds of thousands of trees, worth about £3m a year in a forestry region of about 12,500 acres.

The scientists are based at the Natural Environment Research Council's Institute of Terrestrial Ecology. They concluded that winds averaging 40mph, quite common in northern Britain, could fell trees the trunks and roots of which appeared strong enough to resist winds twice that speed.

The team, led by Dr Ronnie Milne at the institute's Edinburgh research station, blames this on so-called wind waggle: if gusts coincide with a tree's natural swaying frequency, the trees can be subjected to forces strong enough to break or uproot them.

The team is developing mathematical models of how trees bend, to find ways of reducing losses.

WORLD COMMODITIES PRICES

LONDON MARKETS

NICKEL PRICES climbed to six-year highs in dollar terms on the London Metal Exchange yesterday in response to what traders described as "a broad front of consumer demand." They noted in particular sustained offtake by the Japanese stainless steel industry. As chart resistance points were breached speculative demand added to the upward impetus pushing cash position to £3,585 a tonne at the close, up £160 on the day and £215 on the week so far. The LME lead market also gained ground as a strong surge of trade and speculative buying and shortcovering pushed prices through established resistance levels. The cash position advanced £12.50 to close at £380 a tonne, while the three months quotation gained £13 at £361.50 a tonne.

SPOT MARKETS

Crude oil (per barrel FOB January)		+ or -
Dubai	$15.60-5.70	-0.10
Brent Blend	$17.85-7.75y	-0.225
W.T.I.(1 pm est)	$18.63-8.67	-0.155

Oil products (NWE prompt delivery per tonne CIF)		+ or -
Premium Gasoline	$178-180	
Gas Oil	$161-163	+1
Heavy Fuel Oil	$87-88	+1
Naphtha	$151-153	
Petroleum Argus Estimates		

Other		+ or -
Gold (per troy oz)♣	$476.75	+3.00
Silver (per troy oz)♣	696c	+12
Platinum (per troy oz)	$509.50	+4.25
Palladium (per troy oz)	$121.00	+5.00
Aluminium (free market)	$1690	-10
Copper (US Producer)	113-118c	-0.625
Lead (US Producer)	42.00c	
Nickel (free market)	290c	+5
Tin (European free market)	£3870	-50
Tin (Kuala Lumpur market)	17.00r	-0.22
Tin (New York)	321.00c	-2.00
Zinc (Euro. Prod. Price)	$880	
Zinc (US Prime Western)	$44.375	
Cattle (live weight)†	101.57p	+2.82*
Sheep (dead weight)†	194.41p	+7.57*
Pigs (live weight)†	72.37p	-0.37*
London daily sugar (raw)	$195.40w	+2.80
London daily sugar (white)	$202.20w	+1.70
Tate and Lyle export price	£215.00	+0.50
Barley (English feed)	£109.50y	
Maize (US No. 3 yellow)	£134.50	
Wheat (US Dark Northern)	£91.75y	+0.50
Rubber (spot)♥	61.50p	-1.00
Rubber (Jan) ♥	63.00p	-1.00
Rubber (Feb) ♥	63.25p	-1.00
Rubber (KL RSS No 1)	260.50m	-0.50
Coconut oil (Philippines)§	$490.00s	+7.50
Palm Oil (Malaysian)§	$360.00	
Copra (Philippines)§	$320.00y	-5.00
Soyabeans (US)	$144.50	+1.00
Cotton "A" index	77.40c	+1.25
Wooltops (64s Super)	493p	

£ a tonne unless otherwise stated. p-pence/kg. c-cents/lb. r-ringgit/kg. w-Dec/Jan. s-Jan/Feb. y-Nov/Dec. y-Dec. † Meat Commission average fatstock prices. * change from a week ago. ♥ London physical market. § CIF Rotterdam. ♣ Bullion market close. m-Malaysian/Singapore cents/kg.

COCOA £/tonne

	Close	Previous	High/Low
Dec	1093	1119	1115 1091
Mar	1127	1153	1149 1125
May	1146	1171	1167 1148
Jly	1166	1192	1190 1166
Sep	1185	1209	1205 1185
Dec	1210	1237	1233 1210
Mar	1233	1261	1251 1233

Turnover: 5821 (8891) lots of 10 tonnes
ICCO indicator prices (SDRs per tonne). Daily price for November 25: 1452.27 (1471.36); 10 day average for November 26: 1437.80 (1436.82).

COFFEE £/tonne

	Close	Previous	High/Low
Nov	1221	1235	1232 1220
Jan	1253	1266	1264 1252
Mar	1274	1289	1286 1275
May	1296	1310	1307 1295
Jly	1315	1326	1325 1317
Sep	1340	1364	1348 1344
Nov	1365	1375	

Turnover: 2287 (1969) lots of 5 tonnes
ICO indicator prices (US cents per pound) for November 24: Comp. daily 116.47 (116.72); 15 day average 115.74 (115.82).

SUGAR $ per tonne

Raw	Close	Previous	High/Low
Dec	176.40	170.80	176.00 171.00
Mar	179.40	173.80	179.80 174.00
May	179.60	174.80	179.80 175.00
Aug	180.40	175.60	180.80 175.40
Oct	181.00	176.80	180.80 177.40
Dec	183.00	180.00	
Mar	186.00	182.80	186.00

White	Close	Previous	High/Low
Mar	211.20	206.80	211.00 206.80
May	215.20	210.80	215.00 210.70
Aug	223.00	215.50	220.00 215.30
Oct	223.00	215.50	216.00 215.00
Dec	224.00	217.00	217.00 217.00
Mar	228.00	223.00	
May		226.00	

Turnover: Raw 3700 (3087) lots of 50 tonnes; White 1434 (1228).
Paris- White (FFr per tonne): Mar 1186, May 1210, Aug 1245, Oct 1250, Dec 1260, Mar 1295.

GAS OIL $/tonne

	Close	Previous	High/Low
Dec	161.75	162.00	162.25 160.50
Jan	161.00	161.75	162.00 160.50
Feb	158.50	159.75	159.75 158.50
Mar	154.75	156.00	156.00 154.75
Apr	151.50	154.00	154.00 151.50

Turnover: 4545 (4320) lots of 100 tonnes

GRAINS £/tonne

Wheat	Close	Previous	High/Low
Jan	115.00	114.35	115.05 114.85
Mar	117.00	116.40	117.15 117.00
May	119.30	118.50	119.40 119.00
Jly	121.75	121.15	121.80 121.55
Sep	102.15	101.75	102.15 101.80
Nov	104.05	103.50	104.05 103.80

Barley	Close	Previous	High/Low
Jan	107.80	107.45	107.85 107.75
Mar	109.75	109.25	109.80 109.75
May	111.60	111.00	111.60 111.40
Sep	98.00	98.00	
Nov	100.00	100.00	100.00

Turnover: Wheat 529 (182), Barley 71 (88) lots of 100 tonnes.

LONDON METAL EXCHANGE (Prices supplied by Amalgamated Metal Trading)

	Close	Previous	High/Low	AM Official	Kerb close	Open interest
Aluminium, 99.7% purity ($ per tonne)						Ring turnover 0 tonne
Cash	1690-710	1705-15		1690-700		
3 months	1670-90	1665-75		1660-80		2,383 lots
Aluminium, 99.5% purity (£ per tonne)						Ring turnover 23,575 tonne
Cash	935-8	950-2	945	945-7		
3 months	917-8	924-5	920/916	922-3	917-8	56,706 lots
Copper, Grade A (£ per tonne)						Ring turnover 53,175 tonne
Cash	1580-2	1540-2	1610/1580	1610-12		
3 months	1357-8	1297-8	1360/1337	1347-8	1352-3	78,208 lots
Copper, Standard (£ per tonne)						Ring turnover 0 tonne
Cash	1450-70	1480-5		1480-500		
3 months	1335-45	1290-5		1325-35		29 lots
Silver (US cents/fine ounce)						Ring turnover 10,000 ozs
Cash	693-6	665-8	695/685	686-90		
3 months	705-8	697-700		702-4	705-8	820 lots
Lead (£ per tonne)						Ring turnover 15,500 tonne
Cash	379-81	367-8	370	368-9		
3 months	361-2	348-9	366/347	360.5-1.5	364-5	12,606 lots
Nickel (£ per tonne)						Ring turnover 2,915 tonne
Cash	3560-70	3400-10	3620/3400	3620-30		
3 months	3493-4	3369-70	3506/3410	3440-5	3487-502	8,196 lots
Zinc (£ per tonne)						Ring turnover 4,200 tonne
Cash	484-5	485.5-6.5		484.5-5.5		
3 months	484-5	485-5.5	486/483	484-4.5	485-6	14,886 lots

POTATOES £/tonne

	Close	Previous	High/Low
Feb	102.50	102.60	
Mar	90.50	91.00	90.00
Apr	150.10	150.80	151.00 150.00
May	164.00	164.00	164.80
Nov	86.00	82.50	
Feb	99.00	94.50	

Turnover: 131 (198) lots of 100 tonnes.

SOYABEAN MEAL £/tonne

	Close	Previous	High/Low
Dec	146.50	144.00	146.80
Feb	143.20	141.50	143.00
Apr	138.90	138.80	139.00 138.50
Jun	128.70	128.50	
Aug	126.50	128.50	
Oct	127.00	128.00	
Dec	128.50	130.00	

Turnover: 336 (40) lots of 100 tonnes.

FREIGHT FUTURES £/index point

	Close	Previous	High/Low
Jan	1240.0	1219.0	1244.0 1220.0
Apr	1274.0	1267.5	1286.0 1271.0
Jly	1134.0	1130.0	1140.0 1134.0
Oct	1230.0	1220.0	1230.0
BFI	1168.0	1159.0	

Turnover: 386 (136)

WOOL
Prices in Australia were barely steady after the rise of the past two to three weeks, reports Wool Record. Even fine merinos, which have for a long time led the upward trend in prices, levelled out. Market strength is nevertheless considered very sound in the longer term, with sales to the world trade so far this season unusually high and offerings in the remainder consequently low. Bradford business has been quiet but since order books are well filled and production very high this is not causing anxiety. Currency fluctuations continued to make pricing and trading difficult from day to day. The Australian Wool Corporation market indicator was A$9.32 (A$9.08 a week ago) while top quotations in Bradford were unchanged or fractionally down from earlier in the week.

LONDON BULLION MARKET

Gold (fine oz)	$ price	£ equivalent
Close	476½-477	265¼-265¾
Opening	479-479½	266½-267
Morning fix	478¾	267½
Afternoon fix	476½	266¾
Day's high	479-479½	
Day's low	474-474½	

Coins	$ price	£ equivalent
US Eagle	490-495	273-275½
Mapleleaf	490-495	273-275½
Britannia	490-495	273-275½
Krugerrand	475-478	264-266
1/2 Krug	248-257	138¼-143¼
1/4 Krug	123-131	68½-73
Angel		
1/10 Angel		
New Sov.	112-113	62½-63
Old Sov.	112-113½	62½-63¼
Noble Plat	529-539	294½-300

Silver fix	p/fine oz	US cts equiv
Spot	383.85	688.50
3 months	392.45	701.45
6 months	400.35	713.55
12 months	418.40	742.90

LONDON METAL EXCHANGE TRADED OPTIONS

Aluminium (99.5%)	Calls		Puts	
Strike price $ tonne	Jan	Mar	Jan	Mar
1650	72½	79	49½	95
1675	59½	68½	62	109
1700	48½	59	75½	124½

Copper (Grade A)	Calls		Puts	
Strike price $ tonne	Jan	Mar	Jan	Mar
2500	215½		139	
2550	190		163	
2600	167		189½	

Copper (Grade A)	Calls		Puts	
Strike price £ tonne	Jan	Mar	Jan	Mar
1375	91		29	
1400	75½		38½	
1425	62		49½	

US MARKETS

The precious metals finished on a firm note, reports Drexel Burnham Lambert. Silver led as continued buying interest held prices steady. Most notable was liquidation of the December contracts, with positions switched into forward contracts. Copper reached new contract highs for the second day running, as continued fears over supplies prompted general buying. Crude oil was under pressure throughout the day from local and trade selling, but short-covering pared losses. Coffee eased on light trade selling in the face of commission house buying. Cocoa came under pressure from origin-type selling, but industry scale-down interest was noted. Sugar was very strong reflecting constructive fundamentals with the trade a noted buyer. The soya complex was firm - oil on reports of a typhoon approaching India, meal on commercial price-fix buying. The beans, too, were steady, but new crop contracts were under pressure on reports of rain in growing areas. Maize was firm reflecting a possible pick-up of physical business, while wheat eased on profit-taking as the market underwent a correction to recent strength.

New York

GOLD 100 troy oz.; $/troy oz.

	Close	Previous	High/Low
Nov	476.6	474.9	476.9 476.9
Dec	478.9	475.4	478.3 475.0
Jan	480.0	476.5	0 0
Feb	482.9	481.4	484.4 481.4
Apr	488.6	487.1	490.0 487.5
Jun	494.5	492.9	496.0 493.2
Aug	500.6	498.9	0 0

ORANGE JUICE 15,000 lbs; cents/lbs

	Close	Previous	High/Low
Jan	171.50	168.75	171.50 168.75
Mar	169.80	168.55	170.45 166.00
May	169.40	168.50	170.20 168.15
Jly	169.15	168.25	169.25 168.25
Sep	168.70	166.00	168.00 167.75
Jan	161.00	159.75	0 0
Mar	161.00	159.75	0 0

COCOA 10 tonnes;$/tonnes

	Close	Previous	High/Low
Dec	1860	1877	1880 1855
Mar	1863	1883	1880 1846
May	1890	1910	1904 1880
Jly	1920	1941	1929 1920
Sep	1949	1971	0 0
Dec	1986	2005	2002 1991
Mar	2017	2033	2040 2010

COPPER 25,000 lbs; cents/lbs

	Close	Previous	High/Low
Nov	119.00	113.55	118.50 118.50
Dec	118.50	111.30	119.80 113.20
Jan	114.00	107.90	114.00 113.50
Mar	109.00	103.30	110.60 105.30
May	101.50	98.20	102.80 98.80
Jly	97.50	92.90	98.20 96.00
Sep	95.80	91.50	96.00 93.00
Dec	94.70	90.60	95.50 92.80
Jan	94.55	90.50	0 0
Mar	94.30	90.30	98.20 98.50

COFFEE "C" 37,500lbs; cents/lbs

	Close	Previous	High/Low
Dec	127.13	126.90	127.25 126.40
Mar	130.99	130.85	131.30 130.25
May	132.80	132.60	133.00 132.15
Jly	133.95	134.00	134.50 133.90
Sep	136.30	135.63	0 0
Dec	137.25	136.75	137.25 137.25
Mar	138.00	137.87	138.00 138.00

PLATINUM 50 troy oz; $/troy oz

	Close	Previous	High/Low
Dec	506.6	506.0	0 0
Jan	510.6	509.0	519.0 508.0
Apr	518.9	517.1	527.0 517.0
Jly	527.1	525.1	534.0 527.0
Oct	535.3	533.1	542.0 540.0
Jan	543.8	541.8	0 0

SILVER 5,000 troy oz; cents/troy oz

	Close	Previous	High/Low
Nov	692.8	691.5	0 0
Dec	693.0	692.0	702.5 691.0
Jan	697.7	696.5	699.0 699.0
Mar	707.4	706.0	717.0 705.0
May	717.2	715.2	724.0 715.0
Jly	727.0	724.4	735.0 724.0
Sep	737.2	734.0	744.0 744.0
Dec	752.5	746.8	760.0 751.0
Jan	757.1	759.4	0 0

SUGAR WORLD "11" 112,000 lbs; cents/lbs

	Close	Previous	High/Low
Jan	7.40	7.36	7.35 7.35
Mar	7.93	7.75	7.98 7.79
May	8.02	7.79	8.04 7.83
Jly	8.04	7.82	8.05 7.86
Oct	8.06	7.88	8.06 7.92
Jan	8.20	8.03	0 0
Mar	8.41	8.22	8.36 8.27

COTTON 50,000; cents/lbs

	Close	Previous	High/Low
Dec	70.09	70.85	71.40 70.00
Mar	70.45	71.23	71.70 70.30
May	70.95	71.50	72.20 70.95
Jly	71.13	71.80	72.25 71.06
Oct	65.10	65.50	65.85 65.00
Dec	65.10	64.10	64.80 63.35

CRUDE OIL (Light) 42,000 US galls $/barrel

	Close	Previous	High/Low
Jan	18.62	18.80	18.75 18.56
Feb	18.53	18.66	18.64 18.49
Mar	18.51	18.64	18.59 18.49
Apr	18.48	18.60	18.55 18.47
May	18.46	18.55	18.48 18.44
Jun	18.46	18.42	18.46 18.42
Jul	18.44	18.40	18.44 18.35
Aug	18.30	18.45	18.30 18.30
Sep	18.30	18.30	0 0
Oct	18.30	18.25	0 0

HEATING OIL 42,000 US galls, cents/US galls

	Close	Previous	High/Low
Dec	56.75	55.45	55.90 55.40
Jan	55.00	54.80	55.14 54.85
Feb	54.20	54.20	54.35 54.00
Mar	52.05	52.10	52.10 51.85
Apr	50.00	50.30	50.15 50.00
May	49.00	49.10	49.00 49.00
Jun	48.50	48.75	48.50 48.25
Jul	48.30	48.75	48.30 48.30

INDICES

REUTERS (Base: September 18 1931 = 100)

Nov 24	Nov 23	mnth ago	yr ago
1704.3	1695.9	1668.4	1811.9

DOW JONES (Base: September 18 1931 = 100)

Spot	130.62	129.72		118.92
Futures	134.47	133.13		117.80

Chicago

SOYABEAN OIL 60,000 lbs; cents/lb

	Close	Previous	High/Low
Dec	18.24	18.03	18.26 17.97
Jan	18.44	18.23	18.48 18.16
Mar	18.81	18.61	18.85 18.51
May	19.10	18.88	19.15 18.80
Jly	19.30	19.10	19.35 19.00
Aug	19.30	19.12	19.30 19.10
Sep	19.35	19.20	19.35 19.15
Oct	19.32	19.15	19.35 19.25
Dec	19.47	19.38	19.49 19.30

SOYABEAN MEAL 100 tons; $/ton

	Close	Previous	High/Low
Dec	214.2	212.7	214.6 210.2
Jan	205.6	203.8	205.8 202.5
Mar	198.2	196.7	198.5 195.6
May	190.6	189.7	190.7 188.0
Jly	188.7	186.2	188.9 184.5
Aug	186.0	185.5	186.0 184.0
Sep	184.5	184.0	184.5 182.0
Oct	180.0	181.0	181.0 180.0
Dec	179.6	180.5	182.6 179.5

WHEAT 5,000 bu min; cents/60lb-bushel

	Close	Previous	High/Low
Dec	301/0	305/0	305/4 301/0
Mar	312/6	315/0	316/0 312/2
May	309/0	309/6	310/4 308/0
Jly	296/2	297/6	298/0 296/0
Sep	300/0	300/4	302/4 300/0
Dec	309/0	308/4	310/0 309/0

LIVE HOGS 30,000 lb; cents/lbs

	Close	Previous	High/Low
Dec	44.90	44.97	45.15 44.80
Feb	44.07	44.25	44.45 44.00
Apr	40.02	40.05	40.35 39.87
Jun	42.65	42.57	42.80 42.50
Jly	43.12	43.10	43.25 42.90
Aug	42.12	42.02	42.25 42.00
Oct	39.02	39.05	39.15 39.02
Dec	39.85	39.80	39.85 39.75

MAIZE 5,000 bu min; cents/56lb bushel

	Close	Previous	High/Low
Dec	189/2	187/2	189/2 186/6
Mar	195/4	193/2	196/2 193/0
May	200/6	198/2	201/4 198/0
Jly	205/4	202/2	206/0 202/2
Sep	202/2	200/0	202/4 200/0
Dec	198/6	196/6	198/6 0
Mar	204/4	201/2	205/0 203/2

PORK BELLIES 38,000 lbs; cents/lb

	Close	Previous	High/Low
Feb	56.05	56.87	57.00 56.85
Mar	55.72	56.30	56.56 55.80
May	57.45	57.60	57.80 56.35
Jly	56.70	56.65	57.10 56.15

SOYABEANS 5,000 bu min; cents/60lb bushel

	Close	Previous	High/Low
Jan	600/0	597/0	600/6 593/4
Mar	607/4	604/4	609/0 601/4
May	612/6	606/6	614/0 606/4
Jly	615/6	609/6	616/0 607/4
Aug	614/6	608/4	614/6 607/0
Sep	592/4	592/4	594/4 591/0
Nov	589/0	590/2	591/4 586/4
Jan	596/0	596/0	596/0 593/4

LIVE CATTLE 40,000 lbs; cents/lbs

	Close	Previous	High/Low
Dec	66.22	66.37	66.40 66.05
Feb	63.05	63.10	63.25 62.80
Apr	65.05	65.15	65.17 64.80
Jun	64.97	65.10	65.25 64.95
Aug	62.95	62.92	63.15 62.65
Oct	62.30	62.25	62.50 62.25
Dec	63.95	63.70	63.96 63.50

9 Commodities and Agriculture

Commodity trading is still surrounded by a somewhat professional mystique, although private investor interest is growing rapidly in the US and European centres. But the experience of world inflation, and then of deflation, has given commodity markets a special importance even for those who never expect to trade in them.

Basic resources, such as oil, tin, copper, lead and zinc, are the lifeblood of the world's manufacturing industries, and prices for them respond quickly to changing views on economic prospects. Industrial buyers may begin to stockpile these commodities because they believe the business cycle is about to turn upwards — or because they fear that inflation is about to push prices higher. The same is true of the soft commodities, like coffee and sugar, which now supply a world manufactured food industry. The past fifteen years have brought crises in the oil and gas and the metal markets as inflation fears have waxed and waned. The FT has responded by expanding its coverage of the global markets in commodities, and by endeavouring to give its readers more information on the background factors which drive prices.

By their very nature, commodity markets are world markets, and often respond more quickly to world events than do domestic equity or even bond markets. This means that during times of world tension, trends in commodity markets will appear on the front page of the newspaper, often at the end of the news-report on the area under strain. During the Seventies, oil prices were hardly off the front pages as the OPEC nations sought to boost crude oil prices and the Western countries grappled with the inflationary implications of the oil price surge.

Commodity markets, however, have to be watched in times of calm as well as times of tension. For the day-to-day run of world commodity markets and the comment of factors affecting them, the FT's coverage appears on its Commodities and Agriculture pages. The daily coverage is a mixture of prices, market comment and news-reports of events likely to affect supply and demand for major commodities.

The prices sections are headed by reports on the previous day's trading in London and in the US markets. And here we have two significant anomalies. First, the US markets are essentially futures markets, offering price quotations for delivery several months ahead, while the London markets for the base metals — copper, lead, nickel and zinc — quote a cash price which is actively traded, as well as a three-month delivery price. Moreover, for largely historical reasons, these same base metals are quoted in £ per tonne in London, but in cents per pound (lb) in the US.

By way of leavening the weight of market statistics, the columns of London prices are headed by two useful items. The Reuters Daily Index of UK Staple Commodity Prices (Reuters Indices) is a geometric average of 17 primary commodities, weighted by their

WORLD COMMODITIES PRICES

LONDON MARKETS

THE LONDON Metal Exchange copper market went from strength to strength yesterday with forward prices reaching 2¾-year highs in sterling terms and fresh 7-year highs in dollar terms. Having reversed the downturn of late last week with a £46.50 rise on Monday cash grade A copper advanced another £52 to £1,541 a tonne, only a few pounds short of the all-time high reached two weeks ago. Dealers attributed the market's renewed strength to bullish chart patterns and continuing concern about the availability of metal for immediate delivery. Supply worries were highlighted by news of a further 3,000 tonnes fall in the already depleted stocks held on the New York's Comex, they added. London cocoa futures also rose yesterday, though on a much more modest scale and from a much lower base.

SPOT MARKETS

Crude oil (per barrel FOB January)		+ or -
Dubai	$16.74-6.76	-0.025
Brent Blend	$17.87-7.93y	-0.04
W.T.I.(1 pm est)	$18.78-8.83	
Oil products (NWE prompt delivery per tonne CIF September)		+ or -
Premium Gasoline	$178-180	
Gas Oil	$160-162	+1
Heavy Fuel Oil	$86-87	+3
Naphtha	$151-153	+1
Petroleum Argus Estimates		
Other		+ or -
Gold (per troy oz)♦	$473.75	+3.50
Silver (per troy oz)♦	686c	+15
Platinum (per troy oz)	$505.25	+11.50
Palladium (per troy oz)	$116.00	+2.00
Aluminium (free market)	$1700	+50
Copper (US Producer)	114⅝-17c	-⅛
Lead (US Producer)	42.00c	
Nickel (free market)	282c	+2
Tin (European free market)	£3920	-20
Tin (Kuala Lumpur market)	17.22r	-0.09
Tin (New York)	323.00c	-1.50
Zinc (Euro. Prod. Price)	$820-870	
Zinc (US Prime Western)	$44.375	
Cattle (live weight)†	100.96p	+1.96*
Sheep (dead weight)†	192.07p	+3.92*
Pigs (live weight)†	70.70p	-1.80*
London daily sugar (raw)	$192.80w	-1.60
London daily sugar (white)	$200.50w	-1.90
Tate and Lyle export price	£214.50	+0.50
Barley (English feed)	£109.50y	
Maize (US No. 3 yellow)	£134.50	-0.50
Wheat (US Dark Northern)	£91.25y	+1.00
Rubber (spot)♥	62.50p	+0.75
Rubber (Jan) ♥	64.00p	+0.75
Rubber (Feb) ♥	64.25p	
Rubber (KL RSS No 1)	261.00m	+0.50
Coconut oil (Philippines)§	$482.50s	
Palm Oil (Malaysian)§	$360.00	
Copra (Philippines)§	$325.00y	
Soyabeans (US)	$143.50	+0.50
Cotton "A" index	76.15c	+0.45
Wooltops (64s Super)	493p	

£ a tonne unless otherwise stated. p-pence/kg. c-cents/lb. r-ringgit/kg. w-Dec/Jan. s-Jan/Feb.

COCOA £/tonne

	Close	Previous	High/Low	
Dec	1119	1096	1123	1107
Mar	1153	1129	1155	1136
May	1171	1148	1175	1156
Jly	1192	1165	1194	1174
Sep	1209	1184	1210	1197
Dec	1237	1209	1238	1225
Mar	1261	1234	1260	1250

Turnover: 8991 (5864) lots of 10 tonnes
ICCO indicator prices (SDRs per tonne). Daily price for November 24: 1471.56 (1447.84) .10 day average for November 25: 1438.82 (1434.86) .

COFFEE £/tonne

	Close	Previous	High/Low	
Nov	1235	1230	1238	1225
Jan	1268	1262	1273	1256
Mar	1289	1283	1295	1281
May	1310	1305	1312	1302
Jly	1328	1330	1334	1323
Sep	1364	1360	1364	1362
Nov	1375	1375		

Turnover: 1969 (1203) lots of 5 tonnes
ICO indicator prices (US cents per pound) for November 21 :Comp. daily 116.72 (116.93) ; 15 day average 115.52 (115.29).

SUGAR ($ per tonne)

Raw	Close	Previous	High/Low	
Dec	170.80	169.40	171.00	168.20
Mar	173.80	173.80	175.40	171.80
May	174.80	174.40	175.60	173.00
Aug	175.80	175.00	176.40	174.00
Oct	178.80	176.40	178.00	176.00
Dec	180.00	178.20		
Mar	182.80	183.80		
White	**Close**	**Previous**	**High/Low**	
Mar	206.80	207.00	207.00	206.00
May	210.80	211.00	210.80	209.50
Aug	215.50	215.90	215.40	214.00
Oct	215.50	216.00	215.50	214.00
Dec	217.00	217.00	216.00	
Mar	223.00	223.00	220.00	
May	226.00	226.00		

Turnover: Raw 3087 (2216) lots of 50 tonnes; White 1228 (1507).
Paris- White (FFr per tonne):Mar 1179, May 1206, Aug 1250, Oct 1250, Dec 1280, Mar 1290.

GAS OIL $/tonne

	Close	Previous	High/Low	
Dec	162.00	160.50	162.25	160.25
Jan	161.75	160.25	162.00	159.75
Feb	159.75	158.50	161.00	159.00
Mar	156.00	154.50	156.75	156.00
Apr	154.00	153.00	155.00	154.00

Turnover: 4320 (6004) lots of 100 tonnes

GRAINS £/tonne

Wheat	Close	Previous	High/Low	
Jan	114.35	113.95	114.50	113.60
Mar	116.40	115.90	118.45	115.50
May	118.50	117.90	118.50	117.65
Jly	121.15	120.75	121.15	120.25
Sep	101.75	101.75		
Nov	103.50	103.70	103.50	
Barley	**Close**	**Previous**	**High/Low**	
Jan	107.45	106.90	107.45	106.70
Mar	109.25	108.80	109.25	108.95
May	111.00	110.55	111.00	110.65

US MARKETS

Precious metals opened higher on follow-through buying, reports Drexel Burnham Lambert. Continued trade buying of the December contract against forward positions helped steady the markets before profit-taking and local selling eased prices. Copper saw fundamentals reassert themselves as fears of declining stocks led to short-covering which touched off stops as the market rallied sharply again. Crude oil rallied on fund buying and short-covering but met resistance at the highs from light trade and commission house selling. Coffee fell in early trading but recovered on dollar weakness. Cocoa finished higher on short-covering, industry interest and East European price-fix buying. Sugar eased on commission house selling but closed higher following trade buying. Cotton was higher on trade buying. Cattle futures were mixed, spread activity being the main feature despite higher cash prices. Hogs and pork bellies were higher on the day reflecting firmer cash prices and despite fears of a bearish cold storage report. Wheat was firm on confirmation of buying by Morocco and interest from China and the Soviet Union

New York

GOLD 100 troy oz.; $/troy oz.

	Close	Previous	High/Low	
Nov	474.9	475.4	0	0
Dec	475.4	476.0	478.2	473.4
Jan	478.5	479.1	0	0
Feb	481.4	482.1	484.3	479.5
Apr	487.1	487.8	490.2	485.3
Jun	492.9	493.8	495.5	491.2
Aug	498.9	499.6	500.5	495.9

ORANGE JUICE 15,000 lbs; cents/lbs

	Close	Previous	High/Low	
Jan	168.75	167.50	169.40	166.80
Mar	168.55	166.65	168.70	166.25
May	168.50	166.25	168.50	166.05
Jly	168.25	166.25	0	0
Sep	168.00	166.60	168.00	168.00
Jan	159.75	159.50	0	0
Mar	159.75	159.50	0	0

COPPER 25,000 lbs; cents/lbs

	Close	Previous	High/Low	
Nov	113.55	108.30	112.30	112.30
Dec	111.30	106.40	112.00	113.20
Jan	107.90	103.60	105.00	105.00
Mar	103.30	99.90	103.40	100.70
May	96.20	92.40	96.60	93.20
Jly	92.90	89.00	93.10	90.00
Sep	91.50	87.70	90.50	89.95
Dec	90.60	86.80	92.00	87.90
Jan	90.50	86.80	0	0
Mar	90.30	86.40	91.50	89.70

COCOA 10 tonnes;$/tonnes

	Close	Previous	High/Low	
Dec	1877	1868	1880	1870
Mar	1883	1864	1885	1872
May	1910	1894	1913	1901

COFFEE "C" 37,500lbs; cents/lbs

	Close	Previous	High/Low	
Dec	126.90	127.40	127.00	126.10
Mar	130.85	130.80	131.00	129.75
May	132.60	132.55	132.65	132.00
Jly	134.00	134.13	134.25	133.30
Sep	135.63	135.75	0	0
Dec	136.75	137.38	137.00	137.00
Mar	137.87	138.50	0	0

PLATINUM 50 troy oz, $/troy oz

	Close	Previous	High/Low	
Dec	505.0	509.4	512.0	512.0
Jan	509.0	511.7	514.5	506.0
Apr	517.1	519.8	521.5	515.0
Jly	525.1	527.6	528.5	524.0
Oct	533.1	535.8	536.0	533.5
Jan	541.8	544.1	0	0

SILVER 5,000 troy oz; cents/troy oz

	Close	Previous	High/Low	
Nov	691.5	694.2	687.0	687.0
Dec	692.0	695.0	701.0	681.0
Jan	696.5	699.5	0	0
Mar	706.0	709.2	716.0	695.0
May	715.2	718.8	726.0	705.0
Jly	724.4	728.0	732.0	715.0
Sep	734.0	737.9	741.0	727.5
Dec	748.8	753.1	757.0	746.0
Jan	753.4	757.9	0	0

SUGAR WORLD "11" 112,000 lbs; cents/lbs

	Close	Previous	High/Low	
Jan	7.35	7.25	7.35	7.24
Mar	7.75	7.72	7.80	7.63
May	7.79	7.78	7.84	7.70
Jly	7.82	7.81	7.85	7.74
Oct	7.88	7.88	7.93	7.80
Jan	8.03	8.03	0	0
Mar	8.22	8.19	8.17	8.17

COTTON 50,000; cents/lbs

	Close	Previous	High/Low	
Dec	70.85	68.98	71.00	69.50
Mar	71.23	69.87	71.40	70.10
May	71.50	70.23	71.70	70.60
Jly	71.80	70.40	71.80	70.80
Oct	65.50	64.90	65.50	65.50
Dec	64.10	63.50	64.30	63.75
Mar	0	64.80	0	0

CRUDE OIL (Light) 42,000 US galls $/barrel

	Close	Previous	High/Low	
Jan	18.80	18.95	18.98	18.75
Feb	18.68	18.82	18.84	18.64
Mar	18.64	18.77	18.76	18.59
Apr	18.60	18.72	18.70	18.55
May	18.55	18.63	18.62	18.50
Jun	18.42	18.48	18.44	18.40
Jul	18.40	18.47	18.50	18.40
Aug	18.45	18.38	18.45	18.40
Sep	18.30	18.50	18.30	18.30
Oct	18.25	18.30	18.25	18.25

HEATING OIL 42,000 US galls, cents/US galls

	Close	Previous	High/Low	
Dec	55.45	55.85	56.15	55.45
Jan	54.80	55.25	55.45	54.80
Feb	54.20	54.60	54.75	54.20
Mar	52.10	52.55	52.60	52.10
Apr	50.30	50.80	50.80	50.30
May	49.10	49.70	49.55	49.25
Jun	48.75	49.50	48.75	48.75
Jul	48.75	49.50	48.75	48.75

INDICES

REUTERS (Base: September 18 1931 = 100)

Nov 23	Nov 20	mnth ago	yr ago
1695.9	1700.1	1689.0	1814.9

relative importance to international trade. Based at 100 in September 1931, the index now stands in the 1655 plus area. The daily column shows the closing index for the previous day, together with the level one month earlier and one year ago.

The Dow Jones Commodity indices, more recent arrivals, first appeared in January 1982. The DJ Spot Commodity Prices Index (Spot) and the DY Commodity Futures Index (Futures) take in 12 commodities including gold and soyabeans, both extensively traded in US futures markets. Both were replacements for previous indices, so the base dates have been kept at December 1931. Both indices stood at around 130 in September 1987, and in both cases comparable figures are given for the previous session, for one month and for one year ago.

ORANGE JUICE 15,000 lbs; cents/lbs

	Close	Previous	High/Low	
Jan	161.20	162.10	162.00	160.40
Mar	159.40	160.00	159.70	158.40
May	158.75	159.50	159.90	158.70
Jly	158.60	159.00	0	0
Sep	158.50	158.95	158.25	158.25
Jan	154.50	155.00	154.00	154.00
Mar	154.50	155.00	0	0

INDICES

REUTERS (Base: September 18 1931 = 100)

Nov 17	Nov 16	mnth ago	yr ago
1691.7	1700.5	1640.1	1610.7

DOW JONES (Base: September 18 1931 = 100)

Spot	128.61	127.62		118.95
Futures	131.60	130.47		118.25

MAIN PRICE CHANGES

‡ Unquoted. † Per 75-lb flask. c Cents a pound. * Cotton outlook. w Oct-Nov. y Nov. z Dec. t Nov-Dec.

	Oct. 14 1987	+ or —	Month ago
METALS			
Aluminium........			
Free Market......	$1230/140	+30	$1735/755
Copper.............			
Cash Grade A....	£1212	+12	£1092.5
3 months........	£1169	+6	£1077.5
Gold Troy oz......	$460.5	+0.75	$458.5
Lead Cash.........	£366	—4	£387.5
3 months........	£356.5	—3	£370.75
Nickel			
Free Mkt...........	257/277c	+5	240/260c
Palladium oz	$134.25	+0.5	$137.50
Platinum oz.......	$577.75	+4.75	$582.25
Quicksilver†	$295/305	....	$300/310
Silver troy oz. ...	468.05p	—2.20	$463.35
3 months	480.10p	—1.70	474.80p
Tin			
free Mkt..........	£4160/180	—5	£4130/160
Tungsten	$51.16	....	$55.47
Wolfram 22.0lb...	$38/50	....	$40/57
Zinc..................	£457	—4.5	£453.25

Beneath the market indices appears a list of Main Price Changes in London. This column rounds up the more important of the prices shown in greater detail elsewhere in the prices columns. Consequently, the table acts as a summary of market trends for the reader in a hurry.

The separation of London prices from those traded in the US does not change the fact that the principal UK commodity markets are now international rather than domestic. In other words, commodity prices in London are driven by the behaviour of investors throughout the world. Many will switch their operations between London, New York and other centres at great speed and London prices are unlikely to move out of step for very long. The point is often underlined in the London Commodity Markets Report, which will refer to the influence of prices and trading in the US — and also to currency movements which make London either more or less desirable for the global investor.

LONDON METAL EXCHANGE (Prices supplied by Amalgamated Metal Trading

	Close	Previous	High/Low	AM Official	Kerb close	Open Interest
Aluminium, 99.7% purity ($ per tonne)						Ring turnover 500 tonne
Cash	1705-15	1690-710		1700-10		
3 months	1665-75	1650-70	1642/1632	1660-70	1665-75	2,321 lots
Aluminium, 99.5% purity (£ per tonne)						Ring turnover 13,950 tonne
Cash	950-2	934-8	958/957	965-6		
3 months	924-5	906-7	927/903	926.5-27	924-5	59,995 lots
Copper, Grade A (£ per tonne)						Ring turnover 32,875 tonne
Cash	1540-2	1488-90	1540/1515	1514-5		
3 months	1297-8	1264-5	1301/1277	1289-90	1299-300	78,205 lots
Copper, Standard (£ per tonne)						Ring turnover 0 tonne
Cash	1480-5	1420-30		1455-70		
3 months	1280-5	1240-50		1265-80		29 lots
Silver (US cents/fine ounce)						Ring turnover 0 ozs
Cash	685-8	668-71		686-9		
3 months	697-700	680-3		697-700	695-700	598 lots
Lead (£ per tonne)						Ring turnover 13,375 tonne
Cash	367-8	361-3	373	372-2.5		
3 months	348-9	343.5-4	352/347	351.5-52	348-8.5	12,719 lots
Nickel (£ per tonne)						Ring turnover 2,076 tonne
Cash	3400-10	3365-75	3385/3380	3385-90		
3 months	3369-70	3338-48	3380/3355	3365-6	3380-90	8,052 lots
Zinc (£ per tonne)						Ring turnover 7,450 tonne
Cash	485.5-6.5	481-3		484.5-5.5		
3 months	485-5.5	479-80	486/484	484.5-5.5	485-6	15,139 lots

POATOES £/tonne

LONDON BULLION MARKET

Beneath the London Markets column and the Reuter and Dow Jones indices, are the brief price reports on the individual markets (see page 87.)

Although prices are still quoted in sterling in the base metal markets, discounting aluminium, and in silver and some soft commodities, dollar prices are quoted in other sectors — notably the oil and gold markets, which are essentially international markets. Prices for the metals are London Metal Exchange quotations. After each metal price, the text gives total turnover on the exchange, and quotes the 'final kerb' or very latest trading levels. Gold and silver prices are fixed daily by the major participants, but then traded normally. Soft commodities are traded for future delivery.

The onset of commodities futures trading has already brought daily quotations from the London Metal Exchange Traded Options Market, and from the market in gas oil futures operated by the International Petroleum Exchange.

POTATOES £/tonne

	Close	Previous	High/Low
Feb	102.00	101.30	102.00
Mar	91.00	92.00	
Apr	150.30	148.90	150.90 149.00
May	163.80	161.80	
Nov	75.00	75.00	
Feb	90.00	90.00	

Turnover 244 (226) lots of 100 tonnes.

SOYABEAN MEAL £/tonne

	Close	Previous	High/Low
Dec	141.00	140.50	141.00
Feb	139.50	185.00	140.00 139.50
Apr	138.00	137.50	137.00
Jun	128.00	129.00	128.00
Aug	126.00	127.00	
Oct	127.00	127.00	
Dec	129.00	129.00	

Turnover 535 (53) lots of 100 tonnes.

FREIGHT FUTURES £/Index point

	Close	Previous	High/Low
Jan	1189.0	1189.0	1189.0 1175.0
Apr	1240.0	1232.0	1240.0 1215.0
Jly	1090.0	1104.5	1090.0 1090.0
BFI	1155.5	1154.0	

Turnover 202 (142)

WOOL
After a very brief setback Australian wool prices rose strongly again this week, reports Wool Record. The emphasis was again on finer merinos where increases were

LONDON BULLION MARKET

Gold (fine oz)	$ price	£ equivalent
Close	463¾-464¼	262-262½
Opening	464½-465	263¾-264¼
Morning fix	464.20	263.60
Afternoon fix	463.70	263.17
Day's high	464½-465	
Day's low	462½-463	

Coins	$ price	£ equivalent
US Eagle	477½-482½	269½-273
Mapleleaf	477½-482½	269½-273
Britannia	477½-482½	269½-273
Krugerrand	463½-466½	261¾-263¾
1/2 Krug	241-250	136-141¼
1/4 Krug	119-127	67¼-71¾
Angel	473-478	268-271
1/10 Angel	47-52	27-29¾
New Sov.	109-110	61½-62¼
Old Sov.	109-110½	61½-62½
Noble Plat	516-525	293¾-299¼

Silver fix	p/fine oz	US cts equiv
Spot	378.35	666.25
3 months	386.85	678.85
6 months	395.05	691.15
12 months	412.70	719.55

LONDON METAL EXCHANGE TRADED OPTIONS

Aluminium (99.5%)	Calls		Puts	
Strike price $ tonne	Jan	Mar	Jan	Mar
1650		93½		

The (Shipping) Freight Futures sector quotes daily prices, as well as brief comment on shipping contracts fixed during the previous session.

Meat prices are reported both by the UK Meat and Livestock Commission and from major markets. And a Potato market is also reported daily in the FT.

The US price sector is divided between the markets situated in New York, the NY Mercantile, the NY Commodities Exchange, and the Coffee, Cocoa and Sugar exchange, and those in Chicago, the Chicago Board of Trade, and the Chicago Mercantile Exchange.

The Chicago markets, reflecting their location and tradition, trade live cattle and hogs, markets with no counterpart in the UK. But the city also remains the leading centre for trading grains and soyabean.

After ploughing through this mass of statistics, it is worth glancing again at the market trading reports which head the Commodities and Agriculture page. As both the London and US reports make clear,

	Close	Previous	High	Low
Nov	692.8	691.5	0	0
Dec	693.0	692.0	702.5	691.0
Jan	697.7	696.5	699.0	699.0
Mar	707.4	706.0	717.0	705.0
May	717.2	715.2	724.0	715.0
Jly	727.0	724.4	735.0	724.0
Sep	737.2	734.0	744.0	744.0
Dec	752.5	746.8	760.0	751.0
Jan	757.1	753.4	0	0

SUGAR WORLD "11" 112,000 lbs; cents/lbs

	Close	Previous	High	Low
Jan	7.40	7.35	7.35	7.35
Mar	7.93	7.75	7.98	7.79
May	8.02	7.79	8.04	7.83
Jly	8.04	7.82	8.05	7.86
Oct	8.05	7.88	8.06	7.92
Jan	8.20	8.03	0	0
Mar	8.41	8.22	8.36	8.27

COTTON 50,000; cents/lbs

	Close	Previous	High	Low
Dec	70.09	70.85	71.40	70.00
Mar	70.45	71.23	71.70	70.30
May	70.95	71.50	72.20	70.90
Jly	71.13	71.80	72.25	71.05
Oct	65.10	65.50	65.85	65.00
Dec	65.10	64.10	64.80	63.35

CRUDE OIL (Light) 42,000 US galls $/barrel

	Close	Previous	High	Low
Jan	18.62	18.80	18.75	18.58
Feb	18.53	18.68	18.64	18.49
Mar	18.51	18.84	18.59	18.49

	Close	Previous	High	Low
May	190.6	189.7	190.7	188.0
Jly	186.7	186.2	186.9	184.5
Aug	186.0	185.5	186.0	184.0
Sep	184.5	184.0	184.5	182.0
Oct	180.0	181.0	181.0	180.0
Dec	179.6	180.5	182.5	179.5

WHEAT 5,000 bu min; cents/60lb-bushel

	Close	Previous	High	Low
Dec	301/0	305/0	305/4	301/0
Mar	312/6	315/0	316/0	312/2
May	309/0	309/6	310/4	308/0
Jly	296/2	297/6	298/0	296/0
Sep	300/0	300/4	302/4	300/0
Dec	309/0	308/4	310/0	309/0

LIVE HOGS 30,000 lb; cents/lbs

	Close	Previous	High	Low
Dec	44.90	44.97	45.15	44.80
Feb	44.07	44.25	44.45	44.00
Apr	40.02	40.05	40.35	39.87
Jun	42.65	42.57	42.80	42.50
Jly	43.12	43.10	43.25	42.90
Aug	42.12	42.02	42.25	42.00
Oct	39.02	39.05	39.15	39.02
Dec	39.85	39.80	39.85	39.75

MAIZE 5,000 bu min; cents/56lb bushel

	Close	Previous	High	Low
Dec	189/2	187/2	189/2	186/6
Mar	195/4	193/2	196/2	193/0
May	200/6	198/2	201/4	198/0
Jly	205/4	202/2	206/0	202/2
Sep	202/2	200/0	202/4	200/0
Dec	198/6	196/6	198/6	0
[illegible]	[illegible]	[illegible]	[illegible]	[illegible]

these are highly professional and very active markets. While some traders represent end-users of the commodity, many are more speculative — more prepared to jump in and seize an opportunity to buy or sell.

Commodities, whether hard or soft, take some time and investment to produce and can be expensive to store. If a sudden storm flattens the soyabean crop in the US, there will not necessarily be more soyabean waiting around for delivery. Commodity prices can rise and fall sharply in response to factors which may upset the most carefully made plans. For this reason, commodities brokers try even harder than traders in other markets to foresee the future and to offset their risks. They are keen to find out how the Spring corn planting progressed out on the North American Prairies, because they know that the result will begin to influence corn prices before the crop is harvested. For similar reasons, traders in the metal markets need to know whether Pechiney of France intends to increase production of aluminium at its plant in Montreal, Canada. It is information of this nature that the FT publishes in the editorial areas of the Commodities and Agriculture page. The newspaper has about 100 overseas correspondents to draw on for this kind of information and maintains a regular flow of news and comment from the chief commodity-producing nations of the world. On the national level, correspondents will report the estimates for annual crop production issued by the government specialists in the producer countries. Such estimates will need updating if climatic, or similar disasters threaten.

Much of the FT's coverage of commodity producers and markets aims to examine the background factors which may affect future trends, rather than the reporting of day-to-day developments. Many factors clearly hinge on political developments either in the producer country or elsewhere. Examples of this would include reports on the moves within the European Community to reduce grain surpluses, or the constant review of world trade trends by the members of the General Agreement on Tariffs and Trade. Other factors involve a counterplay between a commodity and its price. Higher prices for copper, for example, would stimulate higher production, which might mean the re-opening of closed mines.

The susceptibility of commodity markets to a wide range of domestic and international factors means that references to them will be found in almost every sector of the newspaper. With the world now increasingly linked by instant electronic communication, commodity markets, like securities markets, are likely to become even more active — and thus even more widely reported.

Whaet and rice, which have benefited from the new technology, are consumed by the better off

Agriculture

Poorest lose out

NDIA'S AGRICULTURAL chievements since Indepen- ence are frequently praised in e West Foodgrain production as almost tripled in 40 years, roductivity has more than dou- led India, unlike Africa, no lon- er fears famine Indeed, it main- ins large buffer stocks of food

The achievements are real and npressive But all is not rosy in dia's garden In the first place, oor or indifferent monsoons in cent years have underlined its ontinued vulnerability to dverse weather In spite of the pread of irrigation, 70 per cent f agricultural land remains ain-fed and therefore impossible "drought proof"

Poor weather has resulted in he stagnation of agricultural utput Foodgrain production eaked at 152.4m tonnes in 1983/ 4 and has slid downhill since ast year's crop is estimated at 49-150m tonnes, slightly worse han the previous year's The utturn in drought-hit 1987/88 vill be considerably worse, possi- ly 135-140m tonnes

Yet India's population contin- es to expand remorselessly Foodgrain production of at least 25m tonnes will be required by he turn of the century, if India s to feed a population that by hen may number 1bn

How meaningful is India's resent claim of food self-suffi- iency? Not very, according to ome critics Mr Krishna Raj, the ditor of the left-wing Economic nd Political Weekly, says India an claim self-sufficiency only ecause "so many people are oor"

There is, after all, an obvious contradiction in saying that ndia has all the food it needs when it is also admitted that nearly 40 per cent of the popula- ion (some 300m people) are elow an absolute poverty line n other words cannot afford to neet minimum nutritional stan- lards

If these millions had sufficient ncomes to buy the food they needed and wanted, India clearly would not have buffer stocks It would, like the USSR, be importing heavily The surpluses are no more than a measure of the gross inequality in purchasing power that disfigures the country.

Professor B B Bhattacharya, of the Delhi Institute for Economic Growth, has pointed out that although food production has increased substantially since independence, it has not brought significantly higher consumption "The per capita per day net availability of foodgrains has in fact declined from 480 grams in 1964-65, the peak achieved during the planning period, to 450-470 grams in subsequent years" In bad monsoons, it has fallen as low as 410 grams

The mismatch between food production and consumption reflects the limitations of the Green Revolution of the 1960s. The introduction of new high yielding seeds, the much greater use of fertilisers and pesticides, and improved farming techniques have allowed India to maintain growth of agricultural product at 2½-3 per cent a year, even though opportunities for increasing the acreage were mostly exploited by the mid-1960s

But it has not brought balanced agricultural growth. The benefits of new technology and higher investment in irrigation have been largely limited to the affluent states of Punjab, Haryana and Western UP in the North West, and to parts of Tamil Nadu in the South - in other words to about only one quarter of the total cultivated area

But India's poor are concentrated in the three-quarters of the country that remains undeveloped They cannot afford to buy grain from the rich states, which are talking about exporting their surpluses The problem is accentuated because the crops - principally wheat and rice - that have benefited from the new technology are those consumed by the better off Production of coarse cereals and pulses - staples of the poor - has stagnated by comparison

The extent of regional disparities is illustrated by the fact that 75 per cent of the total increase in foodgrain output between 1981/82 and 1985/86 was accounted for by higher production in the three states of Punjab, Haryana and Uttar Pradesh. While yields in these states rose by around 27 per cent over the period, they stagnated in poor states like Gujarat and Rajasthan

The prosperous high-yielding states are consuming around 90 per cent of government subsidies for agriculture, according to Professor K Subbarao, of the Institute for Economic Growth. As he argues, rather than stimulating more output at a higher marginal cost in states like Punjab, the Government should do more to encourage low-cost production in poorer regions "What we need," he says "is cost-reducing technological progress"

Mr Srinivasa Sastry, the Agriculture Secretary in Delhi, responds to these criticisms by arguing that it was logical to strive first for self-sufficiency and to worry about geographical imbalances later The Government is trying to promote development of the poorer regions. The launching of the Special Rice Production Programme in six eastern states in 1984/85 is beginning to show results Its aim is to raise productivity from 1-1.5 to 2 tonnes per hectare. (Punjab already produces 3 tonnes per hectare.)

Efforts are also being made to spur faster growth of the poorer-performing crops In 1986, Mr Rajiv Gandhi launched a "Technology Mission on Oilseeds" This will aim to improve crop technology farm support systems and price incentives in 180 districts spread over 17 states

Food security at the household, rather than merely the national, level, however, is likely to require a much bigger shift in resources from richer to poorer states than presently seems politically feasible In particular, it awaits a massive extension of irrigation

Michael Prowse

Forestry

Dangerous depletion

LANCE AT A TREE in India nd if it is near a road or a illage, the chances are it will be isshapen The lower branches ay well have been lopped off r sale as firewood Wood is an iormously important energy ource in rural India, and this is ne of the reasons why its for- sts have been dangerously epleted in recent decades

Around 23 per cent of India's tal land area 75m hectares is fficially described as "forests" ut the World Bank estimates at owing to increasing deple- on and degredation only about 0m hectares is actually tree-cov- red India has squandered more f its timber resource than any eveloping country in south east Asia, with the possible exception f Malaysia

The scale of deforestation eflects the fact that non-com- nercial energy sources mainly uelwood but also animal dung nd agricultural wastes account or 80 per cent of rural house- olds energy consumption and vell over 50 per cent of India's otal energy consumption

The pressure on the forests eems set to intensify By the ear 2000, the total annual fuel- wood demand may have dou- led If industrial timber demand s added in, the total wood equirement by then could mount to the equivalent of 20- 0m hectares of mature planta- ion

The Government recognises he imperative need to prevent urther degradation of the offi- ial forests Over the years it has earnt that this is best done by ncouraging the active participa- ion of local communities "Social forestry" projects, which re backed by the World Bank, im to increase the production of uelwood on farm, village and ommunal lands The hope is hat if the rural poor can be put n a position to satisfy their own uelwood requirements they will top ravaging the reserved for- sts

To date social forestry projects have had mixed results Individual farmers have proved keen foresters between 1979 and 1984 over 500m seedlings were planted on individual plots in the state of Uttar Pradesh alone This contrasted with a target of only 8m seedlings But attempts to persuade villagers to establish communal woodlots have flagged badly

But the wood produced by individual "farm foresters" has not been used to meet the local fuel needs of the poor Instead, it has been sold for profit on the commercial market And the degredation of the forests has continued

Thus although social forestry projects are boosting India's total wood production, they are not yet doing much to meet the needs of the poor Many of the new foresters are very far from being marginal farmers eking out a subsistence living

Indeed one doctor with a eucalyptus planation in the village of Anwarpur in Uttar Pradesh seemed to look at trees in much the way that certain Manhattan physicians look at Wall Street stocks He said he had no intention of planting any more eucalyptus seeds because the prices had topped out and he could make a much better return with more conventional agricultural crops Having made his point, he proceeded to entertain a visiting World Bank team to drinks in the shade of a pleasant grove of poplars

It is hard to help the really poor in Indian villages because they lie at the bottom of a rigid social hierachy Landless labourers stand to get little benefit from a community woodlot scheme if the village leaders sell the wood commercially and use the cash to further their own pet projects To counter this type of problem, state forestry departments, with World Bank guidance, are pushing the concept of "micro planning"

A micro-plan, says Dr Ajit Banerjee, a Bank forestry specialist, starts by establishing "the land, leadership and financial resources of a village" In drawing up a plan, officials talk to all sections of village society and try to establish their needs The aim is to persuade the village leaders to agree an equitable distribution of the eventual harvest before the seeds are planted

Micro-planning also aims to bend technology to meet the needs of the rural poor rather than vice versa The technically most efficient strategy for example, might be to harvest a plantation only every seven years and allow no pruning in the interim. But this would not be an optimal social strategy because it would ignore villagers' ongoing fuelwood needs

This new approach makes a lot of sense in theory But it is far from clear that it will work in practice Farm forestry caught on because it appealed to the self-interest of individual farmers A micro-plan that serves the interests of a whole community calls for effective cooperation, a commodity that may be in shorter supply

But Dr Banerjee points out that a communal forestry project on a scale much larger than anything contemplated in village microplans has already proved a great success In 1972, 450 families in 11 villages in West Bengal were persuaded to co-operate in rehabilitating 1300 hectares of totally degraded government forest

The rehabilitation scheme made allowance for their continuing firewood needs and, more importantly offered them a 25 per cent share in all future produce The villagers are now the happy owners of a $2.4bn stake in what is the some of the most luxurient forest in West Bengal. Each family can thus expect an income in perpetuity of around $700 a fortune in rural India

If India really wants to turn the tide of deforestation, suggests Dr Banerjee, it must promote ambitious communal projects of this type.

Michael Prowse

Drought no longer means national (though it can still mean personal) disaster

Efforts to combat monsoon failure

THE DROUGHT that has afflicted India this year is quite possibly the most severe since 1877. The rainfall pattern between June and early September was more adverse than in 1965 - the worst drought year since Independence. In many regions the summer kharif crop was devastated.

But whereas droughts under the British Raj spelled mass starvation, deficient rainfall after 40 years of self-rule represents at the national level no more than a serious economic setback.

India, in spite of a projected shortfall of almost 15 per cent in food production (as compared with targets), will not require massive food aid of the kind supplied by the US in the mid-1960s. The spread of irrigation and the use of high-yielding seeds have helped amass a buffer stock of foodgrains which peaked at around 23m tonnes in the summer (it is now down to 17m tonnes). Imports of some items, such as edible oils, have shot up; the overall impact on the balance of payments could be negative to the tune of $1bn-$1.5bn over a period of 12 months.

No section of Indian society has been able fully to insulate itself from the drought. Prosperous city dwellers and foreign tourists admittedly have experienced little more than mild inconvenience - power cuts, price rises and occasional shortages of particular items.

But for millions of marginal farmers and landless labourers, the drought has spelled personal disaster. Coming, as it has, after three morale-sapping years of poor monsoons, it is forcing many small farmers to sell their livestock (those animals that have not already perished), abandon their land and vainly seek work in the congested urban districts. Drought is cruelly underlining the scale of Indian income inequalities.

Desert-like conditions in western states like Rajasthan and Gujarat have ironically gone hand-in-hand with chronic flooding in eastern states such as Bihar and West Bengal. As always, India's problem is less a shortage of water than its maldistribution.

Officials in Delhi have been reluctant to make firm estimates of the drought's full economic impact. Hopes that the rabi (winter) crop will make up much of the ground lost in the summer appear to be fading. This is despite the fact that winter crops are less dependent on rainfal than summer crops.

The Government is putting into effect emergency relief measures that will cost around R20bn in 1987/88. This is being paid for out of the budget contingency reserve, the cutting back of other spending programmes, and special surcharges on taxes paid by the wealthy. However, it is far from clear that the resources being set aside are sufficient or that the relief will actually reach the most needy.

The drought is putting the subsidised public food distribution system to its most severe test yet.

Although the number of "fair price" outlets has risen sharply during the 1980s, the geographical coverage is still patchy. Nobody doubts, however, that India is better placed than ever before to combat monsoon failure.

MP

Waiting for the evening ration of water around a dried-up well in Hassanpur

Bomb alerts bring Belfast to standstill

BY OUR DUBLIN AND BELFAST CORRESPONDENTS

TRAFFIC was brought to a halt in Belfast last night as security forces dealt with more than 20 bomb alerts.

Hi-jacked vehicles were used to block roads near police and military bases, and near the airport.

Earlier in the day it had emerged that changes in extradition procedures worked out by the Irish and British governments were likely to be delayed.

Meanwhile both governments faced embarrassing criticism when the attempted extradition of a Belfast man to Northern Ireland ran into problems.

Mr Paul Anthony Kane, 33, was arrested in Co. Longford in the republic on Monday along with Mr Dermot Finucane. Both had escaped during the Maze prison breakout in Northern Ireland in September 1983.

A warrant for Mr Kane's arrest was issued by Belfast Crown Court yesterday. But by the time it reached the Gardai (Irish police force) his period of detention had lapsed and he had been set free.

On his release, Mr Kane went to his solicitor's office in Cavan town. Later he was re-arrested.

The changes in extradition procedures are now unlikely to make the December 1 deadline imposed by Dublin following opposition objections to some of the provisions.

However, the European Convention on Terrorism will automatically be ratified next Tuesday while the Dail (Irish parliament) debates amendments to an earlier law providing the safeguards sought by Mr Haughey's Government.

Under the terms of the amended act, the Irish Attorney-General will scrutinise extradition warrants provided by his British counterpart.

However, the opposition parties have demanded parliamentary time to discuss the implications of the arrangement.

Mr Kane was captured the day after the Maze escape in 1983 and returned to prison where he was serving an 18-year sentence for attempted murder and firearms offences. However, the sentence was quashed in July last year by the Northern Ireland Court of Appeal.

Mr Kane, who was then being held on charges connected with the escape, obtained bail in October last year but failed to appear at any subsequent court hearings.

In Belfast last night a train was set on fire at Central Station and a police patrol was attacked with a hand grenade. Firebombs exploded on two buses, but there were no casualties in any of the incidents.

A police spokesman blamed the IRA. "We are seeing their answer to current problems - punish the public."

Nations to act on N Sea pollution

BY DAVID FISHLOCK, SCIENCE EDITOR

AGREEMENT to reduce North Sea pollution was reached in London last night at an eight-nation ministerial meeting.

The environment ministers from nations surrounding the sea agreed that the dumping of harmful toxic wastes, the incineration of toxic wastes and the dumping of ships' wastes in the North Sea should be banned.

Mr Nicholas Ridley, UK Environment Secretary, as chairman of the second international conference on pollution of the North Sea, described the two-day meeting as a great success and a major step forward in combating North Sea pollution.

Although the conclusions of the conference were not legally binding, they were a common declaration of political will, Mr Ridley said.

Among the more contentious issues on which ministers reached unanimous agreement was the immediate end to the dumping of garbage from ships.

Incineration of toxic waste is to be drastically reduced by 1991 and ended by 1994. Dumping of solid industrial wastes deemed to be harmful will be banned from the end of 1989.

The present ceiling on toxic contamination is to be reduced.

Lord Belstead, representing Britain at the conference, said that from the end of 1989 only dumping of liquid wastes would be permitted in the North Sea.

The conference also agreed to reconcile national objectives for water quality with those for atmospheric emission limits.

On radioactive wastes and emissions, it agreed unanimously that no polluting practice would be adopted by any nation.

Britain is not required to make further reductions in emissions and effluents from British Nuclear Fuels' Sellafield reprocessing plant in Cumbria beyond those already in prospect.

Britain will form a scientific task force next year to seek a greater understanding of the complexities of the North Sea.

In a £6.8m project over five years, the Natural Environment Research Council plans to produce a computer model that will predict the behaviour of the sea's tides, currents and winds.

The conference agreed that a third ministerial meeting on North Sea pollution should be convened in the Netherlands in the early 1990s.

Shell Expro likely to cut another 300 to 600 jobs

BY MAURICE SAMUELSON

ANOTHER 300 to 600 jobs are expected to disappear at Shell Expro, the operator for the Shell and Esso North Sea joint venture, on top of the 700 shed in the past year. The cuts will all be by natural wastage, voluntary redundancy or redeployment.

They are partly a response to last year's oil-price collapse but the company says they also expect a continuing fall in North Sea oil output from its peak levels.

Mr Peter Everett, managing director, told staff yesterday that the organisational review was intended to prepare "for the long-term challenges of the 1990s" when total oil production would fall as older, larger fields declined.

The review will concentrate on the London, Aberdeen and Lowestoft offices and may be extended to the St Fergus, Mossmorran and Bacton gas plants.

Offshore platforms will be exempt, having recently been affected by a restructuring of shift patterns and introduction of new working practices.

US bank to complete purchase of broker

By Stephen Fidler, Euromarkets Correspondent

SECURITY PACIFIC, the Los Angeles-based commercial bank, said yesterday that it intended to buy out minority shareholders of Hoare Govett, the UK stockbroker, in which it took a controlling stake in December 1984.

It also announced a streamlining of management and the merging of all the equity, debt and banking business of its international merchant banking operations into one firm, Security Pacific Hoare Govett (Holdings). Hoare Govett will disappear as a separate entity.

The firm said it would not leave any business areas and no lay-offs would result from the moves, although a few executives might resign. Mr Anthony Greayer, chief executive of Hoare Govett, has already resigned.

Security Pacific currently owns about 85 per cent of Hoare Govett. The minority stake is held by about 120 executives of the firm.

The stockbroker was valued at $78m when Security Pacific took control. The price to be paid for the remaining shares will be in line with this. The move was contemplated in the 1984 deal and the transaction is expected to be completed next month.

Mr Richard Westmacott, chairman of Security Pacific Hoare Govett (Holdings), said the move had been under discussion before last month's stock market collapse. However, while not prompted by the crash, the announcement had been hastened by speculation that the Californian bank was looking for a buyer for Hoare Govett.

He said that, in common with other market-makers, Hoare Govett had lost money in the crash. He declined to say how much.

Until the crash the firm's equity business had been "quite outstanding", he said. The firm thus expects to be profitable for the second half of the year, though results will probably be down on last year.

Mr Westmacott said the streamlining had resulted in there being only one chief executive position rather than two. Mr Greayer had been "very dignified in accepting the situation", he said.

Security Pacific, the sixth-largest bank holding company in the US with assets of $74bn (£41.2bn), recently acquired a 30 per cent stake in Burns Fry, the Canadian investment dealer. A representative of Burns Fry will sit on the new company's board.

FKI Babcock to close Lincoln plant

By Ralph Atkins

FKI BABCOCK, the engineering and electrical group, is closing its Babcock Robey boilermaking factory in Lincoln with the possible loss of up to 270 jobs.

The closure is part of a rationalisation plan announced after the £416m takeover of Babcock International by FKI Electricals in July. Operations are to be transferred to Stone International, FKI Babcock's industrial boilermaking division in Oldbury, West Midlands.

The decision emerged less than 24 hours before today's announcement of interim results for FKI Babcock.

At the time of the Babcock International takeover in July, Mr Tony Gartland, FKI Babcock chief executive, said that a rationalisation programe was required. There was speculation that the group would sell the energy division of Babcock, of which Babcock Robey is part.

In 1986 the division accounted for about 24 per cent of Babcock International's turnover and made an operating profit of £4.18m.

Andrew Taylor reports on the challenge to BPB Industries' near-monopoly market

Writing is on the wall for plasterboard fight

IT IS particularly appropriate that BPB Industries and Redland, two of Britain's biggest building material producers, should have both decided to publish half yearly results today.

The two companies are central figures in an intriguing battle for market share of one of Britain's fastest-growing building materials markets.

BPB Industries' near monopoly over British plasterboard sales is being challenged by Redland, which 11 weeks ago announced it was establishing a plasterboard manufacturing joint venture with CSR, an Australian building materials, sugar and resources group.

The aim of the new venture is to capture up to 30 per cent of the British plasterboard market. At least two other Continental plasterboard manufacturers are planning to start operations in the UK.

Eternit TAC, a Belgian company, proposes to import up to 10m sq m of plasterboard a year, equivalent to about 6 per cent of total British sales this year.

Knauf, West Germany's biggest plasterboard manufacturer, is seeking planning permission to build a factory in south-east England.

Sales of plasterboard in Britain, likely to be about 150m sq m this year, have risen by more than a fifth since 1975.

It is widely used for the interior walls of houses and is increasingly being used in commercial developments, where its acoustic and fire-resistant properties make it ideal for lift voids and shafts.

Contractors like it because it arrives on site prefabricated and ready for use. It is a dry product, less messy to use than wet-wall plaster techniques.

However, Sales of plasterboard in Britain and on the Continent lag well behind consumption in North America. Sales per head in the US are more than three times those in the UK.

Mr Malcolm Brown, building analyst for stockbroker James Capel, forecasts that western European plasterboard sales could increase from 460m sq m in 1986 to 725m sq m by 1995. British sales, he says, could rise from 136m sq m last year to 200m sq m by 1995.

BPB is Europe's biggest plasterboard manufacturer with an estimated 50 per cent of the European Community market. It is market leader in France and it became Germany's second-biggest producer in April when it acquired Rigip's plasterboard and gypsum interests.

BPB's share price has fallen by more than 35 per cent since Redland announced its joint venture. Redland's share price by comparison had fallen 29 per cent by yesterday morning and the FT Actuaries building materials index by just over 27 per cent.

BPB has been Britain's only plasterboard manufacturer since 1968, when ICI closed its Billingham plant in Cleveland. Its share price, therefore, was always going to be vulnerable to an outbreak of competition in the UK.

Brokers say that one advantage BPB has over its British market rivals is that it mines and quarries its own rock gypsum and produces its own liner board, both of which are used to manufacture plasterboard.

Redland and CSR plan to import Spanish gypsum and probably Swedish liner board, which some observers say could make it vulnerable to currency fluctuations and supply disruption.

The joint venture recently acquired a 44.9 per cent stake in Norgips, a Norwegian plasterboard manufacturer, and intends to import plasterboard until the first of two proposed British plants opens around 1990.

Eternit TAC, a Belgian company, also plans eventually to build a British manufacturing plant. In the meantime it has taken over the Essex-based import and distribution facilities of Lafarge Coppee, a large French building materials group.

Coppee, which this year will import just over 2m sq m of plasterboard into the UK, less than 2 per cent of total sales, says that strong demand for plasterboard in France has made it difficult for it to increase its share of the British market.

Knauf, a privately owned company, from Iphofen, northern Bavaria, is the latest company to emerge as a potential threat to BPB's British sales.

It is seeking planning permission from Swale Borough Council to build a plasterboard plant on 32 acres of vacant land near Sittingbourne, Kent.

Mr Jamie Stevenson, building analyst with stockbroker Wood Mackenzie, says that, judging by the scale of the application, Knauf is planning a plant with a capacity of about 20m sq m.

He forecasts that this could represent more than 10 per cent of the British market by 1990. Knauf, if it goes ahead with its plans, is likely to import Spanish gypsum but to use locally produced liner board.

The news that Knauf was seeking planning permission hit BPB's shares again on Tuesday when they fell another 25p to 248p.

The stock market appears to be taking the view that increased competition might be good news for plasterboard customers but may not be quite so good for shareholders of some of the companies involved.

PLASTERBOARD DELIVERIES IN WESTERN EUROPE (m square metres)

Country	1985	1986	1987*	1995*
UK	122	136	150	200
France	130	135	145	240
W. Germany	60	60	64	80
Italy+	8	9	10	36
Nordic Countries	50	54	56	65
Benelux	24	24	28	33
Austria	19	19	20	27
Spain	5	6	9	20
Switzerland+	3	3	4	5
Ireland	14	14	14	19
TOTAL	435	460	500	725

*James Capel estimates. +Imported. No indigenous capacity in Italy until 1990

Kleinwort chairman named

By David Lascelles, Banking Editor

MR DAVID PEAKE is to become chairman of Kleinwort Benson, the merchant banking group, in succession to Mr Michael Hawkes who reaches the bank's retirement age of 60 next month.

Mr Peake, 53, is vice-chairman of the company and non-executive chairman of Kleinwort Benson Investment Management, its subsidiary.

He trained with Banque Lambert in Brussels and worked with Schroders for several years before joining Kleinwort in 1963. There, his experience has been mainly in banking and international capital markets.

Yesterday, he said he intended to pursue the policies of Mr Hawkes, which are to make Kleinwort an investment-banking group of global stature.

Kleinwort will also rationalise its group structure. This currently vests principal management authority in Kleinwort Benson, the operating company, rather than in its publicly-quoted holding company, Kleinwort Benson Lonsdale.

Mr Peake will be chairman of Kleinwort Benson but will succeed Mr Robert Henderson as chairman of the holding company when he retires next year.

Mr Hawkes will become executive deputy chairman of the holding company. There he will be in charge of deploying capital resources and risk-management worldwide.

The executives at the head of Kleinwort's main operating divisions will also join the holding company board.

Tax relief for 1,800 donors

By Philip Stephens, Economics Correspondent

MORE than 1,800 schemes have been established during the last 18 months providing tax relief for charity donations which are deducted directly from employees' pay packets, Mr Peter Lilley, the Economic Secretary to the Treasury said yesterday.

The payroll giving scheme allows employees to receive tax relief on contributions of up to £120 per year.

Mr Lilley said it had led to an upturn in donations.

Policy change for north urged

BY IAN HAMILTON FAZEY, NORTHERN CORRESPONDENT

MANCHESTER Chamber of Commerce and Industry - one of the largest bodies representing the private sector in the north - is calling for fundamental changes in the Government's regional policy to help business, particularly manufacturing, to create wealth before jobs.

The chamber, which set up an economic committee a year ago to develop a growth strategy for the north-west, published the committee's first paper yesterday. This says that regional assistance is mainly directed at employment levels, not growth.

"Grants have been used to preserve jobs or postpone redundancies rather than to invest in long-term growth. This is a social policy. The Government has no regional economic policy," the paper says.

Arguments about whether there really is a north-south divide are described as diversions from the real problem, which is seen as the over-concentration of wealth and investment in one corner of the UK - London and the south-east.

"The north-west, which already provides 11 per cent of UK gross domestic product and 28 per cent of UK manufacturing output, could contribute more to the national economy if its economic potential were understood in the capital," the committee says.

It believes that natural economic forces will drive investment northwards in the long run, provided they are allowed to operate by the removal of distortions, such as Government failure to carry out five-yearly revaluations of rateable property since 1973, which has given taxpayers in the south-east a regional subsidy.

The paper attacks a south-eastern bias in air transport as a distortion that has penalised all other regions and inconvenienced millions of passengers.

It says another is the Government's employment and purchasing policies, which have produced a concentration of manpower in London, where costs are highest.

Moving large departments out of London is seen as an important means of correcting the imbalance.

The paper also says that the Scottish and Welsh Development Agencies cost the rest of UK taxpayers more than £100m a year in subsidies and distort economic forces even more.

The main advantage of the agencies is not providing financial aid but their coherent policy towards business, with co-ordination of government departments and ministerial spokesmen in the Cabinet.

A mechanism for similar co-ordination could be achieved elsewhere if some Cabinet ministers also had responsibility for an English region as well as for their own department, it says. However, the impact would be limited if the centralism of the Civil Service remained untouched.

New car sales rising sharply

BY JOHN GRIFFITHS

NEW CAR sales in the UK have been accelerating sharply this month in spite of the stock market downturn.

Industry figures yesterday showed sales in the first 20 days of November up 15.31 per cent on the same period of 1986, itself a year of record sales totalling 1.92m.

The increase for the current month is one of the biggest, in percentage terms, of any period this year. Sales would now have to collapse below last year's levels to not reach the 2m sales mark for the first time.

Ironically, the biggest threat to reaching this target is from within the industry - the labour stoppages at Ford, the market leader. The company said last night that it had lost output of 11,000 cars, mainly Sierras and Sapphires.

The industry figures showed 104,334 cars sold in the first 20 days of this month, compared with 90,482 last year, bringing sales for the year to date to 1,885,519.

The figures come amid a fierce debate over car sales next year. At a conference organised by the UK trade publication Motor Trader, Mr Arthur Way of the Economist Intelligence Unit said that until the stock market turned down, the EIU had been forecasting a 2.5 per cent fall in new car sales to 1.92m from this year's expected 2m units. A 5 per cent fall to 1.85m units with a further drop to 1.75m the following year was now more likely.

Mr Peter Batchelor, Vauxhall's sales and marketing director, predicted a fall to 1.9m units next year, dropping to 1.5m in 1989. "After that there will be slow growth which could result in an annual market as high as 2.5m in the year 2,000."

● The Peugeot 405 saloon, UK production of which is getting under way at Peugeot Talbot's plant at Ryton, near Coventry, has been elected Car of the Year by the award's international panel of 57 judges.

Brokers' body can seek recognition

BY ERIC SHORT

REGISTERED insurance brokers with life, pension and other financial services operations that are comparatively small will be able to receive authorisation under the financial services legislation through the Insurance Brokers' Registration Council.

The council has been given clearance by the Securities and Investments Board to seek to become a recognised professional body.

Under the 1977 Insurance Brokers' Registration Act, firms operating as insurance brokers must be registered with the council for general, life and pensions business.

Under the financial services legislation, life and pensions business has to be authorised, usually by the Financial Intermediaries, Managers and Brokers Regulatory Association or through a recognised professional body.

Insurance brokers operating mainly in general insurance already provide most of the required information for authorisation to the Insurance Brokers' Registration Council.

It would be convenient for these brokers to be authorised by the same route as they are registered and this may now be possible.

About 1,360 brokers would be eligible.

Head for equality commission

By Jimmy Burns, Labour Staff

MRS JOANNA FOSTER, a leading member of the Industrial Society, one of Britain's largest private sector training bodies, has been appointed chairman of the Government's Equal Opportunities Commission.

Mrs Foster is head of the Pepperell Unit, the Industrial Society's equal opportunities division. She was previously employed by the society in helping to train young people and has worked in management relocation counselling in the US and France.

She will succeed Baroness Platt of Writtle who retires on April 30 after five years as EOC chairman.

The appointment of Mrs Foster, 48, who publicly claims no particular party allegiance, breaks with a 10-year tradition at the EOC. Her two predecessors, Baroness Platt (Conservative) and Lady Lockwood (Labour), were drawn from the voluntary sector and local government and were life peers with links to the Government in power at the time.

Mrs Foster said yesterday that she hoped to use her practical experience of working with the Industrial Society to promote equal opportunities as a "mainstream" employment issue.

"This is not an issue that can be marginalised any more. We need to think how best to capitalise on our skills and improve the competitiveness of British industry," she said.

The EOC was established under the 1975 Sex Discrimination Act. Its duties are broadly defined as helping to eliminate discrimination and promoting equality of opportunity.

Men and Matters, Page 36

BT likely to lose monopoly on call-boxes

By Lynton McLain

THE BT monopoly on public phone boxes is expected to be broken with the introduction of competition. Mr John Butcher, undersecretary for trade and industry, said yesterday that the Government had decided that call-box users should have more choice and that BT must now "face the spur of competition."

A report in September from Oftel, the Office of Telecommunications that has supervised and monitored BT since it was privatised, said BT's level of performance in providing call-box services was "not acceptable."

Professor Brian Carsberg, the director general of Oftel, is considering how to introduce competition. Mr Butcher said Prof Carsberg was to advise the department on ways to increase choice for the consumer in call-box provision.

The Department of Trade and Industry said Oftel's report on the subject was expected "shortly."

The options to be considered by Oftel include allowing Mercury, BT's sole competitor, to provide a public call-box service and liberalising the rental of payphones in shops, restaurants and other public places. At the moment their provision in these establishments is strictly regulated.

Michael Dixon examines the Government's proposals for a further shake-up in the National Health Service

Charges to be extended for dental treatment and eye tests

THE END of free eye tests and dental checks, and higher charges for National Health Service dental treatment were signalled by the Government yesterday as part of its scheme for developing the UK's primary health care services.

The proposed scheme, set out in a new Health and Medicines Bill and a supporting white paper, contains a range of options for health authorities to make money by running shops and selling services and facilities to the private sector. It also contains measures to tighten up the management of NHS employees, including family doctors and dentists.

Although the £5.08bn a year public cost of the family practitioner service is to be increased by a total of £570m during 1988-91, the Government said the extended charges and other money-raising activities were indispensable to its plan for developing primary health care. The plan's main objectives are:

● To make services more responsive to the needs of the consumer.

● To raise standards of care.

● To promote health and prevent illness.

● To give patients the widest range of choice in obtaining high-quality primary care services.

● To improve value for money.

The bill - which would apply throughout England and, with some detailed differences in Wales, and also largely in Scotland and Northern Ireland - would provide direct powers for the widening and raising of charges.

Sight-testing would be privatised for all except children and young people in full-time education, adults on low incomes and people registered as blind or partly sighted who would continue to receive NHS tests without charge.

Those undergoing tests, whether private or free, would have the right to receive a prescription or a statement that a prescription was not necessary. "The optician will not be able to charge for the sight test or for any spectacles required until this has been done," the white paper says.

Exceptions to the charges for dental checks and treatment would include pregnant women, and those who have had a baby in the past 12 months, children and young people in full-time education and low-income adults.

The proposed charge for dental examination is estimated at "under £3" at present-day prices. The generally increased charges for dental treatment would be calculated on a new basis, relating what was paid by the patient to the cost of the service provided.

In the case of family doctors the Government's proposals were strictly factual statements about themselves and their services.

Emphasis was also placed on changing the system for paying NHS general practitioners, so that rewards would be tied more closely to performance, and to provide incentive payments to encourage developments.

The proportion of the doctors' total NHS pay depending on the courses for general practitioners and their associated staff.

A compulsory retirement age of 70 would be introduced for NHS family doctors, although family practitioner committees in England and Wales and health boards in Scotland could continue contracts with older practitioners if circumstances required.

Extended charges are said to be essential to official plans for developing primary health care

mostly "for negotiation with the profession" rather than enforceable by direct powers in the bill. But the white paper states that the outcome of such negotiations with different branches of the NHS would influence how much the branches received in extra public investment.

Measures to increase competition between general practitioners would include easier ways for patients to change their NHS doctor, the provision of more detailed information on the various practices operating in an area and discussions with the General Medical Council with the aim of allowing family doctors - like dentists - to advertise number of people using their particular practice would be raised from the present 47 per cent to "at least 50 per cent in the first instance."

Doctors would also have to meet stiffer conditions before qualifying for the full basic practice allowance, currently £7,850.

Incentive payments would be introduced to encourage such activities as initial health checks and follow-up treatment for newly registered NHS customers, comprehensive services for the elderly, meeting immunisation and vaccination targets, working in run-down and isolated areas, performing minor operations and attending in-service training

The Government would provide extra funds to help with improvements to general practitioners' premises - for which minimum standards would be revised - and invite private financial institutions to develop schemes for providing further capital for such improvements.

Measures to tighten the management of NHS family doctor services - together with other branches of primary health care - would hinge on extensions of the responsibilities and powers of the family practitioner committees and their equivalents.

The committees would be able to take stronger action in response to complaints from consumers, to check on practitioners' performance.

In the case of dentists, the bill would provide powers to change the division of responsibilities between general dental practitioners and the community dental services. The community service would probably provide treatment for children and adults who would otherwise find it hard to obtain treatment.

The NHS contract for dentists would be amended to ensure dentists provided advice on oral hygiene. Subject to the successful outcome of current experiments, dentists could be required to maintain children's oral health at a specified fee per child, rather than charge for each item of service provided.

Under the bill, the Government would be able to impose a compulsory retirement age - not yet determined - for NHS dentists, and to streamline and strengthen the managerial powers of the Dental Estimates Boards. Complaints against the boards would be subject to investigation by the Health Service Commissioner.

Matters for discussion with the dental profession include a new pay system, incorporating incentives for high efficiency and standards, and the appointment of part-time "advisers" to keep watch on NHS dentists.

Community pharmacists, who were put under a new type of NHS contract earlier in the year, would be subject to only a few additional changes. They include the introduction of allowances for pharmacy contractors who take an active part in training other community health workers, keep substantial records of medicines used by individual patients, particularly the elderly, and display health-promotional material.

The Government would also begin negotiations with the pharmacy profession to establish a fund to improve pharmacy services in deprived areas.

Where community nursing services were concerned, the white paper emphasised "that there is no single right way of organising services and the decision about what is appropriate in different localities remains one for the health authority concerned."

The Government nevertheless intends to consult the appropriate professional bodies about a number of proposals, including giving nurses more freedom to prescribe a limited range of items such as ointments.

Promoting Better Health. Cm 249. HMSO. £7.90.

'Buoyant outlook' for advertising

By Feona McEwan

THE OUTLOOK for the advertising industry [illegible]

[illegible] of the 30 top advertising and marketing directors questioned expect the economy [illegible] next year [illegible] similar number are prepared [illegible] increase their 1988 advertising budgets.

The poll was conducted by MORI for Campaign magazine.

10 UK Economic News

While the FT endeavours to cover a very wide range of subjects, it is inevitable that financial and economic news in the UK takes pride of place. The annual Budget Speech, the monthly trade figures, the Retail Price Index (RPI) and the rest of the host of official statistics on which the pundits feed, must all be fully reported in the FT. In this, the paper is no different from the rest of the UK press, or radio and television. The implications of trends in national employment totals, interest rates or inflation are not confined to readers of the FT.

The aim of the paper is to report all significant UK economic statistics as they appear, but to devote substantial resources and editorial space to explaining them. This often means putting the figures into context by publishing a graph showing how the relevant trend has been moving over the previous quarter of year. When the trend shows signs of changing direction, whether for the good or the bad, the FT will publish an article by the specialist staff explaining what appears to be happening.

The highlight of the year is the Budget Speech by the Chancellor of the Exchequer, which always provides the supreme test for the British press as journalists race to insert the Budget provisions in the first editions. For the FT, there is one important factor. The Chancellor does not begin his speech to the House of Commons until mid-afternoon, usually around 3.30 pm, and invariably spends the first hour or so in a general review of economic prospects. This was

Financial Times Thursday March 19 1987

ECONOMIC VIEWPOINT

Aftermath of the Budget

By Samuel Brittan

MY SECOND thoughts about the Budget relate not so much to the Chancellor, but to the Opposition, including among the Opposition the BBC interviewers and presenters.

There is, heaven knows, enough about which to castigate the Government from a social market point of view. There are so many ways by which the Government could both make more use of market forces—in the jobs, housing, import and other markets—while doing more to help the worst off and the victims of change. If one is looking for disincentives and traditionally believed to be a device to allow the financial markets to close before hearing the substance of the Speech.

This argument will become hard to maintain as London moves ever faster into the 24-hour markets now near at hand in the real world. At present, however, most London markets are effectively closed before the Chancellor gets down to serious business and the City's considered response is held over until the next day. Nevertheless, the FT reports on the major financial markets are not written until after the reporters have telephoned round the traders' offices to find out what reaction is likely when the City opens for business the following morning. Although the Budget Speech will not be completed until late in the newspaper's day, full details of the Chancellor's proposals will be carried in the first edition on the following morning, together with comment from FT specialist writers on the likely effects and implications of the various measures.

The Budget as a whole will inevitably be the subject of a leading article, setting out the paper's view of its strong and weak points. The article will be written after the newspaper has sounded opinion in the City and at Westminster — but it will represent the view of the FT.

It is also usual to invite outside contributors, academics, business figures or leading politicians, to write articles on, or shortly after, Budget Day, offering their own views. In such cases, articles are clearly ascribed to the writer, whose status is explained so that readers know that his views are not necessarily those of the FT.

The newspaper expects to publish the full text of the Chancellor's Speech as soon as possible, usually on the morning after its delivery in the House of Commons. And the Budget proposals will be discussed at greater length in the days following.

The final hurdle in the Budget coverage will come in the following week when the House of Commons discusses the Speech. While the outcome of the Speech has to be a success for the Government — the alternative would be its resignation — the Budget Debate is always reported closely in the UK press.

The excitements of Budget Day come only once a year, but official economic data are disclosed by Government departments weekly, monthly, and sometimes quarterly. The FT publishes all the important statistics relating to the progress of the economy. For readers' convenience, the chief statistics are combined into a table headed 'UK Economic Indicators' (see opposite), which is published in each Thursday's paper.

UK ECONOMIC INDICATORS

ECONOMIC ACTIVITY-Indices of industrial production, manufacturing output (1980=100); engineering orders (1980=100); retail sales volume (1980=100); retail sales value (1980=100); registered unemployment (excluding school leavers) and unfilled vacancies (000s). All seasonally adjusted.

	Indl. prod.	Mfg. output	Eng. order	Retail vol.	Retail value	Unem-ployed	Vacs.
1986							
2nd qtr.	109.7	104.0	97	121.3	154.0	3,203	175.6
3rd qtr.	110.9	105.0	96	123.7	158.7	3,202	200.2
4th qtr.	111.1	107.4	98	126.5	194.3	3,141	213.0
1987							
1st qtr.	111.9	107.4	95	125.4	157.0	3,073	210.4
2nd qtr	112.5	109.4	93	128.3	166.0	2,965	226.1
3rd qtr	114.3	111.4		131.8	171.8	2,827	241.3
April	112.5	109.0	94	130.0	169.0	3,018	217.7
May	113.1	109.5	93	125.4	161.3	2,952	230.5
June	111.9	109.8	93	129.4	167.3	2,925	233.7
July	114.2	111.1	93	131.2	173.7	2,876	235.2
Aug.	115.0	111.8	98	132.5	171.0	2,829	236.9
Sept.	113.6	111.2		131.6	171.0	2,773	246.6
Oct.				132.9		2,714	261.4

OUTPUT-By market sector; consumer goods, investment goods, intermediate goods (materials and fuels); engineering output, metal manufacture, textiles, leather and clothing (1980=100); housing starts (000s, monthly average).

	Cnsmer goods	Invest goods	Intmd. goods	Eng. output	Metal mnfg.	Textile etc.	Housg. starts*
1986							
1st qtr.	103.9	100.8	114.9	101.1	109.1	103.1	14.6
2nd qtr.	105.3	101.1	115.7	102.6	119.6	104.1	19.5
3rd qtr.	106.4	101.2	117.5	103.3	108.5	103.2	19.4
4th qtr.	108.5	103.3	116.0	105.4	115.0	104.8	15.5
1987							
1st qtr.	108.1	103.2	117.8	105.2	113.8	101.9	17.4
2nd qtr	111.1	102.0	117.5	105.8	119.1	105.8	19.6
3rd qtr	113.0	104.9	119.3	108.1	120.6	107.9	19.0
February	109.1	103.2	118.5	105.0	120.0	102.0	18.6
March	107.9	104.7	118.6	107.0	115.0	101.0	20.8
April	110.7	102.8	117.8	105.0	115.0	106.0	18.1
May	111.6	102.6	118.7	106.0	119.0	106.0	20.4
June	111.1	103.6	116.1	106.0	123.0	106.0	20.2
July	112.8	104.2	119.4	107.0	120.0	108.0	20.3
Aug.	113.6	104.8	120.3	108.0	124.0	109.0	17.4
Sept.	112.6	105.7	118.1	109.0	118.0	107.0	19.4

EXTERNAL TRADE-Indices of export and import volume (1980=100); visible balance; current balance (£m); oil balance (£m); terms of trade (1980=100); official reserves.

	Export volume	Import volume	Visible balance	Current balance	Oil balance	Terms trade	Reserve US$bn
1986							
2nd qtr.	121.9	129.1	-1,608	+146	+765	102.5	19.20
3rd qtr.	122.6	139.0	-2,891	-910	+621	103.2	22.43
4th qtr.	130.5	144.0	-2,725	-960	+785	100.9	21.92
1987							

The largest batch of statistics, published monthly, consist of:

Retail Prices Index (RPI): Published by the Department of Employment, this quotes prices from the previous month for a weighted basket of items which includes food and clothing, mortgages and rents, and public utility charges. The RPI is compared with that for the previous month and also interim of a year-on-year comparison.

The RPI is the best snapshot guide to the progress of the rate of inflation in the UK and is often quoted simply as 'the inflation rate'. In addition to its use as an economic measure, the RPI is often regarded as the basis for real wage growth and for comparisons between UK inflation and that elsewhere in the world.

Retail sales: An index for the volume and value of retail sales published by the Department of Trade, referring to the previous month. It is followed within a few weeks by revised figures giving important data on instalment credit. Thus, while its immediate application may be for the retail trade, this index also discloses important trends in consumer credit which are linked to inflationary trends.

Producer prices: Two indices, from the Department of Industry, showing costs and output prices for the manufacturing industries in the previous month. An important signal to future price trends at the retail level.

Earnings: A closely-watched index on average earnings and basic manual wage rates published by the Department of Employment. An important guide to cost pressures on industry and also, by comparing it with the RPI, to trends in the standard of living.

Balance of Payment figures: The Department of Trade's statistics on the UK current account for the previous month. Once the dread of UK Governments because of the implications for the sterling exchange rate, the monthly trade figures cover both visible trade (goods) and invisibles (services, profits and dividends). Oil-trading is expressed separately.

Central Government Borrowing: Published by HM Treasury, this shows how the Government's financing plans are progressing. More importantly in recent days, it shows how much the Government needs to borrow in the domestic capital markets, a crucial figure in the determination of interest rates in the market-place.

UK Official Reserves: HM Treasury statistics showing the country's reserves of gold and of foreign currency, expressed in US dollars. Watched closely for indications of official intervention in the foreign exchange markets, to influence the sterling rate of exchange. However, the authorities can disguise any intervention operations to some extent.

Money Supply: The Bank of England figures for liabilities and assets of the UK banking system, together with an estimate of trends in the monetary aggregates. Simultaneously, the London clearing banks disclose their total deposits and advances — the 'bank lending figures'. These statistics together provide significant evidence on the trends of the money supply in the UK.

Unemployment: The Department of Employment statistics on unemployment, relating to the middle of the month of publication. The figures are expressed both as a total and as an adjusted figure excluding seasonal variations and school leavers. Also excluded are:

Cyclical Indicators: Published by the Central Statistical Office, these are four composite indices composed of economic data intended to identify developing trends in the UK economy.

Tax and Price Index: Published by the Central Statistical Office on the same day as the RPI, and adjusting it to take account of changes in UK taxation.

Published on a quarterly basis are:

Gross Domestic Product (GDP): The key statistic on UK economic activity, in the form of Central Statistical Office data on output. Quarterly figures are regarded as estimates and are followed a month later by further estimates and then, very shortly afterwards, by a full breakdown of UK economic activity in the quarter.

Balance of Payments: Revised figures for the three months, taking in invisible transactions and estimates of capital movements.

Public Sector Borrowing Requirement (PSBR): Fuller, and more significant, details of PSBR, and regarded as key statistics in the Government's financial policies.

Fixed Investment: The Department of Industry figures on fixed capital investment by British industry, expressed at constant 1980 prices. An indication of longer-term factors in industrial competitiveness.

Consumers' Expenditure: Estimates of consumer spending, expressed in 1980 prices.

Other statistics published quarterly in the FT include a Quarterly Analysis of Bank Advances (by the Bank of England), Company Liquidity (Dept of Industry), Stocks, (DTI), and Industrial and Commercial Companies Finance (Central Statistical Office).

Most of these statistics have considerable significance in the UK financial markets, and their influence on trends in the fixed interest, share, option and currency markets will be explained in the relevant market reporting columns.

Government offices are not the only source on statistics. Many industry associations produce figures indicating progress in their own particular sector. The Building Societies, for example, publish monthly and quarterly statistics of lending totals and also of house price trends. The construction industry reports on business trends, and industrial purchasing officers on price trends in the UK. The Confederation of British Industries publishes regular surveys of its members' assessment of economic trends, with particular reference to near-term plans. Such reports will usually be published in the FT, where they are treated as news-stories: that is to say, that the FT reporter will contact the association concerned and endeavour to expand the statistics if possible.

Because of their significance to the financial markets, it is inevitable that the major economic data should be the subject of research at the major City houses. The banks and large securities houses are constantly warning their clients of possible future trends in the UK trade figures, of Gross Domestic Product. And, inevitably, some of these forecasts will then affect trends in the financial markets.

For this reason, the FT reporters will draw readers' attention to economic forecasts from the City. Some of these forecasts will surface in the UK securities or money market reports, where price trends can be clearly traced to forecasts of impending economic data by widely-recognized specialists.

Sometimes, the City houses express their forecasts in a semi-public fashion, by sending copies of their analysts' reports to the press for

Nomura House, 24 Monument Street, London EC3R 8AJ 01-283 8811

Building society to invest £600m in rented homes

BY ANDREW TAYLOR

NATIONWIDE ANGLIA, Britain's third largest building society, yesterday announced plans to invest £600m in private rented housing during the next five years.

The money will be loaned to Quality Street, a joint venture property company that the building society has established with four former

ments might be able to attract.

He hoped to persuade the Treasury to allow capital grants to be made available to private companies involved in social housing "in the same way that grants are made to voluntary housing associations."

The building society has a 25 per cent stake in Quality Street. The remaining shares are held by the four the former Glasgow

review. If the report is considered worthy of inclusion, the FT will publish it — at the same time making it clear that this is a view expressed by the firm named, and not by the FT or by the Government body which will issue the official figures.

EUROPEAN NEWS

Rain dampens ardour of Italian strikers

By John Wyles in Rome

ITALY'S first four-hour general strike for three years just about managed to keep afloat yesterday despite nationwide cloud bursts and a strong wave of indifference among many industrial workers.

The rains drove some open air rallies indoors, thus blunting the unions' hopes of many televisual demonstrations of widespread support. As on previous occasions, estimates of the actual response to the strike call varied wildly, with the unions talking about 85-90 per cent backing among industrial workers and individual employers reporting much less. But the unions did acknowledge a much lower response among public employees and softer support among many southern industrial workers.

Fiat claimed that "hardly 20 per cent" of its workforce had supported the stoppage - slightly less than in the last such exercise in 1984. The unions claimed a 34 per cent backing. But the company reported that 64 per cent of Alfa Romeo workers had stopped work at the Arese plant near Milan ... Pomigliano ... the pa... union membership has traditionally been much higher at Alfa than at Fiat.

Elsewhere, Montedison said that about half its employees in petrochemicals had supported the strike.

In their speeches to rallies around the country leaders of the three union confederations claimed that the stoppage was a clear demonstration of union strength despite the depredations wrought by unemployment, internal divisions and political setbacks.

Their purpose in calling the stoppage was to drive home rank-and-file opposition to the Government's proposed 1988 budget, which they claim is sacrificing employment, social welfare and development in the south in an unbalanced attempt to reduce the public sector deficit.

But the union action had no discernible impact on the lower house of Parliament yesterday, which delivered a resounding vote of confidence in the Government headed by Christian Democrat Mr Giovanni Goria. This puts the five-party coalition ...

Moscow to reform prices from 1990

By Patrick Cockburn in Moscow

THE SOVIET Union will introduce a new system of wholesale prices from 1990 and retail prices from 1991, according to Mr Valentin Pavlov, the chairman of the State Committee for Prices (SCP).

Mr Pavlov, appointed last year to reorganise the Soviet pricing system, is the latest and most senior Soviet economic official to explain to the public through the trade union daily Trud - that traditional subsidies are eating into the budget and must be cut.

The Government is evidently concerned at the hostile public response earlier this year to plans to change the system of keeping the price of basic foodstuffs and accommodation low.

On average Soviet consumers pay half what it costs to produce the food, Mr Pavlov says.

Explaining the history of subsidies in the Soviet Union and the cheap food policy, Mr Pavlov says the first state subsidies were introduced for food in 1965. They have risen together

Commission sounds knell of steel quota...

By William Dawkins in Brussels

THE STEEL package unveiled yesterday by the European Commission is its final card in the last round of what will be a heated and bloody game.

The proposals are for a gradual run-down over the next six months to three years of the steel output controls which govern around 60 per cent of all European Community steel output and which have protected the industry since 1980.

Initial unofficial reactions suggest that few players on either side of the table like the Commission's hand. Descriptions of the proposals yesterday ranged between "practically insane" from one diplomat, to "a big disappointment" from one steel official.

The package is the Commission's response to a report by a panel of independent experts urging a phased abandonment of steel quotas on the grounds that the industry is unlikely to agree voluntarily to the 30m tonnes worth of plant closures needed to slim capacity in line with demand. It will be presented to a key meeting of industry ministers on December 8. If member states fail to agree on the proposals, the entire quota system would lapse automatically on December 31.

Under the scheme, prepared by Mr Karl-Heinz Narjes, Mr Peter Sutherland, and Mr Abel Matutes, the three Commissioners responsible for the sector, quotas for wire rod and merchant bars, products for which demand is relatively strong, would be scrapped at the end of the year. Production limits for hot rolled coil, which account for 10m tonnes of overcapacity, would go next July 1, though the impact would be softened with a 2.5 per cent enlargement in hot rolled coil quotas for the second quarter of 1988.

That leaves heavy sections and heavy plate, representing roughly another 10m tonnes of surplus production capacity between them. They would also be liberalised in July. The Commission is, however, prepared to let quotas for those two products run until the end of 1990 if the industry comes forward with "guarantees" of adequate closures by March 15 next year.

Brussels reckons that demand is so weak for heavy plate and heavy sections, which are sold mainly to the depressed construction, shipbuilding and offshore industries, that they deserve special treatment. It has no such sympathy for hot rolled coil producers, despite the fact that they account for the biggest single chunk of surplus capacity. Orders for that product jumped 30 per cent in April, thanks to a revival in demand from car manufacturers, which use flat steel for body panels.

The big integrated producers will feel that Brussels wants to drag them into a liberalised quota-free market far too fast, and that ending quotas will plunge them into a chaotic price war. Steel users, backed by a British Government wedded to an immediate end to quotas, see the package as a weak and unsatisfactory compromise.

In the middle stand the smaller independent producers, who yesterday gave a guarded welcome to the prospect of a gradual transition to a free market, but feel that the Commission's plan does not do enough to encourage closures. "We can live with it. However, there should be more financial ... the dismantling of ... ernments should be ... disburse aid under ce... tions for effective clo..." Mr Pol Boel, preside... European Independe... works' Association.

Eurofer, the "club" o... grated steelmakers, pro... official reaction yester... many members feel th... not recovered enough to ... a free market and t... upturn in orders highlig... Brussels is only tempo... Commission official a... yesterday: "The market ... strong at the moment and ... what led us to produce ... like this. We could not ... taken this opportunit... another time."

One diplomat pointed out ... announcing a gradual run-... for quotas was illogical in th... would only create confusion ... the markets for the prod... involved during the transitio... period. The real joker in ... Commission's pack, however, ... the risk that the whole sche... could get stuck on a technical ... in the Council of Ministers.

The package would normal... get by on a majority vote. But ... includes a proposal to transfe... cash from the EC's general bud... get to its coal and steel funds to ... help cushion the social impact of ... closures - and this needs unanimous support under EC voting rules.

BRUSSELS COMPLETES MACHINERY STANDARDS PROPOSALS

THE Commission yesterday approved a streamlined system of industrial standards for engineering machinery, writes William Dawkins.

The draft directive means that any attempt by national authorities to hinder free circulation of a vast range of machines and industrial equipment made in other member states will contravene EC law. This is the most far reaching set of industrial standards to be drawn up under the Commission's "new approach" to standardisation. It covers just over half an engineering machinery market worth Ecu200bn (£140m) annually.

The aim is to ensure that groups of products conforming to basic performance and safety minima are guaranteed free access to any member state's market. In the past, industrial standards were set by deciding criteria for every component of individual products, a process which led to complex standards that were often out of date by the time they were decided.

Yesterday's proposal, which is not expected to be ready for adoption by member states before the end of next year, also aims to tidy up the plethora of national technical regulations which block free trade in the sector. Different member states have notified Brussels of 80 national draft regulations on machine safety over the past three years, of which nearly a quarter are contrary to EC free trade laws, said Commission officials.

OVERSEAS NEWS

Financial Times Thursday September 10...

Fears for Sri Lanka peace accord

By Mervyn de Silva in Colombo

THE first signs of friction between Sri Lanka's rebel Tamil leaders and the Indian peace-keeping force on the island have surfaced following bitter fighting between rival rebel groups.

A memorandum listing Tamil complaints including partisan actions by the Indian military has been sent to the commander of the Indian peacekeeping force, Major-General Harkirat Singh, by the Tamil liberation "Tigers," the key separatist group.

"We hope this does not mean that the peace accord has started to fray at the edges," a Sri Lankan government spokesman said yesterday.

The letter followed a spate of incidents in the northern and eastern provinces, the areas which are accorded semi-autonomous status under the July peace agreement designed to end years of ethnic strife.

In the northern Jaffna peninsula and the eastern areas of Vavuniya, Mannar and Trincomalee, at least 13 people have died in the past few days, mostly in internecine fighting between rival rebel groups.

The Tigers say they lost seven "comrades" and accuse the rival PLOTE ... having ambush... them. But more ... also accuse the ... of being "par... some cases of ... nived" with the ...

In a stiff re... Dixit, the India... sioner in Colo... peace-keeping ... absolutely impa... filling its obliga... peace accord.

The Tigers ... tested that Sri ... lese police are ... north and east, ... of Indian troops ... ave instigated ... e Tamil grou... A spokesman ... Jaffna clain ... thorities were ... Tamil les... epted "Indi... sensitive ... ninistrative ... run the affa... east until ... are ...

Sayed Kamaluddin reports on relief programmes and political fallout after the worst disaster in 40 years

Bangladesh counts out the grain as more floods strike

IN THE Bangladesh village of Asadanga near Jessore, an old man tried to reach a small boat carrying reporters around one of the areas devastated by the country's worst flood in 40 years: "Shelter, fuel, food," he shouted.

These basic needs were multiplied hundreds of thousands of times in the past two weeks after the Ganges and Brahmaputra rivers gave way to monsoon storms last month.

The man had been left behind by younger family members who had gone to a flood relief centre. His task was to ensure that their cattle and those of their possessions that had not been lost to the elements were not in turn lost to thieves.

Army and civil officials had evacuated thousands of marooned people, but thousands like the old man have been living in flooded, make-shift dwellings on bamboo platforms which they share with their cattle. Many of the dwellings do not have a roof to protect the victims from the continuing rains.

A further 50,000 people were forced to seek refuge in temporary camps in the past two days after heavy rains caused a second wave of floods in the north of the country.

The worst-affected by the new deluge were Sirajganj and Pabna districts where the Padma, Brahmaputra, Mahananda and other rivers again ...

Survivors line up for rice and wheat at a relief camp.

Officials in Sirajganj said the new flooding would set back efforts to rehabilitate millions of people ravaged by the earlier floods. Many would be cut off from relief supplies, they said.

The first wave killed more than 700 people and destroyed crops and property worth $1.3bn, according to official figures.

Another 200 people had died of diarrhoea and dysentery because they drank contaminated water and ate rotten food.

Bangladesh's Health Minister, Mr Salahuddin Quader Chowdhury, said more than 2,500 medical teams were fight...

Many of the stranded people were unable to find a dry patch to cook nor could they reach the gruel kitchens run by the administration.

Such conditions are common in huge areas of the south-western district of Jessore and the northern district of Rangpur.

The flood has damaged an estimated 1.6m tonnes of foodgrains and more than 2m houses, about half of them beyond repair. Some officials fear that the crop losses could reach 3m tonnes.

Major-General Sadequr Rahman Chowdhury, chief relief co-ordinator and principal staff officer to the president, ... sheets for building shelters and foodgrains.

Bangladesh is a country which, even at the best of times, is unable to feed itself.

The government's target for foodgrain production for 1987-88 is a record 17.5m tonnes. It recently announced a programme for importing 2m tonnes of foodgrain, nearly two-thirds under grants from donor countries.

However, even if its efforts to recoup between 300,000 and 400,000 tonnes by quickly replanting the rice crop after the flood waters recede are successful the total food gap would still be around 3.2m tonnes, the biggest ever.

The presence of the army in the relief operations, together with the government's decision not to involve local politicians ...

There have, however, been a number of demonstrations to protest at what some see as inadequate relief operations. Opposition political parties have organised marches to demand more and speedy relief distribution.

President Hossain Mohammad Ershad, who has visited a number of areas affected by the flood, had to face one such demonstration in Sirajganj late last month.

Local newspapers reported that thousands of flood-survivors demonstrated in the southern port city of Chittagong on Tuesday demanding food, clothes and jobs. Similar marches were held earlier in Dhaka and other places amid fears that the floods might invite a famine.

The country's planning commission is diverting some of its resources under the annual development programme for creating rural employment and the rehabilitation of rural infrastructure. Emphasis would be given to projects in transport, water resources, agriculture, health, education and communication sectors which were hit hard, officials said.

Just more than half the current-year's annual development programme funds of £980m would be made available in the form of project assistance.

Reconstruction and rehabili... are expected to create a large number of jobs in the rural areas in the next three months.

From December 1 through to the end of March those in need would be provided with 500 grams of foodgrain per head each day.

Maj-Gen Sadequr said that for this purpose a special allocation of 180,000 tonnes of foodgrains would be made, in addition to an earlier allocation of 38,000 under the annual development programme.

Meanwhile, the eight-party and seven-party opposition alliances led by Mrs Sheikh Hasina Wajed and Begum Khaleda Zia respectively and the orthodox right-wing Jamaat-e-Islami are going ahead with their programme to "siege the capital" on October 7. They plan to demand the president's resignation for his "failure to handle the flood situation."

President Ershad, addressing a rally in the flood-swept northern town of Debiganj on Tuesday dismissed charges by opposition leaders that many people had starved to death after the floods.

"No one has died from starvation as a result of quick and timely supplies of food and arrangements for post-flood rehabilitation," he was quoted as saying.

He warned that anyone trying to disrupt relief supplies or make political gains out of ...

Mercede... sacks bla... workforc... in S Afric...

By Anthony Robinson in Johannesburg

MERCEDES BENZ ... Africa, the wholly-owned ... sidiary of West Gern... Daimler Benz, yesterday s... its entire 2,800 black la... force after striking wo... rejected an ultimatum to re... to work. The East London p... which assembles Merce... trucks and cars as well ... Honda cars has been stri... bound since August 4.

The dismissals follow wee... of negotiations over uni... demands for a minimum hour... rate of Rand 5. The compan... originally offered a 20 cents a... hour increase to R3.70 an hou... as part of an industrial counci... award for the industry which ... was then invalidated by the ... government because it included ... a provision making May Day a ... paid holiday.

The company subsequently raised its offer to R3.96 and added another 8 cents to compensate for a reduction in the working week from 44 to 43 hours bringing the minimum monthly wage to R750. It also undertook to reduce the working week to 40 hours without loss of pay within the next two years.

Senior management officials last night blamed the union for intransigence, pointing out that the company had made three ...

Financial Times Thursday November 19 1987

AMERICAN NEWS

●Congress report blasts dishonesty and deception

Iran-Contra affair showed confusion at the highest level

●Never again must NSC engage in covert operations, say committees

The following is an edited version of the executive summary of the 690 page congressional report on the Iran-Contra affair

Starting in 1983 Congress imposed increasingly restrictive laws on US aid to the Contra rebels in Nicaragua.

The President felt strongly about the Contras, and he ordered his staff, in the words of his National Security Adviser, to find a way to keep the Contras "body and soul together." Thus began the story of how the staff of the White House advisory body, the National Security Council, became an operational entity that secretly ran the Contra assistance effort, and later the Iran initiative.

The action officer placed in charge of both operations was Lt Col Oliver L. North.

Between June 1984 and the beginning of 1986, the President, his National Security Adviser and the NSC secretly raised $34m for the Contras from other countries. An additional $2.7m was provided for the Contras during 1985 and 1986 from private contributors.

The first contributions were sent by the donors to bank accounts controlled and used by the Contras. However, in July 1985, North took control of the fund and - with the support of two National Security Advisers (Robert McFarlane and John Poindexter) and, according to North, CIA director William Casey - used those funds to run the covert operation to support the Contras.

At the suggestion of William Casey, North recruited Richard V. Secord, a retired Air Force major-general with experience in special operations. Secord set up Swiss bank accounts, and North steered future donations into these accounts. Using these funds, and funds later generated by the Iran arms sales, Secord and his associate, Albert Hakim, created what they called the Enterprise, a private organisation designed to engage in covert activities on behalf of the US.

The Enterprise, functioning largely at North's direction, had its own aircraft, pilots, airfield, operatives, ship, secure communications devices, and secret Swiss bank accounts.

For 16 months, it served as a secret arm of the NSC staff, carrying out with private and non-appropriated money, and without accountability or restriction imposed by law on the CIA, a covert Contra aid programme.

By executive order and National Security decision directive issued by President Reagan, all covert operations must be approved by the President personally and in writing. By statute, Congress must be notified about each covert action.

The covert action directed by North, however, was not approved by the President in writing. Congress was not notified about it. And the funds to support it were never accounted for.

The cover up

The Administration went to considerable lengths to avoid notifying Congress.

While the President was denying any illegality, his subordinates were ...

Key players in the Contra scandal: from left, Oliver North, John Poindexter, Robert MacFarlane, Richard Secord, William Casey

... up. Several of his advisers had expressed concern that the 1985 sales violated the Arms Export Control Act, and the "cover story" had been agreed on if these arms sales were ever exposed. After North had three conversations on November 18 1986, that the legal problems with the 1985 Israeli shipments, he, Poindexter, Casey, and MacFarlane all told conforming false stories about US involvement in the shipments.

On learning that the President had authorised the Attorney General to gather the relevant facts, North and Poindexter shredded and altered official documents on November 21 1986, and later that weekend. On November 25 1986, North's secretary concealed classified documents in her clothing and, with North's knowledge, removed them from the White House.

According to North, a "fall guy" plan was proposed by Casey in which North and, if necessary, Poindexter, would take the responsibility for the covert Contra support operation and the diver...

Justice Department official, assisting the Attorney General's fact-finding inquiry, found a "diversion memorandum" that had escaped the shredder.

Prior to the discovery of the diversion memorandum, each interview by the Attorney General's fact finding team had been conducted in the presence of two witnesses, and careful notes were taken in accordance with standard professional practices. After discovery of the diversion memorandum - which itself gave rise to an inference of serious wrongdoing - the Attorney General departed from the standard practices.

Iran

The NSC staff was already engaged in covert operations through Secord when, in the summer of 1985, the government of Israel proposed that missiles be sold to Iran in return for the release of seven American hostages held in Lebanon in the process of improved ... Iran ...

... covert action also took operational control of implementing the President's decision on arms sales to Iran.

The President did not sign a finding for this covert operation, nor did he notify Congress. There followed a series of arms for hostages swaps between the US and Iran in late 1985 to September 1986, using unidentified intermediaries in Tehran.

In February 1986, the US, acting through the Enterprise, sold 1,000 TOW missiles to the Iranians. The US also provided the Iranians with military intelligence about Iraq. All the remaining American hostages were supposed to be released upon Iran's receipt of the first 500 TOWs. None was. The difference between what the Enterprise paid the US for the missiles and what it received from Iran was more than $6m. North directed part of this profit for the Contras and for oth...

... ity that would act throughout the world while evading congressional review.

In September and October 1986, the NSC staff began negotiating with a new group of Iranians, the "Second Channel," that Albert Hakim had opened, in part, through promises of bribes. Once again, the Administration insisted on release of all the hostages but settled for less.

The decision to designate private parties to carry out the arms transaction had other ramifications. There was virtually no accounting for the profits from the arms deal. All told, the Enterprise received nearly $48m from the sale of arms to the Contras and Iran, and a contribution directed to it by North.

Conclusions

The common ingredients of the Iran and Contra affairs ...

... tra affairs shows a seriously flawed policy making process. There was confusion and disarray at the highest levels of government.

● The Iran-Contra affair was characterised by pervasive dishonesty and inordinate secrecy.

● The NSC staff turned to private parties and third countries to do the government's business. Funds denied by Congress were obtained by the Administration from third countries and private citizens.

●The solicitation of foreign funds by an Administration to pursue foreign policy goals rejected by Congress is dangerous and improper.

●The confusion, deception and privatisation which marked the affair were the ...

intelligence and conduc... operations - a departure ... proper functions.

●Administration officia... ing no elected office rep... showed disrespect for Co... efforts to perform its co... tional oversight role in f... policy.

● Who was responsible ... central figure was Lt Col ... who co-ordinated all of the ... ities and was involved i... aspects of the secret operatio...

But he had the exp... approval of Admiral John P... dexter and at least the tacit s... port of Robert MacFarlane ... addition we believe that the ... liam Casey encouraged Nor... gave him direction, and p... moted the concept of an ext... legal covert organisation.

Nevertheless, the ultima... responsibility for the events ... the affair must rest with th... President. If the President di... not know what his National ... Security Advisers were doing, he ... should have. It is his responsibility to communicate unambiguously to his subordinates that they must keep him advised of important actions they take for the Administration.

It was the President's policy - not an isolated decision by North or Poindexter - to sell arms secretly to Iran and to maintain the Contras.

Several of the President's advisers lied, shredded documents and covered up their actions. These facts have been on the public record for months, but the President has yet to condemn their conduct.

11 International Economic News

Business journals are now filled with references to the 'globalization' of markets, or the 'internationalization' of trade. Business has been international for a very long time, but the process has been speeded up, in the public consciousness at least, by the application of electronic communication to the world's commodity and securities markets. Now that these markets are on the brink of round-the-clock trading, the old newspaper divisions between 'home' and 'foreign' affairs are breaking down.

Because of its orientation towards business and financial affairs, the FT has always maintained a strong coverage of foreign countries and their political and economic developments. Indeed, the paper's overseas coverage has expanded over a period when other UK newspapers have tended to reduce the role of their foreign correspondents. This has stood the FT in good stead as it has moved to respond to the requirements of a business readership which is increasingly concerned with rapid coverage of global affairs.

The FT has fifty full-time foreign correspondents, based in offices outside the UK, and also retains one hundred part-time correspondents abroad — these are usually locally-employed journalists, often star writers for the leading newspapers in their own countries. Full-time correspondents usually remain on station for a number of years, and will often have spent some time working on the newspaper's foreign desk in London. There are FT offices in Japan, the US — both New York and Washington — and in all the major Western European countries. The FT also has full-time staff journalists in Moscow and Warsaw, as well as in Canada, South Africa, Hong Kong, and in Scandinavia and the Middle East.

But news from any one country can affect the rest of the world in many ways, and the FT foreign pages draw on the expertise of the paper's London-based specialist writers. They may fly out to the scene of the action, supplementing the operation of the locally-based correspondents.

Developments in science or technology, to take an obvious example, usually need to be assessed by comparison with similar developments elsewhere. FT readers will want to know whether the nuclear plant under construction in the Far East will be significantly different from plants already in operation elsewhere. A military conflict in a little-known area of the world must be considered from the viewpoint of the major powers, or perhaps for the evidence it provides of the performance of military equipment already installed in the NATO arsenals.

So the FT foreign pages are not entirely filled with news-reports by intrepid reporters based in foreign countries. Articles by the paper's scientific, diplomatic, financial and industrial writers help to round out the straightforward news-reporting. The policy of the paper is to supply readers with a constant flow of news from foreign countries, accompanied by comment and feature articles which help to place each new development into context, and enable readers to formulate their own judgement on the significance of the news. Readers' priorities may differ widely — an export manager, a research scientist and an investment fund adviser must all be able to find in the FT information to satisfy their various needs.

Moreover, the FT's coverage of non-UK events must now be addressed to a readership which is increasingly non-UK in residence, as well as by birth. The status of the FT means that its foreign correspondents may often be read as closely in their host country as at home in the UK.

On a daily basis, foreign news is sub-divided into pages on European, American, Overseas News and World Trade News. The names speak for themselves. American News pages cover the United States, but also Canada and the South American nations. The World Trade News pages focus on cross-border deals as well as on the international institutions which endeavour to control or regulate them. The foreign news pages appear at the front of the paper, immediately after page one. But the paper also often carries extra foreign pages to cover an important development on the international front. Important meetings of world political leaders or Foreign Ministers, or a scheduled meeting of Foreign Ministers or world bankers, all have been granted substantial extra coverage in the FT — as well as outbreaks of tension or actual military conflict in the world's more sensitive trouble spots.

Even the normal flow of news does not always divide itself up quite as neatly as newspapers would like. Developments inside the European Community may be covered on the FT's European News pages, but clearly have a life and significance of their own. Consequently, when important matters are afoot in Brussels, the FT's European pages will be weighted heavily in that direction.

The American pages may sometimes be dominated by events in the United States, inevitably in view of the significance for the world of political, social or economic developments in that country. But the South American countries have assumed major importance for the other industrialized nations because of their substantial debts. While international debt negotiations usually make the front page of the *Financial Times*, the paper's foreign pages carry a steady flow of information on the economies and political fortunes of the major debtor countries.

EUROPEAN NEWS

Genscher warning on short-range weapons

By David Marsh in Bonn

THE West German Foreign Minister, Mr Hans-Dietrich Genscher, has delivered a clear warning to other Nato countries on the need for fresh arms control negotiations on reducing the Soviet superiority in short-range nuclear missiles aimed at the Federal Republic.

He said in an interview there was "no doubt" that Nato foreign ministers would honour their commitment in June to press for follow-on talks after the conclusion of a superpower accord to eliminate intermediate-range weapons(INF).

His remarks were made in the light of indications that the US and Britain in particular are in no hurry to start talks on reducing arsenals in Europe to tactical nuclear weapons. Both countries have made it clear that once the INF accord is signed further reductions in nuclear weaponry in Europe could disrupt further Nato's nuclear defence strategies.

West German worries have been increased by the recent meeting of Nato's Nuclear Planning Group which discussed plans to upgrade short-range missiles in Europe.

Farm ministers deal

BY TIM DICKSON IN BRUSSELS

PREPARATIONS for next month's summit of European Community heads of state received a major setback in Brussels yesterday when EC farm ministers unexpectedly adjourned their negotiations on new ways to control farm spending.

The meeting will reconvene in Brussels on Monday but in the absence of any significant progress this week diplomats and Community officials were last night pessimistic about the chances of an early agreement.

Firm decisions on the European Commssion's proposals to cut back Community support to farmers when production targets are exceeded are being widely seen as an essential precondition of support from member states for Commission President Mr Jacques Delors' request for a substantial increase in the EC's own resources.

That was why this week's meeting of the Farm Council was expected to turn into a marathon session, clearing the way by this weekend for foreign ministers of the 12(who start their Council on Monday) to complete their preparation of the summit agenda.

Mr Waurits Toernaes,the Danish chairman of the Council, appeared yesterday to succumb to French ar pressure for a in the proceed indicating his the meeting s the rest of the

Mr Francoi French Farm address the today on the tisation of C state owned Mr Ignaz Kiec man counterp appointment members of t ment in Stras

Yesterday's clearly infuri

MEPs back tougher cur

BY QUENTIN PEEL IN STRASBOURG

THE European Parliament yesterday voted by a large majority for even tougher controls on farm spending in the European Community than currently proposed by the Commission - including a special tax on agriculture to finance any budget overrun.

The hardline plan for reform of the Common Agricultural Policy, with strong support for the Commission's plans to impose specific production controls in each farm sector, confirmed the Parliament's conversion from its former role as a fervent farm lobby. It was adopted as part of a whole package of parliamentary ... by EC leaders at their summit in Copenhagen next month.

The MEPs gave broad support to the plans tabled by the Commission, which link reform of the CAP to an increase in long-term national contributions to the EC budget. The plans also include a new system for calculating those national contributions, to shift the burden more on to the richest member states with the highest gross national product, and doubling the cash available for social and regional spending in economically-backward regions.

They voted by 286-37, with 30 abstentions, for the report of Spanish Socialist Enrique Baron ented to the C by Lord Plun president.

Apart from on farm spen trast to the a ment's agric the key char MEPs is for put even gr fairer burder tions. The P whole finar based on G coming from agricultural and the b added tax.

The prese contributio

In reporting day-to-day developments in foreign countries, the FT has to make judgements on the relative interest of its readers in the different countries of the world. Is the latest forecast for the Gross National Product of the United States of equal significance as the opening of a new shopping centre in a small town in Brazil? Clearly not, and sometimes FT foreign correspondents themselves feel hurt by the cruel decisions made by the London newsdesks. But the paper tries to set out a formula, stating which news will always be reported from each country, and which must take its chance with the competing news of the day. This means that on a quiet day, the Brazilian supermarket opening may have a chance of appearing in the FT — but not on a busy day.

In the case of political coverage, this means that important developments will always be reported, as will shifts in the political background which could lead to future changes in the government. In practice, this means coverage of:

**

OVERSEAS NEWS

Queensland Premier fac

BY CHRIS SHERWELL IN CANBERRA

r Joh: loss of support

SIR JOH Bjelke-Petersen, the maverick National Party Premier of Queensland, faces one of the toughest tests of his 20-year state leadership today, one day after summarily sacking three members of his Cabinet.

A special meeting of National Party members of the state parliament is scheduled for this morning and is widely expected to oust the 76-year-old Sir Joh, and replace him with a new party head.

But he says he will refuse to resign the premiership, and this could force a showdown in which the Governor of Queensland, Sir Walter Campbell, would have to choose between Sir Joh and any new National Party leader to form a government. This could embroil the Queen in a constitutional crisis, and may entail an early state election.

The crisis comes just over a year after Sir Joh won a state election victory in Queensland in which the National Party won power without help from its erstwhile allies in the Liberal Party.

The victory encou Sir Joh to start an mately disastrous "pu Canberra". His cam almost destroyed the tion with the Liberals federal level, but wrecked in July wh Bob Hawke, the L Party Prime Ministe returned to power fo toric third term in election.

Sir Joh's trouble since been compoun revelations from an set up to investiga year allegations th Queensland Gove

ny Hawkins on a successful experiment in currency liberalis

Lagos grasps the currency nettl

EVIDENT success of Niger- foreign currency auctions the past 14 months may vince African governments the risks of trade and pay-

rate - handling official transactions, predominantly debt-servicing; the second-tier market, or the free auction system for commercial transactions; and two parallel markets.

Naira
against US$ (N per $)
6.0
Merger 3/7

tive monetary poli played a vital role in because bidders ha upfront for foreign Tight liquidity and h est rates have helped ket demand fo exchange. When in

1) Elections — both those for national governments and, where relevant, for local or state governments.

2) Political Parties: Readers want to know how the various Party Conferences, both Government and Opposition, were carried off. What new policies were adopted or proposed. The names of new leaders, or potential leaders — to be followed up in FT feature articles.

3) Government policies: Both domestic and foreign policy changes need to be examined for international implications, or for global trade and finance.

Of course, this summary presents a rather tidier picture of foreign reporting than actually exists. Not every country presents such a neat example of parliamentary government.

In that case, the foreign correspondent may have to look to street riots, protest meetings or to local press coverage in order to catch the

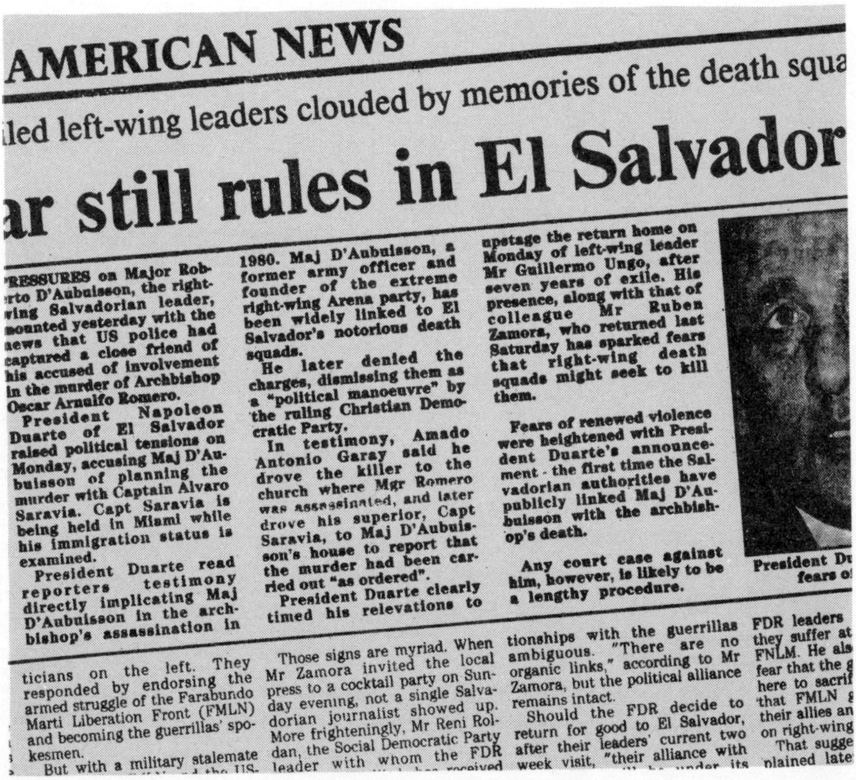

AMERICAN NEWS

led left-wing leaders clouded by memories of the death squa

ar still rules in El Salvador

RESSURES on Major Roberto D'Aubuisson, the right-wing Salvadorian leader, mounted yesterday with the news that US police had captured a close friend of his accused of involvement in the murder of Archbishop Oscar Arnulfo Romero.

President Napoleon Duarte of El Salvador raised political tensions on Monday, accusing Maj D'Aubuisson of planning the murder with Captain Alvaro Saravia. Capt Saravia is being held in Miami while his immigration status is examined.

President Duarte read reporters testimony directly implicating Maj D'Aubuisson in the archbishop's assassination in 1980. Maj D'Aubuisson, a former army officer and founder of the extreme right-wing Arena party, has been widely linked to El Salvador's notorious death squads.

He later denied the charges, dismissing them as a "political manoeuvre" by the ruling Christian Democratic Party.

In testimony, Amado Antonio Garay said he drove the killer to the church where Mgr Romero was assassinated, and later drove his superior, Capt Saravia, to Maj D'Aubuisson's house to report that the murder had been carried out "as ordered".

President Duarte clearly timed his relevations to upstage the return home on Monday of left-wing leader Mr Guillermo Ungo, after seven years of exile. His presence, along with that of colleague Mr Ruben Zamora, who returned last Saturday has sparked fears that right-wing death squads might seek to kill them.

Fears of renewed violence were heightened with President Duarte's announcement - the first time the Salvadorian authorities have publicly linked Maj D'Aubuisson with the archbishop's death.

Any court case against him, however, is likely to be a lengthy procedure.

President Du
fears o

ticians on the left. They responded by endorsing the armed struggle of the Farabundo Marti Liberation Front (FMLN) and becoming the guerrillas' spokesmen.

But with a military stalemate

Those signs are myriad. When Mr Zamora invited the local press to a cocktail party on Sunday evening, not a single Salvadorian journalist showed up. More frighteningly, Mr Reni Roldan, the Social Democratic Party leader with whom the FDR

tionships with the guerrillas ambiguous. "There are no organic links," according to Mr Zamora, but the political alliance remains intact.

Should the FDR decide to return for good to El Salvador, after their leaders' current two week visit, "their alliance with

FDR leaders
they suffer at
FNLM. He als
fear that the
here to sacrif
that FMLN
their allies an
on right-wing
That sugge
plained late

flavour of the political scene. Some governments are reticent about discussing their policies in public, or disclosing them to the rest of the global community. FT correspondents will seek regular briefings with government ministers at which they can raise matters of importance to FT readers and the world at large. Correspondents will also report on comments by government leaders in the local press, and will keep a sharp eye on personnel changes in official circles.

Political coverage, then, may vary according to the country in view. In the case of the major democracies, where information is publicly available, and policies are decided by some process of public debate and election, the reportage of events can often stand on its own — with the background significance explained later in a feature article. But when seeking information on countries which either because of size or political system send out less information to the world, readers may need to pay more attention to the FT's background features. The paper tries to review each country at regular intervals, both by means of articles in the Foreign pages and also by Special Supplements. It is in these articles that political developments can be considered in depth, and reference made to factors less easy to report on a day-to-day basis.

A similar policy is followed in the case of the economic news from outside Britain which is a major area of interest to FT readers. The paper aims to report the significant economic data from major countries on a regular basis. Such data may be published monthly, quarterly or annually. Among the statistics printed in the FT will be:

Gross Annual Product (GAP): the most fundamental economic statistic concerning any national economy. Major countries usually publish forecasts, which may be updated during the year. When the actual figure is released, it is often subject to revisions, which will also be published in the FT.

Inflation statistics: including retail prices, producer prices and consumer spending statistics. These have become major guides to economic progress, especially among the major industrial nations which saw the prosperity of the 1960s and 1970s vanish as prices spiralled upwards.

Money Supply data: Statistics on Government borrowing, or potential borrowing, are also major guides to the outlook for inflation and, more significantly, for local interest rates. Under this

WORLD TRADE NEW

; to end tariffs on ird World goods

A

; will scrap or significantly uce duties on semi-processed products made from se materials and cut by up to per cent duties on finished iducts.

ustoms duties on fresh or ni-processed tropical fruits I nuts, spices, essential oils I vegetable materials will be minated or significantly reced. Processed tropical farm oduce will also face lower dus.

At the non-tariff level the EC offering to do away progresely with restrictions such as port quotas on all tropical oducts, except for fresh banas.

These measures would affect ughly 7 per cent of EC imrts, while the products coved are estimated to provide out 40 per cent of the developing countries' export revees.

Agreement to table the offer was reached only on Monday among the 12 EC governments with Bonn holding out longest. West Germany and Denmark are the two countries likely to be most heavily affected.

The EC offer is conditional on other industrialised countries, in particular the US and Japan, and the more advanced developing countries agreeing to "share the burden".

Third World countries which are dominant suppliers of raw materials to world markets are called on to curb measures restricting exports.

World trade in tropical products and in most cases their prices have declined appreciably, much to the detriment of Third World export earnings.

Efforts in previous Gatt rounds to give priority to liberalising trade in these products failed conspicuously.

Japan and EC head for new liquor clash

BY IAN RODGER IN TOKYO

APAN appears to be heading or a fresh row with the European Community over its taxes on lcohol. Recent reports suggest okyo will refuse to bow to EC omplaints that the taxes discriminate against imported vines and spirits.

Last year Japan's Ministry of Finance proposed a partial reorm of liquor taxes, but the European Commission dismissed hese as unacceptable and filed complaint at the General Agreement on Tariffs and Trade.

A Gatt panel sent a confidenial report on the issue last month to the two parties. Last veek stories appeared in the apanese press claiming the reort condemned Japan's liquor ax system as incompatible with Gatt rules. Mr Andreas van Agt, ead of the EC delegation in Tokyo, said yesterday that 'we do not quarrel' with these reports.

The stories have given details of reforms that the Ministry of Finance apparently proposes to put forward early next year.

Finance Ministry officials have confirmed that they intend to propose revisions, but, according to the press reports, they will be virtually identical to those put forward last December.

That package consisted of the removal of the ad valorem portion of the current two-tier system so that tax would be determined solely on alcohol content. Also, two of the three classes of whiskies would be unified for tax purposes. But the higher class, into which fall most imported whiskies, would still attract a much higher rate of tax.

Those proposals were never enacted because the overall tax reform bill of which they were a part was withdrawn from the Diet (parliament). However, the EC then said they were unacceptable. It seems unlikely that the EC's attitude towards the reforms proposed last year will have changed.

One interpretation of the leaks is that they are related to the campaign to choose a successor to the Prime Minister Mr Yasuhiro Nakasone.

EC set to keep ban on hormones in meat

By Tim Dickson in Luxembourg

THE PROSPECT of a new trade war between Europe and the US loomed closer yesterday when Britain's legal challenge to the EC's ban on the use of hormones in meat production received a serious setback.

The UK, supported by Denmark, took the Community to the European Court last year after the controversial decision by its farm ministers in December 1985 to outlaw five hormones used in the fattening of beef cattle.

The complaint alleges both that the council ignored vital scientific evidence and (more importantly) that the decision should have been taken unanimously, rather than by a "qualified" majority of member states.

Yesterday, however, Mr Carl Otto Lenz, the Advocate-General of the court, proposed in an eagerly awaited opinion that the British application should be dismissed and that the hormone ban should thus be upheld. It is due to come into effect on January 1 next year.

Mr Lenz is not a judge but past precedents suggest that his views are likely to be followed in the final verdict expected before Christmas.

Yesterday's development is not only a major disappointment for the British Government, which claims that vital EC decision-making procedures are at stake. It will also be noted with alarm by the US, which claims that the prohibition was politically motivated and without any scientific justification.

The ban will mean that $130m of American meat exports per year, mostly in the form of offal and produced with the help of hormones, will not be allowed to enter the Community.

Britain's main argument in the case rests on the claim that the European Commission submitted the proposal under the wrong legal base, thereby allowing the decision to be agreed by a qualified majority of ministers. The UK says that this has widespread implications for the way in which key plant and animal health issues could be determined in Brussels in future.

Mr Lenz, however, said that the legal base which was used - the so-called Article 43 of the Treaty of Rome, which covers the Common Agricultural Policy - was wide enough to include non-specific agricultural issues like the health of the consumer.

Lionel Barber

US tra

"TODAY CANADA, tomorro the world," the New York Tim declared in a ringing endors ment of the draft US-Cana free trade pact.

At this early stage, it see fair to forecast that the prosp of a free trade zone betwe North America's two nei bours will enjoy overwhelm support in the US press. Prot tionism rarely finds much vour in the editorial colun south of the Great Lakes and US-Canada outline agreem reached 10 days ago will prove the exception to the ru

So the Reagan Administrat has some powerful allies in forthcoming struggle for pu opinion. In turn, that sho help shape the votes in House of Representatives US Senate needed to gain fi approval of the accord betw two countries whose ann trade already amounts $135bn.

US negotiators, helped b bevy of laywers, are now put flesh on the agreement wi has to be sent in final forr Congress by January 3 1988. House and Senate will have 90 days to approve deal, under a "fast track" me nism set up on the US side negotiating, considering voting on the trade pact.

So much for the politica mospherics: what about substance of the pact?

Despite presidential rhet about historic breakthrou many observers (including US officials who have bri reporters themselves over past week) are reluctan trumpet the pact as an e shaker.

A senior official at the U partment of Agriculture (U

Sumiton

BY RODERICK ORAM IN NE

A US court has ruled that tomo Electric Industries pan has infringed two p held by Corning Glass Wo the US on fibre optic prod

The ruling brought to a long-running battle betwe two companies. Each cla other has been infringing tents. The products con the core of fibre optic for which demand is g strongly in the telecomn tion and computer indust

The practical and fi impact of the ruling is li be limited, however. Su heading also come the consumer and personal credit statistics published by many, but by no means all countries.

Employment statistics: These are important for both political and corporate business reasons. Politically, employment levels are a point of friction between governments and those governed. For the businessman, they are evidence of prospective markets — or plant investment.

Where economic data is concerned, the division between the major industrialized countries and the rest is much sharper. The recurrent slowdowns in world economies over the past decade have deepened the significance of trends in the 'motor' economies — those regarded as the driving force for the others. Consequently, economic data from Japan, the US and the leading countries in the European Community, are reported — and scrutinized — more closely than in the past. Major statistics from these major countries will almost certainly find their way to page one of the FT, but will also require constant comment in the Foreign pages.

Inevitably, great stress is laid on the economic data from the US. This is partly because of the enormous economic importance of the US for the rest of the free world economies — as well as for many of the not-so-free. But it also reflects the openness of the US political system, under which official information is readily, and regularly, available. It also reflects the place in the US political structure of the Federal Reserve Board, which is active in the financial markets, often daily, and makes regular reports to the public and to Congress. By its actions in the US markets, the Federal Reserve influences US interest rates, which are watched keenly throughout the world.

In addition to covering developments in the political and economic areas of major countries, the FT reports regularly on other areas which are of significance internationally. These include labour relations either at major companies or throughout a particular country. Management techniques, consumer habits, even fashion, may be of importance to the businessmen seeking new markets. All are grist to the FT's mill, and will be covered on the appropriate pages.

The World Trade News pages range widely across the field of international trade, reporting and commenting both on individual deals and on inter-nation trade agreements which have wider significance for the industries concerned.

In the European sphere, this includes reporting on trade matters involving the European Community, or between the EC and non-EC countries. The thorny question of alleged dumping by Far Eastern producers of some electronic products has been the subject of regular coverage on these pages. Also reported here are such matters as the development of trade between the Eastern European bloc and the rest of Europe, a subject requiring constant comment on political, as well as purely commercial developments.

While reviews of specific industries within one country will usually be found on the Foreign News pages, there will always be some industries — the Japanese computer industry is an example — which will inevitably be discussed chiefly in terms of world trade, and will therefore appear on the World Trade News pages.

Finally, the pages carry news and comment on the international trade agencies or semi-regulatory bodies. Reports on the US Export-Import Bank (Eximbank) or the General Agreement on Tariffs and Trade (GATT) provide the backcloth to the trade and barter deals reported daily on the World Trade News pages.

Austria	Sch22	Indonesia	Rp3100	Portugal	Esc100
Bahrain	Din0.650	Israel	NS3.50	S Arabia	Rls6.00
Belgium	BFr48	Italy	L1600	Singapore	S$4.10
Canada	C$1.00	Japan	Y600	Spain	Pta125
Cyprus	C£0.75	Jordan	Fils500	Sri Lanka	Rup30
Denmark	DKr9.00	Kuwait	Fils500	Sweden	SKr8.00
Egypt	E£2.25	Lebanon	$L125.00	Switzerland	SFr2.20
Finland	Fmk7.00	Luxembourg	LFr48	Taiwan	NT$85
France	FFr6.50	Malaysia	Rin4.25	Thailand	Bht50
Germany	DM2.20	Mexico	Pes300	Tunisia	Din0.800
Greece	Dr100	Morocco	Dh6.00	Turkey	L500
Hong Kong	HK$12	Netherlands	Fl3.00	UAE	Dh6.50
India	Rup15	Norway	NKr8.00	USA	$1.00

FINANCIAL TIMES

EUROPE'S BUSINESS NEWSPAPER

No. 30,399 Thursday November 26 1987 D 8523 A

Tokyo: Brokers ride out the storm, Page 25

World News

Freedom of expression promised in China

Direct Communist Party control over the arts in China would be eliminated, Vice Minister of Culture Ying Ruocheng promised in the clearest statement by a senior official endorsing freedom of expression.

His comments marked a sharp contrast with traditional party policy towards arts and literature established in the early 1940s by Mao Tse-Tung. **Page 20**

US mayor dies

Chicago's mayor, Mr Harold Washington, 65, died after a heart attack. He was the first black mayor of the country's third largest city. Mr Jesse Jackson, Democratic presidential contender, in Kuwait immediately cancelled plans for a Gulf visit to attend the funeral.

Italians shun strike

Many industrial workers showed indifference to a four hour general strike call by Italian unions. **Page 20**

Moscow prices reform

The Soviet Union would introduce a new system of wholesale prices from 1990 and retail prices from 1991, a senior economic official said. **Page 3**

North Sea clean-up

Agreement to reduce North Sea pollution was reached at an eight nation ministerial meeting in London. **Page 10**

French cheese danger

The sale of five French-produced soft cheeses was halted in Sweden after a dangerous bacteria was found in one of the brands.

Airlines action shelved

The EC postponed a decision on whether to take fresh legal action against nine airlines to force them to abandon cartel agreements.

Red Army terror alert

Japan's ultra-radical Red Army might be planning terrorist attacks against the 1988 Summer Olympics in Seoul, Japanese and Korean newspapers reported.

Nigerian military aid

Nigeria said it had offered military training facilities to ANC guerrillas in South Africa. **Nigerian currency auctions, Page 6**

Ershad faces turmoil

Bangladeshi police were ordered to increase security in main towns while President Ershad faced fresh political turmoil as opposition parties prepared for a new three-day strike against his Government.

E Germans raid library

East German security men raided a church library in East Berlin, seized printing equipment and literature and detained five people connected with an environmental and human rights group. **Page 3**

Yugoslav pay rise

Miners in Bosnia-Herzegovina republic, Yugoslavia, won a 60 per cent pay rise after a five-day strike. **Serbia party clash, Page 3**

Swiss impose visas

The Swiss Government, aiming to reduce illegal immigration, said passengers from 10 nations would need transit visas to pass through Swiss airports. **Page 2**

More Haiti violence

Two people were killed in Haiti, bringing to five the number murdered on the eve of the nation's first presidential elections in 30 years. **Page 6**

Argentine strike call

Argentina's trade union confederation called a 34-hour general strike for December 8 and 9 to protest against President Raul Alfonsin's economic policies.

Beirut camp clash

Heavy fighting flared between Shia gunmen and Palestinian guerrillas defending a Beirut refugee camp.

Business Summary

Primerica to back Triangle buy-out

PRIMERICA, US financial services company and largest independent shareholder in Triangle Industries, leading US manufacturer of metal cans and bottles, will back a controversial $1bn buy-out of Triangle by its two founders and controlling shareholders. **Page 21**

NICKEL PRICES climbed to six year highs in dollars on the London Metal Exchange, helped by speculative demand and

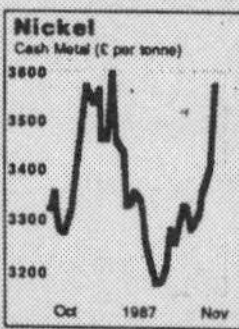

strong buying by Japan's stainless steel industry. The cash position rose £160 to £3,565 a tonne.

WALL STREET: The Dow Jones industrial average closed down 16.58 at 1946.95. **Page 44**

TOKYO: Strong demand for large capitalisation stocks lifted the Nikkei average to close at 23,219.69, up 363.67. **Page 44**

LONDON: Uncertainty over the dollar hit equities and bonds. The FT-SE 100 index closed down 25.0 at 1,664.1 and the FT Ordinary index shed 18.6 to 1,316.6. **Details Page 40**

DOLLAR closed in New York at DM1.6710; FFr5.6662; SFr1.3715 and Y134.90. It closed down in London at DM1.6675 (DM1.875); FFr5.6575 (FFr5.7175); SFr1.3705 (SFr1.3855) and Y134.70 (Y135.50). **Page 33**

STERLING closed in New York at $1.792. It rose in London over 2 cents to $1.7945 and improved to DM2.9925 (DM2.99); to FFr10.1550 (FFr10.1350); to SFr2.46 (SFr2.2550) and to Y241.75 (Y240.25). **Page 33**

NIPPON TELEGRAPH and Telephone, Japan's telecommunications group, reported pre-tax profits up 16.2 per cent in six months to September on the strength of cost-cutting measures and improved marketing. **Page 22**

STATOIL, Norway's state oil company named Mr Jan Erik Langangen, 37, president of Storebrand, Norway's largest insurance company, as its new chairman.

ELECTROLUX of Sweden, world's leading white goods maker showed a 26 per cent jump in profits to SKr604m ($99.5m) in the third quarter on sales up 22 per cent to SKr16.3bn. **Page 23**

BOMBARDIER, Canadian transport and aerospace group, earned C$42m for the first nine months of 1987, up from C$23.3m (US$32m) a year earlier, on revenues of C$1.01bn, against C$715m. **Page 21**

SANDVIK, Swedish cemented carbide and special steels group, showed a 4 per cent rise in nine month pre-tax profits to SKr1.37bn ($225m) on stagnant sales of SKr9.332bn. **Page 23**

HONG KONG Telephone, quoted subsidiary of Britain's Cable and Wireless group, lifted profits by 28 per cent to HK$545.1m (US$69.9m) for half year to September. **Page 22**

NATIONALE-NEDERLANDEN, largest insurance company in the Netherlands, edged net profits up 6 per cent to Fl 463.5m ($245m) from Fl 435.5m a year earlier. **Page 23**

DORBYL, South African heavy engineering company, increased year sales to R1.72bn ($870m) from R1.5bn with pre-tax profit at R77.9m against R64.2m. **Page 22**

VOLVO, Swedish motor, energy and foods group, would consider opening a car plant in the US if the dollar continued to weaken, the company said. **Page 23**

US to halt cruise missile deployment in Western Europe

BY QUENTIN PEEL IN BRUSSELS

THE US has agreed with its Nato allies that no further intermediate range nuclear missiles (INF) will be deployed in Western Europe from December 8 - the date President Ronald Reagan and Mr Mikhail Gorbachev will sign the treaty to scrap these weapons over the next three years.

European governments yesterday unreservedly welcomed the treaty's completion, despite some doubts in West Germany about its contents and disagreements about what should be the next step in arms control.

Mr George Shultz, the US Secretary of State, announced the agreement in Brussels yesterday, where he flew to brief Nato foreign ministers and ambassadors on the outcome of his talks in Geneva with Mr Eduard Shevardnadze, the Soviet Foreign Minister.

The decision to halt deployment, even before the US Congress has ratified the INF treaty, will remove a major political headache for those countries providing bases for cruise missiles - in particular Belgium and the Netherlands, as well as the UK, Italy and West Germany.

The decision means that the Molesworth base in the east of England, scheduled to take 64 missiles, will now not be used. There are already 96 launchers in place at Greenham Common, west of London.

In Belgium, where the Government goes to the polls on December 13, further missile deployment has been a major election issue. Both Belgium and the Netherlands had been strongly resisting US pressure.

Mr Shultz said the decision to halt deployment was not matched by any similar Soviet agreement. They could continue deploying new SS20s until the date of ratification of the INF treaty.

Lord Carrington, the Nato secretary-general, said: "The Council enthusiastically welcomed the INF agreement, and looked forward to its signature and early ratification".

There was a widespread welcome from the Europeans on three fronts: for the decision not to insist on further missile deployment; for the success of the US in negotiating a clearly asymmetrical deal with the Soviet Union, which is removing more than four times more warheads than the US; and for the verification measures agreed to allow for inspection of missile sites - and factory gate inspections at missile manufacturing facilities.

Sir Geoffrey Howe, the British Foreign Secretary, welcoming the agreement, said in a statement that Nato had achieved everything it wanted under the proposed pact.

The terms justified the decision by the North Atlantic Alliance to deploy US-built cruise and Pershing missiles and, he added, "bears witness to the determination and unity of the Nato countries".

The West German Government, parts of which were firmly opposed to the INF deal in its present form only seven months ago, put on a brave face and welcomed the Geneva agreement.

Chancellor Helmut Kohl said he greeted the news that the US

Continued on Page 20
Editorial comment, Page 18

Bonn plans measures to boost domestic growth

BY PETER BRUCE IN BONN

WEST GERMANY plans to make concrete proposals soon on ways to boost domestic economic growth following the US budget deficit agreement, Bonn's Finance Minister, Mr Gerhard Stoltenberg, said yesterday.

Separately, the Bundesbank again signalled its readiness to support the US currency by cutting its interest rate on three-day Treasury bills from 3.2 per cent to 3 per cent.

Mr Stoltenberg said West Germany was now being asked whether it had room to manouvre beyond the measures, including a bigger than planned tax cut next year, that it had agreed to in the Louvre currency accord in February. "Following the American budget agreement, we, the Government and Bundesbank together, are studying this in close contact with our European partners," he said.

But he did not say what new measures were possible and seemed to rule out any deliberate increase in next year's planned budget deficit of nearly DM30bn.

However, while confirming a fundamental easing of West German hostility to calls for additional pump priming economic measures, Mr Stoltenberg warned that in so doing the Government would have to engage in brinkmanship.

He praised last week's budget deficit compromise between the US Administration and Congress and said that it met the most important precondition for quieting the turbulence on world equity and currency markets. "We expect rapid progress towards the appropriate legislation," he added.

Mr Stoltenberg was particularly scathing about charges in the past few weeks, mainly from the US, that West Germany was not doing enough to cut its trade and current account surpluses. The transatlantic debate about which country should do what had "evoked mistrust about the implementation of agreed international co-operation (the so-called Louvre currency accord) and played a decisive role in the slump in world markets."

In a thinly disguised attack on Mr Edzard Reuter, the chairman of the Daimler Benz motor group, West Germany's biggest company, Mr Stoltenberg said that blaming Bonn for following deflationary policies while its budget deficit and the money supply were growing was "completely devious". Mr Reuter, a supporter of the opposition Social Democrats, said in New York last week that the world

Continued on Page 20
Currencies and equities, Section II

A leading economics research group has called for further sharp cuts in British interest rates to cushion the deflationary impact on the UK's economy of the stock market crash and recent rise in sterling. The National Institute of Economic and Social Research said borrowing costs should be cut from 9 to 8 per cent and that a further cut to 7 per cent should be considered by the end of the year or soon after. Page 8.

Brussels proposes phased end to quotas on steel production

BY WILLIAM DAWKINS IN BRUSSELS

THE EUROPEAN Commission yesterday proposed the ending of output controls on most of the steel production under its control by next July and the liberalisation of the rest by the end of 1990.

Brussels' call for a step-by-step end to the seven-year-old system of steel quotas is a serious blow to Eurofer, which represents the major integrated steelmakers.

The group has lobbied fiercely to retain the full range of quotas for another three years. The quotas help to support prices for 60 per cent of the community's 130m tonnes annual steel output.

The 17-man Commission agreed at its full meeting that quotas should stop at the end of the year for wire rod and merchant bar, representing just over 20 per cent of EC steel output.

But the most controversial part of the package is proposed liberalisation for hot and cold-rolled coils, accounting for roughly 30 per cent of output, by July 1988.

These account for the hard core of 10m tonnes out of the industry's 30m tonnes of total surplus capacity and represent the sector where the industry has found it hardest to come up with voluntary closures from the big state-owned mills that dominate hot-rolled production.

The remaining products left in the quota system, heavy plate and heavy sections, which represents another 10m tonnes of overcapacity, would also be freed from controls next July, unless the industry comes up with adequate production cuts first.

If the Commission receives firm guarantees of plant closures in heavy plate and heavy sections by March 15 next year, it is proposing to let quotas run on until the end of 1990 on the grounds that demand for those products continues to be depressed, while orders for hot-rolled coil are buoyant.

Commission officials said average capacity utilisation in heavy sections and plates was running at a mere 58 per cent, well below the 75 per cent average achieved by hot-rolled coil producers. That compares with the 80 per cent capacity utilisation rate that Brussels estimates is the minimum for commercial viability.

It was unclear yesterday whether the plan, described by Commission officials as a "soft landing" for the industry will attract a majority of member states when EC industry ministers meet to debate it on December 8.

However, Britain, an aggressive advocate of an immediate return to a free market in steel, is almost certain to vote against it, while the Bonn Government is expected to come under renewed pressure from its steel industry to fight for a three-year quota system.

If industry ministers fail to agree, the whole system automatically ends on January 1.

The package supersedes most parts of an earlier Commission offer of a three-year extension for quotas. That was to have been conditional on the industry coming forward with adequate voluntary capacity cuts, but an independent report presented to Brussels last week found that steel companies had been so protected by quotas that they were unable to make the necessary closures.

However, Commission officials said that the package does include earlier plans to provide roughly Ecu 870m ($1.07bn) from EC social and structural funds to help cushion the impact of the more than 80,000 redundancies which the industry expects to make over the next three years.

Holmes a Court: selling assets

Icahn buys Texaco stake for $348m

By James Buchan in New York

MR ROBERT Holmes a Court, the Australian entrepreneur who has sold off big parts of his business empire since the world stock-market crash last month, has sold half his 10 per cent holding in Texaco to Mr Carl Icahn, the US corporate raider, at a $100m loss.

The $348m deal is new evidence that the Australian may be conducting a sale of assets to meet debt payments at his highly borrowed companies. It also brings new uncertainty to Texaco, the beleaguered US oil group which has taken refuge in bankruptcy from a $10.3bn damages judgement.

Mr Icahn, who controls about 76 per cent of Trans World Airlines, announced yesterday that TWA had bought 12m shares of Texaco from Mr Holmes a Court's Bell Resources for $29 a share. TWA said that it had a right of first refusal and a voting proxy over the remaining 12.1m Bell shares in Texaco.

The purchase gives Mr Icahn, one of the most aggressive and successful US takeover specialists, voting control over 12.3 per cent of Texaco. Mr Icahn is

Continued on Page 20

Icahn: takeover specialist

Saudi Arabia wants to buy minehunters

BY DAVID BUCHAN AND LYNTON MCLAIN IN LONDON

SAUDI ARABIA is seeking to buy eight minehunting ships from Europe in the first concrete response by a non-belligerent Gulf state to deal itself with the growing mine menace in the region.

It has invited bids from Britain, Italy and the French-Dutch-Belgian consortium which makes the Tripartite minehunter to supply eight ships in a contract that, with associated training, could be worth between £250m ($442m) and £300m. From the UK, Vosper Thornycroft is offering its Sandown class single role minehunter, while Intermarine of Italy is putting its Lerici class minehunter forward.

The outcome of the contract competition could have a significant influence on smaller Gulf states like Kuwait, Oman and the United Arab Emirates which are considering buying mine counter-measure equipment.

At present, the detection and destruction of mines in the Gulf, mostly sown by Iran, has been left entirely to the flotillas of the US, the UK, France, Italy, the Netherlands and Belgium.

US and British ships have discovered more than a dozen mines in recent weeks.

The Saudis, who sent out the invitations to tender some six weeks ago, are believed to want to move relatively quickly. The purchase is being given a higher priority than the half dozen submarines Saudi Arabia said last year it was interested in buying and for which several European yards, including Vickers Shipbuilding and Engineering of the UK, have submitted bids. The submarines are not seen as having any direct use in the current phase of the Gulf war.

The flare-up in the Gulf since the summer has produced an upsurge in the Gulf states' interest in mine countermeasures, but the Saudi request for tenders is the first firm move. A contract to build as many as eight ships could take some time to fulfil, although some European governments might be prepared to let the Saudis have a few ships directly out of their naval inventories.

Jordan tries to woo Syria from Iran

BY TONY WALKER IN CAIRO

KING HUSSEIN of Jordan travelled to Damascus yesterday to press for reconciliation between the previously estranged rulers of Syria and Iraq. The immediate aim is to persuade Syria and Iraq to resume diplomatic relations, a move which officials in Jordan have been saying is imminent.

Although the talks are moving slowing, a full reconciliation between Syria and Iraq, which can be two of the Arab world's most implacable enemies, would represent a sea-change in the region with important implications in the war between Iraq and Iran.

King Hussein brought bitter rivals, Presidents Hafez al-Assad of Syria and Saddam Hussein of Iraq, together two weeks ago at an emergency Arab summit in Amman.

This followed a secret meeting between the two leaders of rival wings of the Arab Baath Socialist party held early this year in the Jordanian desert.

King Hussein, with the backing of moderate Arab rulers in the Gulf, is trying to persuade Mr Assad to lessen his support for Iran in the Gulf war.

Damascus's backing for Tehran is seen as the main impediment to the formation of a united Arab front against Iran.

Syria, however, is showing no sign of abandoning its links to Iran. Rather, it seems to be attempting to increase its room for manoeuvre between the Gulf war protagonists, but not at the expense of its relations with Tehran.

Farouq al-Shara, Syria's Foreign Minister, said after the Amman summit that political differences with Iraq "could not be mended with an embrace or a handshake."

"We are not with the censure of Iran, but we are against its occupation of Iraqi territory," Mr al-Shara was quoted as saying. Syria was party to a firm party resolution that condemned Iran's failure to agree to UN calls for an immediate ceasefire in the Gulf conflict.

Arab observers in the region view as promising developments in relations between Damascus and Baghdad since the summit. Respective media have toned down hostile commentaries which were a feature of the relationship.

King Hussein is also expected to visit Baghdad soon in an effort to build on the reconciliation process.

CONTENTS

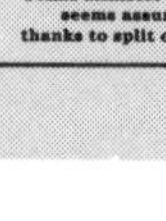

TURKISH POLL TURNS INTO BATTLE FOR SECOND PLACE

Prime Minister Turgut Ozal, who seems assured of victory thanks to split opposition, Page 2

12 National and International Editions

The FT, like the financial and commodity markets it reports to its readers, has moved steadily, extending its horizons from national to international dimensions over the past decades, and will continue to do so over the foreseeable future. The sudden and dramatic setback in world stock markets at the end of October 1987 demonstrated once and for all that global markets are now so closely linked by electronic communications that they respond almost as one to changes in investment sentiment.

The FT was ahead of the trend, in that it began to print an international edition in 1979. Readers inside the UK continue to read a newspaper printed in London, but those elsewhere in the world now read an FT printed in Frankfurt, West Germany, or in New Jersey, US. The newspaper is also interested in printing in the Far East.

The national and international editions of the paper are still 'The FT' in all essentials. The differences between the two would perhaps not be readily apparent, except to the very few readers who see both on the same day. But, with the international edition now providing about 26 per cent of daily circulation, and the proportion of non-UK readers growing by 28 per cent annually, the range of the FT's coverage is expanding rapidly.

Most of the paper's best-known features appear in both editions. Lex, the column featuring high-grade comment on corporate, economic or fiscal developments, covers the full range of the world's trading centres, drawing together new trends in the US, Japan, Hong Kong or the various European centres. The Management pages examine management successes and failures in a similar fashion, seeking to identify those trends of significance throughout the world of business. The same applies to the Technology pages. But there are also aspects of the FT's daily coverage which are more closely linked to events inside the UK, although these may have significance and interest for readers elsewhere. The paper carries a daily page of news on events in the UK labour relations field. And it carries a weekly report on the UK market for commercial property. Against these somewhat domesticated topics, however, must be balanced the paper's strong coverage of the Arts, which, like the Arts themselves, knows no frontiers.

Consequently, when the paper decided to publish and develop an international edition, aimed from the first entirely at readers outside Britain, a shift in newspaper philosophy was required. Many of these readers used English only as a second language; they could not be expected to be familiar with the finer details of business or social life in Britain. Yet they usually shared many common interests, and were usually involved in similar areas of business. So, the international edition, which does not appear in Britain, has to present itself in a different way from the national edition, and sometimes provides extra information.

In the first place, the international paper is 'sectionalized', a concept still new to UK readers, although commonplace elsewhere in the journalistic world. Inside the first section, which looks much like the London-based FT, is a second section, which incorporates all the financial statistical information, including the London Share Service, but also some US share services which are examined later. While Lex stays with the front section, much of the UK and foreign corporate reporting is contained in the second section. The change allows the international edition to shift the emphasis from UK company news to reports on the major overseas companies.

Consequently, the first page of Section II of the international edition will almost invariably be led by reports on US or European companies. News from UK companies will have to compete with these foreign names for the top of the page, and it will be the largest and most internationally-orientated British companies that win out. Smaller UK groups, which may still gain prominence in the London paper, may be relegated to the inside pages of the international edition.

The most significant addition to the international paper is the World Stock Markets page, usually the back page of Section II. Here, the FT publishes daily reports by its own correspondents, on the London and New York securities markets, backed by reports on other world markets either by the local FT correspondents or by the leading newsagencies. The World Stock Markets page has proved a valuable window for reporting the growing inter-relation of the major market-places. The huge setback in stock markets in October 1987 showed only too clearly how selling in New York markets was taken up when Tokyo opened, and then continued in London. In fact, the World Stock Markets page, together with its attendant graphs showing the trend of the various financial centres, now appears in the FT London editions whenever events justify its doing so. As markets become global in scope, so must newspapers.

WORLD STOCK MARKE

AMERICA

as traders wind down

l income rose 1.7
tober, more than
expected, largely
e rise in farm
ubsidy payments
ge increases. Con-
unchanged as

economic data
y has shown the
ent into the late
price collapse in
ape.
rkets will get lit-
e impact of the
n the real econ-
a is released for
nd subsequent
r's run of figures
way to relieving
ut recession next
has helped the
fragile confidence
arket.
e bond market,
e possible infla-
of the substantial
monetary policy
ws strong recent
with some trepi-

ctor in the equity
ase and precious
les. Copper stocks,
particularly dur-
sell-off, have
ounding well,
hortage of copper
prices.
odity Research
res price index
half a point by
esterday after a
in on Tuesday.
stocks, Asarco Inc

lost an early gain of $⅛ to close unchanged at $28⅜ but Inspiration Resources was $⅜ higher at $6⅞ and Phelps Dodge rose $2 to $46¼.

Gold mining stocks were also generally firmer. Battle Mountain, due to open two new mines by the end of this year, rose $¾ to $19¾ while Homestake Mining, which plans to increase output by between 35 per cent and 55 per cent in 1989, added $⅞ to $17⅞.

Tobacco stocks were hard hit in afternoon trading as rumours circulated that new data would be released next month which could hurt tobacco companies trying to defend themselves against liability suits. American Brands lost $1¾ to $41, Philip Morris slumped $4¼ to $89½ and RJR Nabisco lost $2¾ to $48½.

News that investor Mr Carl Icahn has acquired about half of the 9.6 per cent stake in Texaco held by Australian investor Robert Holmes a Court and voting power over the remaining shares boosted Texaco's share price by $1¾ to $30¼.

Bell & Howell recovered from a loss of $⅜ to close $¼ higher at $67¾ after its announcement it had received an offer to acquire its capital stock for $64 per share in cash from the consortium formed by Robert M Bass Group.

Primerica Corp, the financial services concern and specialist retailer, added $⅞ to $27⅞ after news it is selling its stake in Triangle Industries, a manufacturer of packaging and containers, for $124m in cash. Triangle's shares put on $2 to $26.

Canada

TORONTO STOCKS, boosted by a strong advance in gold issues, defied a loss on Wall Street to close higher.

The 300 composite index rose 33.34 to 3028.04 as advances outpaced declines by 519 to 360 on active volume of 33.8m shares.

"The cyclical, economically sensitive stocks are strong," said John Ing of Maison Placements.

"The economy will be much stronger than anticipated in 1988. The resource sector in Canada will be one of the prime beneficiaries."

Golds posted a broad advance. Lac Minerals gained C$½ to C$13⅛, International Corona won C$5¼ to C$53½ and Placer Dome rose C$1¼ to C$18⅜.

Mines also showed strong gains, with Noranda climbing C$⅞ to C$23¼, Alcan Aluminium moving ahead C$⅝ to C$34⅝ and Falconbridge advancing C$1¼ to C$21¾.

Energy issues turned in a mixed performance. Shell Canada fell C$⅜ to C$31⅝ and Texaco Canada was unchanged at C$27⅝.

Although Imperial Oil said it will report record operating and net profits for the year, its class A shares fell C$⅜ to C$53¼.

Nikkei

Tokyo

STRONG DEMAND for big ca
talisation stocks lifted the Nikk
average above 23,000 in Tok
yesterday for the first time
three weeks, *writes Shigeo Nis*
iwaki of Jiji Press.
The market measure gain
363.67 to close at 23,219.69. V
ume rose to 617.90m shares fro
Tuesday's 340.02m. Rises l
falls 682 to 223, with 115 issu
unchanged.
The buying spree was spark
by Wall Street's overnig
advance and Tuesday's co-or
nated interest rate cuts in t
Netherlands, France and We
Germany. The market was al
cheered by the nuclear arms de
between the US and the Soc
Union.
Large-capital steels and sh
buildings drew most intere
with Kawasaki Steel busiest
trade of 113.21m shares. It ro
Y6 to a record Y363.
Nippon Steel, the second bu
est issue as 71.00m shar
changed hands, added Y8
Y439, while Ishikawajima-H
ima Heavy Industries added Y
to Y667, Nippon Kokan Y8
Y348 and Mitsubishi Hea
Industries Y21 to Y639.
Chemical issues returned fr
recent neglect to the limelig
helped by rising demand for e
ylene. Showa Denko ended Y
higher at Y742, Sumitomo Che
ical leapt Y40 to Y800, Mits
Toatsu Chemicals Y56 to Y
and Teijin Y30 to Y785.
Trading houses found fav
on a possible cut in inter

EUROPE

lar takes fizz

Portugal's markets

Bob Kir

Taiwan

NEW YORK

November 25	Price US$	+ or −
AAR	17⅞	−⅛
AGS Computers	15½	+⅛
AM Intl Group	63	−¾
AMCA	7	.....
AMR Corp	32⅜	−⅜
ASA	50½	+1½
AVX Corp	12¾	−½
Abbott Labs	46⅝	−⅞
Acme Cleveland	9⅞	+⅛
Adobe Res	5½	+¼
Advanced Micro	9⅞	−⅛
Aetna Life	46⅛	−2⅛
Ahmanson (H.F.)	14⅝	−¼
Air Prod & Chem	36	+⅜
Alberto-Culver	19¾	+¼
Albertson's	26¾	+⅞
Alcan Aluminium	26⅜	+⅞
Alco Standard	18¼	+¼
Alcoa	48½	+1⅛
Alexander & Al	19⅞	+⅛
Allegheny Intl	5⅛	+¼
Allegheny Power	37	−¼
Allegis	71½	−½
Allied Bancshares	4⅝	−⅛
Allied Signal	30⅛	−1
Allis Chalmers	1⅜	+⅛
Amax	19⅛	+¼
Amdahl Corp	31⅛	+¼
Amerada Hess	23¾	−⅞
Am Brands	41⅜	−1⅜
Am Cyanamid	38⅞	+⅛

November 25	Price US$	+ or −
Cleve Cliffs Iron	15⅛	−¾
Clorox	27½	.....
Coastal Corp	26⅞	+⅞
Coca Cola	38¾	−¼
Coca Cola Ent.	14⅝	.....
Colgate Palm	39½	+⅛
Colt Inds	9¼	.....
Columbia Gas	39	−⅝
Combust'n Eng	26⅜	+⅛
Commonw'th Ed	28⅝	−⅜
Comm Satellite	26⅜	−⅜
Comp Science	49	+⅜
Computervision	8⅜	+¼
Con Agra	24	−1
Cons Edison	43	−⅝
Cons Freight	26¾	−⅜
Con Nat Gas	37	−1
Cons. Paper	53	.....
Cons. Rail	26	+⅝
Consumer Power	13⅝	−⅛
Conti Corp	40¾	−⅞
Conti Illinois	2⅞	.....
Conti Ill.Hldgs	¼	.....
Cont Tel Corp	29	+⅛
Control Data	24¼	+¾
Converg. Techs	3⅛	+⅜
Cooper Inds	49⅝	+⅞
Coors Adolph	18⅛	−¼
Copperweld	7½	−⅛
Corning Glass	50¼	+¾
Corroon & Black	28	+⅛

November 25	Price US$	+ or −
Harcourt Brace	5⅛	+⅛
Harris Corp	25	.....
Harsco	26⅜	+⅜
Hecla Mining	14½	+⅞
Heilaman Brew	40⅛	+⅜
Heinz (HJ)	38½	−⅝
Helmerick & P	19	−⅛
Hercules	45⅝	−¼
Hershey	24⅞	−⅛
Hewlett Pkd	50½	−1⅜
Hilton Hotels	69¼	−½
Hitachi	93⅝	−1⅝
Holiday Inns	19⅞	−⅞
Holly Sugar	72	+1
Home Depot	18	−⅛
Homestake	17¾	+⅞
Honeywell	56½	−1
Hormel (Geo)	21¾	.....
Hospital Corp	31⅝	−⅛
Household Int	41⅞	+⅛
Houston Inds	30⅜	−¼
Humana	19½	−⅜
Hutton (E.F)	27⅝	−⅝
IC Inds	30¾	+¾
ITT	46½	−⅝
IU Int	12¼	+⅜

The International Edition, whether printed in Frankfurt or in New Jersey, has a valuable time-advantage over the London edition when it comes to reporting global markets. The International Edition is able to carry a batch of closing prices from the US stock markets, which arrive too late for the early London edition.

US share prices quoted are composite prices — that is to say, incorporating non-New York trades — for the New York Stock Exchange, and the American Stock Exchange, and also for the National Market System of the National Association of Share Dealers of America (or NASDAQ, to give its market symbol).

One edition of the FT — the Saturday FT — in some ways bridges the gap between national and international editions. All FT readers see the same edition on Saturday, although it is printed both in London and New Jersey. The Saturday FT has a number of special characteristics and indeed, in some ways, its own special readership.

The Saturday FT presents the UK reader with the sectionalized format familiar to those who read the international edition. Buyers of the Saturday paper find, inserted inside Section I, which looks much like any other day's FT, a separate section headed 'Weekend FT'.

Abitibi	[illegible]	
Abitibi Res	0.20	......
AMCA Intl	8¾	......
Agnico Eagle	24¼	+⅞
Alberta Energy	15⅝	+⅛
Alcan Aluminium	34⅝	+1⅛
Algoma Steel	14	−¼
Bank Montreal	25½	......
Bank Nova Scotia	12½	+¼
B.C.E.	36⅜	......
Bombardier	7¾	+⅛
Bow Valley	13⅛	......
BP Canada Res	19	−½
Brascan A	26⅝	+¾
BC Forest	18¾	......
CAE Inds.	6¼	......
CIL Inc	26½	......
Cambior	18¾	+1½
Can Cement Pf	14¼	+¼
Can NW Energy	18	+1½
Can Trustco	[illegible]	
Can Imp Bank	19¾	+¼
Can Pacific	19⅝	−¼
Can Tire A	13	......
Can For	22⅜	+⅝
Chieftain	9½	+⅛
Cominco	13⅝	+1
Conigas Mines	3	+¼
Cons Bathst A	16	−⅛
Coremark Intl	1¾	−
Coscan Dev	9	+¼
Dennison Mines A	4¾	−⅛
Dofasco inc	24⅛	+⅛
Dome Petroleum	0.98	+0.02
Domtar	12⅝	−⅛
Echo Bay Mines	29⅜	+1⅜
Falconbridge	21¾	+1½
Fed.Inds.A	13¾	−⅛
Gendis Inds.A	14½	−¼
Hawker Sid Can	19¼	−¾
Hudson's Bay	18½	......
Imasco	25¼	+¼
Imperial Oil A	53¼	−¾
Inco	23⅜	+⅛
Indal	11	......
Int Pipe	41¾	+¼
Labatt	25¼	+⅜
Lac Minerals	13⅛	+⅝
Laidlaw Trans. B	16⅛	+½
Laurentian Gp	9⅞	......
Lawson Mrdon (Cl.A)	11	−⅛
Loblaw	11¾	+¼
Macmillan Bloedel	20½	+½
Magna Intl	10⅜	+⅛
McIntire Mines	38½	......
Metall Mining	10¾	+1

AUSTRIA

November 25	Price Sch %	+ or −
Creditanstalt	1,940	......
Goesser	2,770	+20
Interunfall	11,000	−100
Jungbunzlauer	6,800	......
Laenderbank	371	+2
Perlmooser	632	+7
Steyr-Daimler	113	......
Veitscher Mag	660	+25

BELGIUM/LUXEMBOURG

November 25	Price	+ or

GERMANY

November 25	Price Dm.	+ or −
AEG	232.5	−2.5
Allianz AG	1,175	+64
BASF	266	−2
Bayer	270	−10
Bayer-Hypo	324	−3
Bayer-Verein	331	−9
BHF-Bank	355	+5
BMW	449	−6
Brown Boveri	294.8	......
Commerzbank	226.5	−2.5
Cont'l Gummi	222.5	−0.5
Daimler-Benz	658	−10
Degussa	330	......
D'sche Babcock	151	−11.9
[illegible]	441.5	−9.5

SPAIN

November 25	Price Pts.	+ or −
Alcazar	560.00	−10
Banco Bilbao	1,380 #	......
Banco Central	1140.00	+70
Banco Exterior	440.00	......
Banco Hispano	600.00	−13
Banco Popular	1250.00	+45
Banco Santander	1013.00	......
Banco de Vizcay	1350.00	+100
Banesto	900.00	......
Dragados	358.00	+18
Hidrola	81.00	−1.7
Iberduero	110.70	−1.3
Petroleos	431.00	+6
Telefonica	156.00	+5.8

The new-style format for Saturday was introduced only two and a half years ago, but it reflected factors recognized over a longer period. For the very nature of FT readership undergoes a sea-change on Saturdays. Not only do more people buy it than on a weekday, but they seem to be different people entirely, much to the dismay of advertising and editorial executives. Some Saturday readers are weekday readers who simply want to receive summaries of the events of the week past and the week pending. These readers want the London Share Price Service, but also the details of trading in corporate fixed interest stocks, which are not widely reported in the daily newspapers. Reporting on the securities markets focuses on the trends over the past week, as well as over Friday's trading session. Extra columns outline the outlook for the major profits statements expected in the following week.

The Saturday edition carries a full report on trading in the Unlisted Stock Market (USM) and on the Third market — both markets intended to provide public quotation for small companies not yet able to take on a full International Stock Exchange Quotation.

But the FT recognizes that Saturday is different from a weekday, even for the reader who may study the paper closely during the rest of the week. Saturday is the day when the most hardened professional investor becomes a family man as well, and turns his attention to a wide variety of financial projects. Unit trusts, pension schemes, school fees, or prospective house purchases all receive more attention from readers on Saturdays than on weekdays. Moreover, these same interests will attract to the Saturday FT many readers who are not regular daily readers of the paper. Consequently, the Saturday FT carries regular columns of comment on the latest unit trust offers, the impending rights or privatization issues, as well as a letters column which aims to advise personal investors.

These aspects of the Saturday FT, which are mostly contained in Section I or in the first few pages of 'Weekend FT', can be described as largely financial in character. But the remaining pages of 'Weekend FT' cater for a much wider range of cultural, leisure or private interests of the weekend readership.

Financial Times Saturday November 21 1987

WEEK

Saturday

• MARKETS • FINANCE & THE FAMILY • PROPERTY • TRAVEL •

Michael Field looks at the Arabs in
finds them still struggling to

Agony of th

"OUR PEOPLE are losing faith in us," said King Hussein of Jordan in his opening address at the Arab summit conference in Amman last week. His comment was remarkable for its bluntness - generally Arabs like to refer to unpleasant facts only in the most oblique fashion - but it was not at all controversial. None of the millions of Arabs who saw the King's otherwise fairly bland speech on television or read it in the newspapers would have disagreed with him.

In the last year or so the Arabs - and the intelligentsia in particular - have been plumbing the depths of despair. They are appalled by the ineffectiveness of their countries on the international stage, by the lack of individual freedom in the Arab world and, above all, by the violence of the region.

The chronicle of bloodshed is long and depressing. Wars at present are being fought in Lebanon, southern Sudan, the Western Sahara, on the Libyan border with Chad, and, most bloodily, on the Iran/Iraq frontier, where the last seven years have claimed a million dead and wounded. In the background the Arab-Israeli conflict

left the Arabs' society immobile and their intellect stultified.

On the economic question - of why $1.5tr has had such limited effect - the answer is summed up by a cynical colleague on this newspaper: "The trouble with oil," he remarked, "is that it doesn't do anything for a country except teach it to enjoy spending the revenues."

In other words, oil revenues are ideal for building infrastructure - ports, airports and roads - and for providing good health services and lavish welfare states. But they do

domestic market is too poor to
products.

It was a mistake, therefore, for an
the Arab world or outside to have s
in the first place that oil wealt
would make the region, or part of it
a productive rather than a consum
What is needed for economic grow
developing country is reasonabl
labour, large and increasingly pr
markets at home or abroad and
neurial initiative, as well as capital
ably in private hands. Most
necessities the Arab world lacks.

The first page of 'Weekend FT' acts as a flagship to the section. Its subject may be the major financial event of the week, but from a wider, usually more international perspective than would be likely in the daily paper. Recent examples have included the implications of the sudden about-turn in world markets. Or it may focus on a major Art Collection — the Gulbenkian Foundation has featured on this page.

'Weekend FT' also carries a substantial weekly review of the housing market, an area covered infrequently in the daily newspaper. But coverage is not restricted to London. Regular reviews are carried of domestic property development throughout the UK, and also abroad. True to its fashion, the FT includes in its housing commentaries the advice on mortgage prospects and loan rates which are often omitted from the property agents' catalogues.

And finally, the Saturday paper carries forward the paper's Arts

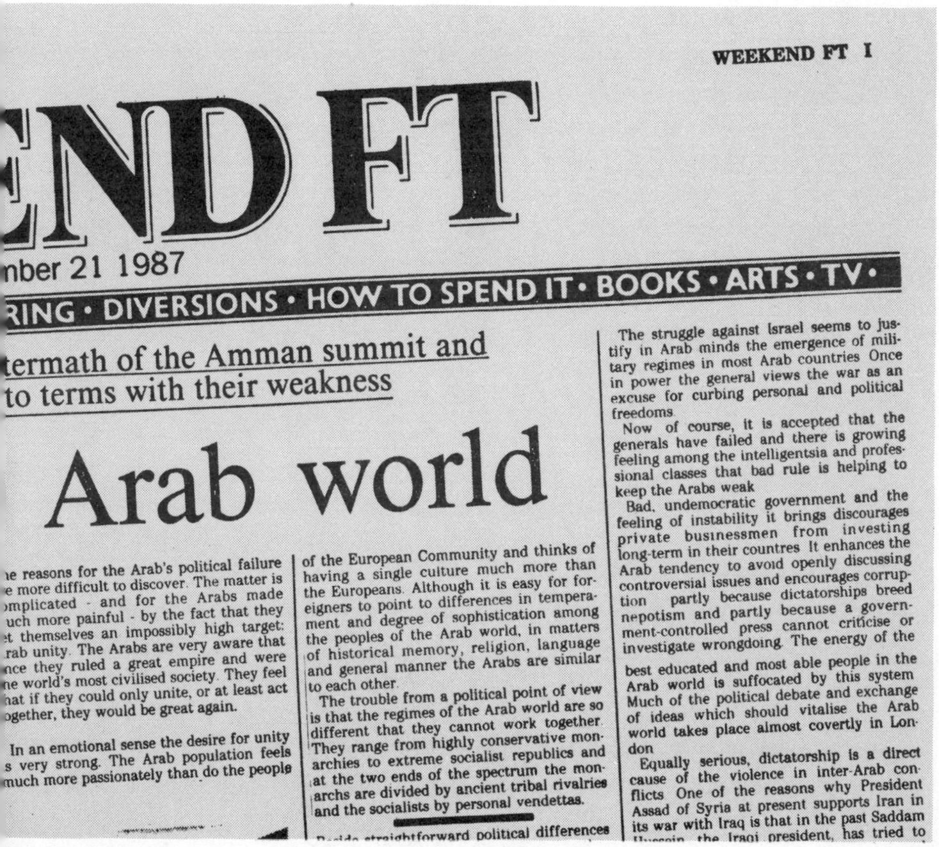

WEEKEND FT I

END FT

nber 21 1987

RING • DIVERSIONS • HOW TO SPEND IT • BOOKS • ARTS • TV •

termath of the Amman summit and
to terms with their weakness

Arab world

ıe reasons for the Arab's political failure e more difficult to discover. The matter is omplicated - and for the Arabs made uch more painful - by the fact that they et themselves an impossibly high target: rab unity. The Arabs are very aware that nce they ruled a great empire and were ne world's most civilised society. They feel hat if they could only unite, or at least act ogether, they would be great again.

In an emotional sense the desire for unity s very strong. The Arab population feels much more passionately than do the people of the European Community and thinks of having a single culture much more than the Europeans. Although it is easy for foreigners to point to differences in temperament and degree of sophistication among the peoples of the Arab world, in matters of historical memory, religion, language and general manner the Arabs are similar to each other.

The trouble from a political point of view is that the regimes of the Arab world are so different that they cannot work together. They range from highly conservative monarchies to extreme socialist republics and at the two ends of the spectrum the monarchs are divided by ancient tribal rivalries and the socialists by personal vendettas.

Beside straightforward political differences

The struggle against Israel seems to justify in Arab minds the emergence of military regimes in most Arab countries Once in power the general views the war as an excuse for curbing personal and political freedoms.

Now of course, it is accepted that the generals have failed and there is growing feeling among the intelligentsia and professional classes that bad rule is helping to keep the Arabs weak

Bad, undemocratic government and the feeling of instability it brings discourages private businessmen from investing long-term in their countres It enhances the Arab tendency to avoid openly discussing controversial issues and encourages corruption partly because dictatorships breed nepotism and partly because a government-controlled press cannot criticise or investigate wrongdoing. The energy of the best educated and most able people in the Arab world is suffocated by this system Much of the political debate and exchange of ideas which should vitalise the Arab world takes place almost covertly in London

Equally serious, dictatorship is a direct cause of the violence in inter-Arab conflicts One of the reasons why President Assad of Syria at present supports Iran in its war with Iraq is that in the past Saddam Hussein, the Iraqi president, has tried to

Roman Glass to blow the mind

The Portland Vase

GLASS OF the Caesars at the British Museum (until March 6) is one of those exhibitions that will permanently change our attitudes. Roman glass has been an underrated glory of the Roman Empire, but now we have in London the unique opportunity to see the Empire's very best surviving pieces together in one place.

Roman glass blends artistic sensitivity with extraordinary technical virtuosity, and the carved scenes have a classic permanence which is sharpened by the fragility of the material. Delicate and fine, it powerfully conveys the wealth of the Roman Empire that produced this Faberge-like work for half a millennium; this exhibition will ensure it is not forgotten again.

It brings together masterpieces from the Corning Museum of Glass, the Romisch-Germanisches Museum in Cologne, the British Museum, and some from Italy. For the first time we can see the Portland Vase next to the only comparable surviving cameo vase, the Blue Vase from Pompeii.

The Portland Vase is the star of the show. It was made in the years when Augustus was consolidating the rule of the Emperors, and it is likely he knew the Vase himself or it was made for his family, its powerful sense of order and noble responsibility suits his ideology well. It is the earliest masterpiece of blown glass - glass blowing had been invented only during the lifetime of Julius Caesar. The Vase was made by putting a gob of blue glass inside a hollow casting of white glass; both were then blown together and afterwards the white was cut to make the designs, which are in relief like the cameo designs of semi precious gemstones.

Deciding who the figures are on the Vase has kept scholars and artists busy since 1600. Rubens hoped to publish it, Wedgwood copied it, Sir William Hamilton bought it and sold it to the third Duke of Portland, who entrusted it to the British Museum in 1810 after it had been damaged by the Duchess of Gordon at his house; his family tried to sell it between the wars at Christie's, where it did not reach the reserve.

Compared with the Portland Vase, the Blue Vase has a bustling fussiness. It's shape is of a wine amphora, and its cameo scenes are of the grape harvest and the pleasures of wine and song. That was not so appropriate for the Imperial household. Two cameo inlays of Ariadne and Dionysus would not have suited either; also from Pompeii, they have a simple vigour: she swoons on Naxos as he appears, the God of Mystery, Vitality and the Grape.

Cameo work was a luxury. So were the cage cups, which are the greatest delight of the whole exhibition and must have been the most expensive glass of antiquity. They are mostly plain glass beakers inside open frames, or cages of glass of different colours. A cup from Cologne has a red, yellow and green cage, and in red is the message in Greek to drink and to live well; the Trivulzio Cup, from near Novara, has the same thought, in Latin, in blue. The cages are so delicate that they look like the spun sugar of the finest pastry basket. But they were not made by moulding or squeezing, but by cutting: many cups must have been broken in manufacture.

The greatest cage cup is the British Museum's Lycurgus Cup, which shows the legendary Thracian King who fought and was defeated by no other God than Dionysus. This seems to show the triumph of Good over Evil, and may symbolise Constantine's great victory over Licinius in 324. The cup is an opaque green which becomes violet in transmitted light: you will see this if you bend down to look at Lycurgus.

Also of the fourth century and explicitly Christian is gold glass, where gold leaf is sandwiched between two layers of glass. The finest piece from Cologne has medallions, including Adam and Eve, and rosettes floating on a sea of blue. Cologne was one of the major glass centres of the Empire: the others were the coast of Syria and Lebanon, the Northern Adriatic and the Naples area. Between Syria and Germany there were close links in glass making - impossible today but feasible to the Romans.

Sea creatures in relief mark yet more fourth century delicacies. Fish swimming on the outside of a clear beaker from Cologne have their mouths and tails and fins picked out in green. The "claw beaker" from Muching in Essex is green throughout with relief lobster claws down the sides.

The exhibition is rounded off by plainer bowls, dishes and jugs which provide the every-day counterpoint to the luxuries. A head flask with big nose and twisted eyes and lips is a forerunner of Toby Jugs, and a broken horse's leg is important as it shows that glass craftsmen could tackle large statues.

Inventinveness, delicacy and expense are the marks of Roman glass. This exhibition is superbly lit and displayed, so that the masterpieces shine like the jewels they are. Sponsored by Olivetti, it has been in Corning and will go on to Cologne, and finally to the Campidoglio in Rome. That hill, with its pimple of Capitoline Jupiter, was the heart of the Empire.

Gerald Cadogan

Antony Thorncroft reports on London's orchestras

Provocative proposals

AFTER YEARS of talk and speculation the Arts Council came up this week with proposals which could transform the London musical scene. Its working party, under the chairmanship of Mr Robert Ponsonby, ex-head of music at Radio Three, into the funding of the four London orchestras blinked at making radical recommendations, but produced ideas that will certainly set numerous cats among pigeons.

The aim is obvious and admirable: the four orchestras, the LSO, the RPO, the LPO and the Philharmonia, will receive the same collective amount of money, (almost £1.8m this season), but it will be concentrated on fewer concerts. The result should be better rehearsed, more imaginative programmes. Basically each orchestra will receive around £13,000 for each of thirty concerts to be played on the South Bank, with the LSO getting the same sum per concert for forty Barbican performances. This represents a drop all round of some fifty concerts in a season.

The new funding policy comes into force for the 1989-90 season, which ensures plenty of time for haggling. Much of it will be with the South Bank and the Barbican. The LSO, the resident orchestra at the Barbican, is receiving £438,000 from the Arts Council this season but is down to play 105 concerts. To make this feasible the City Corporation chips in. Continued City help is essential if the Arts Council's plans are to work.

It is the same on the South Bank, where the LPO, for example, is appearing over forty times this season. The Arts Council is linking its higher subsidy per concert to more rehearsals, preferably in situ. For the South Bank this would involve "dark nights" in the Festival Hall, a negative which would sometimes be surmounted by the orchestras playing repeats of the better rehearsed concerts. However Mr Nicholas Snowman, musical supremo on the South Bank, who shares the Council's aims will have to be persuaded to forgo the revenue that might be sacrificed.

He also has his own ambitions for London's musical scene. He wants "themes," linked series of concerts and concerts linked with National Theatre plays and National Film Theatre movies. He also wants more imaginative programming, which he can encourage by helping with promotional costs and charging less rental for the Festival Hall if orchestras put on enterprising concerts for discriminating, but smaller, audiences. The Arts Council and The South Bank may agree on wanting fewer, better, concerts in London, but which is going to pick up the extra cost and gain the prestige?

There is also the problem of whether the orchestras are prepared to give up concerts. They are only dependent on the Arts Council for around 14 per cent of their revenue. They might persist in playing popular works which, with their high box office returns and few rehearsal needs, can be profitable. But will this earn them black marks from the Council and perhaps a reduction in the number of their subsidised concerts for the next season, after the working of the scheme has been evaluated?

Much still has to be worked out. On the surface there seems little difference in the actual subsidising of the orchestras; they will still receive a sum of money which will disappear into their general funds. There will be no specially promoted Arts Council concerts. The orchestras are fearful that this is a step towards cutting Council expenditure in this sector, by reducing its involvement. It is well known that the Council would prefer to put its cash behind one, or perhaps two, "super" orchestras [illegible] with the London [illegible] tant to shrink [illegible] the City of Birmingham [illegible] Simon Rattle [illegible] ment.

Because the [illegible] successful at generating [illegible] they are [illegible] the Arts Council [illegible] new proposals the [illegible] acknowledging the fact and [illegible] plifying its aid. What is most [illegible] tant in this week's proposals is what was not recommended: there is nothing here which suggests a world class resident orchestra for the South Bank, for example. In practice the horse trading has only just begun.

The orchestras are also concerned that there is nothing in the plans about "incentive funding," the new buzz words. The Council will have £6m to invest in 1989-90 on such funding, which is earmarked for arts groups that succeed in boosting their revenues by their own efforts. The orchestras, which are good at raising support from sponsors, think they deserve a substantial slice of any additional money on offer.

French chanson

THOUGH IT may cultivate a more modest public profile than its contemporary counterpart, the Early Music Network continues to resist the Arts Council's current obsession with devolving to the regions everything but the kitchen sink, and regularly manages to put together enterprising and thoughtful programmes to tour the regions. The Network's London port of call is the Wigmore Hall, and Thursday's visitors there under its auspices were the distinguished French-based Ensemble Clement Janequin.

EMN programmes invariably have an historical and musical coherence that in such varied and wide-ranging territory as the pre-baroque provides valuable points of reference. So the Janequin Ensemble's programme concentrated (as its name might suggest) on the 16th-century French chanson, and on the lyrics of its eponymous composer in particular. What might have seemed potentially a dry, musicologically earnest evening, proved to be anything but that. The group's platform manner, the four singers and lutenist clad in vivid, multicoloured shirts and grouped around a table just as historical research suggests the chansons were originally performed, is refreshingly relaxed, and their singing is extrovert and exuberant.

The quartet of male voices is dominated by the counter-tenor of Dominique Visse. To anyone familiar only with the English brand of that voice, highly refined and soft-grained, Visse's bracing astringency will be a revelation. His bravura vividness gives the Ensemble's accounts their most obvious surface life, but his colleagues proved their own pungency in the programmatic chansons strewn through the evening, especially Janequin's *Le chant des Oyseaulx*, *La chasse* and *La Bataille*, in which the onomatopoeic effects were superbly and virtuosically realised.

Those, though, were essentially the lollipops in a programme that offered a thorough and exquisitely rendered survey of the genre. Just as much care was lavished upon Janequin's more consciously poetic lyrics - the rapt *L'amour, la mort et la vie* and *Quelqu'un me disoit l'autre jour* - and on songs by Costeley, Gentian, Sermisy, Bertrand and Morlaye. Each group was broken with a solo lute interlude, and Claude Debove's discreet accompaniments also underpinned a number of the songs. Altogether a delectable recital.

Andrew Clements

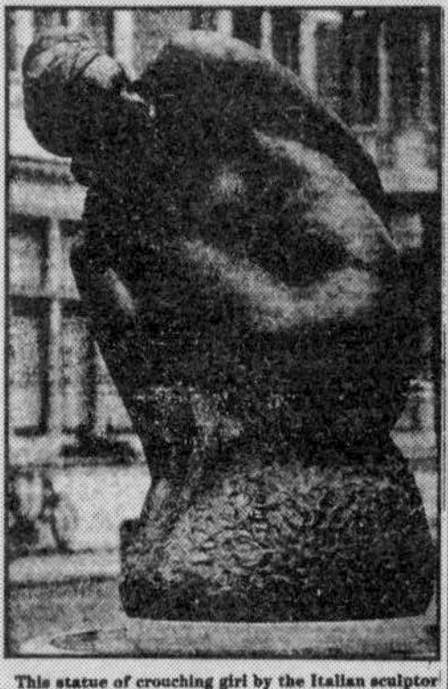

This statue of crouching girl by the Italian sculptor Emilio Greco was unveiled yesterday by the Italian Ambassador in London's Carlos Place. The figure is at the centre of a fountain which was to have been inaugurated by Italian President Cossiga before his State Visit was cancelled. The gift of the fountain coincides with a small exhibition of the work of Greco at the Tate Gallery, London. Born in 1913, Greco is a figurative sculptor most famous for the remarkable bronze doors of Orvieto Cathedral.

Zola's Nana

Alastair Muir

Belinda Davison

IN THE programme note to her adaptation of Zola's *Nana* Olwen Wymark draws an interesting comparison between the gluttonously materialistic Second Empire and our own time. The analogy falls down in one crucial respect: Napoleon III's France had style, and at least paid lip-service to such civilised embellishments of materialism as culture.

Mrs Wymark's neglect of this sense of style sums up the besetting weakness of the production brought by the touring company Shared Experience to the Almeida Theatre in Islington. An attempt to mount a whirling kaleidoscope, an impressionistic phantasmagoria, a sort of Harlot's Progress told as *La Ronde*, becomes a mere jumble, both characterisation and moral issues as smudged and shallow as in a bad comic strip.

Kenny Miller's design gives us a stage ambience from both spectators' and performers' points of view. Scenic flats viewed from the back, three pillars, a piano, candelabra and a row of chairs suggest the theatre - or brothel, as the manager puts it - where everyone is talking about the new sensation, Nana, glorious or untalented, depending on the latest gossip, but apparently perfect for the role of Venus in the mock-Offenbach operetta for extra-artistic reasons.

She appears as a big girl with a diaphanous gown and a leer; the atrocious singing voice which Belinda Davison adopts is well within the tradition of such thespian *grandes horizontales* as Hortense Schneider. This emblematic portrayal is in keeping with the rest of the prancing, stylised production, where an infatuated teenager is invariably depicted without trousers, a prince wears tails and a vest and the round dance of the *demi-monde* is usually performed by caperers in underwear or *deshabille*. (The men, particularly, are embarrassing when getting over their twentieth century idea of thrusting sexiness.)

The impression is of archetypes, symbols and cartoons rather than individuals, not helped by the Dora Bryan-as-cockney-tart accents of Nana's actress friends or the recourse to having Nana occasionally played by other members of the cast for no very good reason. With characters as two-dimensional as this the story soon becomes boringly repetitious as the repellent heroine bankrupts one lover after the other with her insatiable demands. Her tendency to humiliate her besotted admirers is hammered into the ground. Jane Gibson and Sue Lefton, joint directors, remind us of Wedekind's Lulu transformed into a monster,as Nana possessively dominates her trouserless schoolboy and her lesbian lover.

A graphically-depicted bout of shoe-fetishism is followed by a sapphic snog; but it all adds up to earnest *vieux chapeau*. There is something old-fashioned about the energetic miming and leaping, the assumption of many parts by each actor which blurs and confuses the story-line even further. Shared Experience was once a company devoted to clear narrative; this stale, arty gallimaufry marks a sad departure. The ultimate miscalculation is Anthony Ingle's Offenbach pastiche which, as with the lifeless characters, leaves one longing for the real thing.

Martin Hoyle

Radio

Greene fortnight

THE BBC is celebrating a two-week Graham Greene Anthology, but before I get there, I must pay my tribute to two outstanding programmes.

The first is to *Chikamatsu* (Radio 3, Sunday). This was a drama-documentary by Ian Burton on the Japanese playwright Monzaemon Chikamatsu, who wrote Bunraku plays for Gidayu Takemoto, the great *joruri* reciter; the play takes a look at him in the year 1715, when he was 62, Gidayu had died, and had to be replaced. It is no more than a short colour piece, but it contains impressions of two of the company's plays, "Kokusenya Kassen," a famous historical play set in China at the time of the fall of the Ming dynasty, and "Sonezaki Shinju," based on a true story of a double suicide. John Moffatt played Chikamatsu and Anton Lesser the new *joruri*, Masadayu, and there was music on the shakuhachi flute. I thought it beautiful, and one needn't know a lot about Bunraku. Piers Plowright directed.

And then to Peter Barkworth's monologue on Siegfried Sassoon, which he has been giving in the theatre (Radio 4, Monday). This covers the period from Sassoon's childhood in Kent to the end of his wartime experiences. Mr Barkworth spoke it as if to friends at the fireside, the verses running as though they were part of the narrative until he came to "Everyone sang." This was made to ring with the poet's own delight. I have seldom enjoyed a programme more.

The Graham Greene Anthology on Radio 4 includes work in several varieties, prefaced by a commentary on the Greene opus that called in such eminent names that it was promoted to Radio 3. On Saturday, Radio 4 gave a version of the 1939 novel *The Confidential Agent* dramatised by James Saunders - fair enough as a Saturday play, but not really high in the scale of either writer. This is the one about mid-European Droeschke, who comes to England to buy coal for his revolt-torn country and has an affair with Rose, daughter of a coal magnate. Entertainment, yes; art, only just.

But Sunday afternoon brought the start of a three-part *Our Man in Havana*, adapted by Gregory Evans and directed by Brian Miller. Here, with more leisure and an origin in film-script rather than novel, characters and story are altogether more convincing. Jack Watling was a good vacuum-cleaner salesman Wormold, George Pravda a sad set-up spy Hasselbacher.

Beginning last Monday evening, the "Book at Bedtime" is *The End of the Affair*, about faith and faithlessness around Clapham Common, read by Julian Glover and Kika Markham. This is a first-person story, admirable material for such as go to bed at 10.15 pm, and I shall hear as much of it as I can, though it conflicts with the ITN news. Why can't people go to bed at 10.30?

Wednesday brought a sharp change, in the shape of *The Great Jowett*, a comic feature in dramatic form about Benjamin Jowett. Greene wrote this for radio in 1939, when it was directed by Stephen Potter. This week's production was a repeat of a 1980 production directed by Brian Wright, and has Alan Bennett as Jowett. It begins with a guide showing visitors round Balliol. Jowett is hoping to be elected Master of the College ("There's only me"), but the College thinks otherwise and elects Professor Scott ("half a lexicon"). It does not appoint Jowett as Professor of Moral Theology either; apart from anything else, there is alleged blasphemy in his forthcoming work on St Paul. But at least he can be Professor of Greek, and shun his colleagues by choosing his company only at tutorials, one of his students being Swinburne, perpetually drunk. Yet 16 years later he is indeed elected Master, and numbers to his credit such things as the foundation of the Indian Institute (to the annoyance of neighbouring Trinity) and of OUDS. It is all very light in tone, in the manner Greene has used seldom save in his short stories. *The Return of A.J.Raffles* and *For Whom the Bell Chimes*.

Next week, we have *The Third Man* on Saturday, *The Potting Shed* on Monday (an original dramatic work at last), and a dramatised story, *Cheap in August*, on Wednesday. Evelyn Waugh never had it so good.

B.A.Young

Chess No. 697

1 N-R3 (threat 2 N-B4). If QxP; 2 Q-QR8, or if PxP; 2 Q-Q1, or if BxP; 2 Q-KR1. Traps are 1 N-QB6? QxP or 1 B-Q4? PxP or 1 N-B3? BxP or 1 B-N3? P-B5.

Records

Sung with distinction

Elgar: The Dream of Gerontius. Baker, Mitchinson, Shirley-Quirk, City of Birmingham Symphony and Chorus/Rattle. EMI CDS 749549-2 (two CDs).

Bach: Christmas Oratorio. Donath, Lipovsek, Schreier, Buechner, Holl, Leipzig Radio Choir, Dresden Staatskapelle/Schreier. Philips 420 204-2 (three CDs).

Bach: Christmas Oratorio. Rolfe Johnson, Argenta, von Otter, Blochwitz, Baer, Monteverdi Choir, English Baroque Soloists/Gardiner. Archiv 423 232-2 (two CDs).

Mozart: Requiem K.626, Kyrie in D minor K.341. Bonney, von Otter, Blochwitz, White, Monteverdi Choir, English Baroque Soloists/Gardiner. Philips 420 197-2.

ALMOST WITHOUT exception, versions of *The Dream of Gerontius* on record have something distinctive to recommend them. The historical legacy - two versions conducted by Sargent, the earlier with Heddle Nash singing Gerontius, Barbirolli's with Lewis and the young Janet Baker - set a standard which more recent accounts by Britten and Boult in particular convincingly reached. Boult's performance, with Nicolai Gedda a surprisingly successful tenor, was transferred to CD last year, and is the obvious challenger to Simon Rattle's new, spaciously recorded version.

Distinguishing between them leaves no clear-cut recommendation. Both offer comprehensively satisfying accounts with differing though significant shortcomings. The problem with Rattle's performance is his choice of tenor. It is a hard role to cast convincingly, for it seems to presuppose a curiously English hybrid of *Heldentenor* - the *Parsifal* legacy - and oratorio singer, someone capable of combining heroic declamation and liturgical devotion without a trace of sanctimony. Only Richard Lewis in my experience has brought it off with total success. John Mitchinson has the ringing, well-focussed delivery, but lacks an intimate dimension: he is fine at "Sanctus fortis," less secure at "Take me away," stiff and compressed in the crucial dialogues with the Angel in Part 2.

Yet more than adequate compensation is offered by the two known quantities - John Shirley-Quirk's Priest and Angel of the Agony, not as dark-toned as might be but alive to every nuance and harmonic colouring, and Janet Baker's Angel. Of course direct comparison with her earlier recording reveals some vocal wear (though she invariably takes the more demanding vocal alternative when Elgar offers a choice) and one moment of faulty intonation ought to have been retaken, but the way in which she deploys all her resources of colour and inflection is utterly compelling. Her first utterances are absolutely rapt, without vibrato, and rivetting, each subsequent set-piece is presented with perfect economy of expression; there is no superfluous sentiment and no lack of warmth.

Rattle's contribution too is full of marvellous things. There are occasions when he lingers fractionally too long in reflective passages, but the vividness of the orchestral playing, the brightly-lit detail and the sheer elan of the choral singing cannot be faulted. For once the Demons' Chorus is not at all embarrassingly melodramatic; the rhythmic drive and jagged *sforzandi* so characteristic of this conductor provide genuine dramatic bite. The few lapses are at those points where the work itself betrays longueurs; all of Rattle's urgency cannot keep the dramatic thread taut through those.

Had Peter Schreier's account of the *Christmas Oratorio* appeared at any other time, it would have been welcomed almost without reservation. It has the same exceptionally sensitive direction as his earlier recordings of choral music, and in this case he also sings the role of the Evangelist. The performing practices carry no self-conscious aspirations to "authenticity;" the playing of the Dresden orchestra and the singing of the Leipzig chorus are direct and uncomplicated.

While the line-up of singers is a distinguished one, with the contralto Marjana Lipovsek particularly outstanding, it is Schreier's vocal contribution that naturally takes pride of place. It is a marvellously schooled, effortlessly weighted account, phrased immaculately with an acute sensitivity to the sense of the text. If for no other reason, the set should be heard for him.

It is only alongside John Eliot Gardiner's urgent, exemplary performance that Schreier's begins to seem a little pale. With consistently faster tempi Gardiner fits the work neatly on to two CDs; Schreier takes three. Speed is not everything, but the light-fingered attack which Gardiner fosters in his singers and players gives the music a constant, subtly variegated buoyancy.

His Evangelist is Anthony Rolfe Johnson, who lacks much of Schreier's gravitas yet is more personal and involved, if marginally less eloquent. Gardiner's regular stable of soloists furnishes the other roles, voices chosen for their flexible expressive and attention to detail. The result is a highly coherent matching of voice and instruments; the correlation of sound worlds is exact and totally convincing, as it is in his Mozart Requiem with which it shares two soloists, Anne Sofie von Otter and Hans Peter Blochwitz.

Here Gardiner opts to retain Sussmayr's completions; and so presents the Requiem everyone knows rather than adopting the Maunder edition (which expunges everything un-Mozartean) used by Hogwood on his authentic account. Again it is lithe transparency which characterises the account, textures in which bass instruments can make eloquent expressive points without undue emphasis, and consistently swift tempi that never seem too fast yet which strip every vestige of sugary reverence from the music. Fine though it is, the addition of the D minor Kyrie to the disc is neither here nor there; few available versions of the Requiem come close to this for all-round excellence.

Andrew Clements

coverage, which is widely recognized as outstanding in the daily press. The FT has always set a high standard for the Arts, which for this purpose include radio and television coverage.

The combination of national and international editions, together with the wide-ranging coverage of the 'Weekend FT', enables the paper to cater for all its readers' needs under one cover, so to speak. It is the newspaper's answer to those who suggest that it is of interest only to the City businessman.

Conclusion

Like much of Britain, the *Financial Times* has been, and still is, undergoing a process of rapid and substantial change. Some of the changes are historical, and can be traced back to the paper's long-standing policy of extending its coverage beyond the traditional business world. But some changes have come about more abruptly as communication technology has changed the face of newspapers and of the financial services business.

To take first the changes in the FT's coverage. The FT now aims to provide its readers with all the information and comment they have the need — or, perhaps more truthfully, the time — to read. The businessman who needs the cocoa prices also needs to keep up with foreign and domestic political affairs. He probably has an interest in theatre, films, or the Arts and he travels abroad, both on business and pleasure.

It used to be said that the FT was an excellent 'second paper', implying that the most readers also took at least one other UK daily newspaper. That is much less true now that readers are unwilling to pay for more than one newspaper, even if they have time to read a second. Modern man or woman may scan all the daily papers at the office, but tends to be a reader of one — or perhaps two — at home. So, the FT sees itself increasingly as a newspaper which must cover the full range of reader interests.

Not that this represents any sudden change. Since it began its dramatic expansion, some thirty or more years ago, the FT has always written on subjects far removed from the City and its affairs, its coverage of the Arts has long been admired, and has expanded to include films, fringe theatre and television drama. But the paper was well in the vanguard when the other UK newspapers began to carry regular commentaries on farming, fishing, or just plain shopping.

In this sense, the growth of the paper has been organic, without any of the dramas associated with what used to be called Fleet Street, where the *Financial Times* was never situated. There have been few changes in the editorship, and continuity throughout the editorial operation has enabled the paper to hold on to its traditional strengths while tackling new territories.

This has proved an advantage for the paper as it has faced significant changes in direction. The newest territory of all has been that of overseas readership, now the fastest growing area of circulation. The new overseas readers, it was found, wanted access to the FT's existing strengths, rather than to a different paper published only for them.

It was therefore an advantage for the FT to be able to 'grow' its international editions from the existing newspaper, using the same correspondents, and feature-writers as the London editions.

The second area of change has been in that of newspaper technology. Computer typesetting, which arrived on the UK daily newspaper scene with a rush following the move of *The Times* to Wapping, had considerable significance for the *Financial Times*. Computer printing is ideal for the dissemination of the financial data, of which the FT carries a great deal. The paper is now able to print closing prices for most of the major world markets as well as those in London.

As markets become increasingly global, demand for international financial data is likely to become greater. The FT holds a unique position as a disseminator of the data which makes markets run, and will seek to extend this position.

So, as the *Financial Times* moves into its second century, change and expansion will continue. Not, however, at any cost to the paper's base, which will continue to be set firmly in the financial and business community of the UK.

The challenge for the newspaper business for the next decade will be to respond successfully to the internationalization of the business world. The FT is perhaps ideally placed to lead such a response.

Index

Note: Page numbers in italics refer to reproductions from the FT